Why, a stranger may ask, do Canadians flout the laws of geography, history, sound business, continental logic, the mandate of nature itself in a rugged land hard to subdue, cultivate and govern, only to be themselves?

Are they driven by necessity? No, by their own free choice. They choose this land because it is spacious, infinitely varied, full of wonders and unlimited choice . . .

Compressed in sight, sound, scent and the nation's secret heart are certain memories, regrets and hopes known to us alone, to strangers incommunicable. Even if they are far from perfect, we love our native ways and homemade home. There can be no better reason to keep, safeguard and cherish anything of true worth.

THE
UNFINISHED
COUNTRY

BRUCE HUTCHISON

THE UNFINISHED COUNTRY

To Canada with Love and Some Misgivings

Douglas & McIntyre
Vancouver/Toronto

Douglas & McIntyre Ltd., 1615 Venables Street,
Vancouver, British Columbia   V5L 2H1

Canadian Cataloguing in Publication Data

Hutchison, Bruce, 1901–
    The unfinished country

ISBN 0-88894-481-0 (hardcover)
ISBN 0-88894-512-4 (paperback)

1. Canada – Politics and government – 1963– *
I. Title.
FC630.H87 1985   971.064'6   C85-091361-6
F1034.2.H87 1985

Design by Barbara Hodgson
Typeset by Typeworks
Printed and bound in Canada by Imprimerie Gagné Ltée.

In memory of my beloved wife, Dorothy, and my daughter, Joan.

CONTENTS

FOREWORD
AND WARNING

This book is an old Canadian's last attempt to examine the true state of a country that he has known and loved for more than eight decades. After so long a time the examination must abound in prejudice, crochets and misjudgements. Also in hope near the end.

At first glance the book may seem to have no chart or design when the historical sequence of events is deliberately ignored in favour of a roving excursion through the politics, business and society of Canada as I have seen them and, more important, the real life of its people which foreigners, seeing only the surface, rarely understand. They, and even some natives, exaggerate our country's virtues and defects.

The serious student finds a vast library devoted to Canadian affairs. Here the reader will find only the vagrant, changing outlook of a traveller always surprised by an infinite variety of land, thought and folkways.

Doubtless professional scholars, historians and sociologists, if they chance to see it, will reject an amateur's interpretation of the past, present and future while disputing among themselves. But Canada is large enough, its affairs intricate enough, to allow different conclusions, even those of a working newspaperman who has observed some famous history makers at work and found scant resemblance between their private views and their public images.

Since a depth study was far beyond my knowledge I tried, at least, to avoid the misunderstanding of the blind men in the ancient parable who confronted an elephant and took its separate parts for the whole. Instead, seeking the Canadian whole, I concluded that it defied logical analysis and lacked any outward symmetry. A congruent structure, a practical working method, was there all the same but could not be detected from a single viewpoint.

Canada requires shifting observations as a kaleidoscope shifts with every turn. And I am aware, too, that shifting events in a mad world, before this book is printed, are likely to outdate portions of its contents without altering the known record.

What, the reader may ask, is my purpose? What justifies such an effort? Only my belief that the nation is quite unprepared for the hard days ahead, often forgets the vital lessons of experience and needs to be reminded of certain decisions long evaded but now inescapable. Whether this modest purpose has been served, readers can judge for themselves.

Stephen Leacock once introduced a volume of sparkling nonsense with the hint that the author, as well as his kindly friends, deserved a share of credit for the result. He was a genius and could afford his jokes. While asserting no like claim I am happy to thank two men who made my work possible.

Ross Meek, a young follower of my trade whose future is bright, edited the original draft and wisely forced me to undertake laborious revision. I owe special thanks to Vaughn Palmer, a journalist and scholar of high talent, for reading the manuscript, correcting some clumsy passages and offering many invaluable suggestions. For their unfailing affection and support in seasons of trouble, countless others herein named or unnamed have my gratitude in full measure. They probably will not agree with my conclusions but they will understand.

B. H.
Victoria, B.C.
May 1985

1

THE
LONG
JOURNEY

In the summer of 1924 "Honest John" Oliver, British Columbia's premier, a wheezing old gentleman with a crown and beard of white uncombed hair above a distended belly, was riding the Kettle Valley Railway on his last election campaign. Opposite him in the dining car sat a cub reporter from the Victoria *Times* and the Vancouver *Sun* on his first major assignment.

Oliver, unconscious heir to some five thousand years of political experiment, had three years of life before him. The reporter had at least sixty among politicians and still stranger breeds.

What, that once youthful apprentice asks himself, has he learned in the long journey of a lifetime? Not much, but enough to distinguish the paramount question facing Canadians today: Where do we stand in a country and world that no man could imagine yesterday?

A partial answer comes easy, too easy.

Our economic system, based on vast exports of raw materials, does not fit a newly competitive world market; our brave talk of free trade is already voided by import restrictions; our public treasury has been looted by all governments combined, few citizens protesting; our living standard is threatened by the blunders of politics, business and our demand for impossible rewards; our environment is endangered by pollution of air, soil and water; our discontented society is ill prepared to meet a time of change and revolution, peaceful or violent, everywhere, with humanity's existence at the hazard of terrestrial war or even Star Wars.

In short, as we shall see, Canada risks a trap of its own invention. It remains a country affluent, fortunate and wholesome but unfinished and still unknown to a majority of its natives because they have lately ignored the plain facts of their collective life. From a remote distance G. K. Chesterton, the English author, might almost have foreseen the groping Canadian mind today when he wrote that "men must be made to realize, if only by reiteration, how utterly unreal is the real state of things."

Canada's last election in 1984 was a frightening exhibit of reality evaded, the hard, unpopular decisions postponed though not for long—all this in a land of lavish resources, high skills, orderly habits and generous instincts, but a people whose heads were turned by artificial prosperity while they mismanaged their affairs to a point of crisis yet unmeasured or admitted in politics.

The election story needs little retelling here. An old, worn-out, power-drunk Liberal regime was expelled as it deserved to be. Pierre Trudeau's patronage scandal and the deep damnation of his taking off at the very time when his peace mission was capping a strangely mixed lifework brought our eighteenth prime minister to office. Unlike any predecessor, Brian Mulroney had no experience in government. He carried with him more promises than any man could deliver and intended to shrink the apparatus of the state, though in the long run it will keep expanding.

Shabby or triumphant, depending on individual preference, the election was nothing less than a political earthquake. We have still to witness its delayed shocks. It broke the Liberal Party's ancient hold on Quebec, may have doomed Liberalism as a nationwide force and probably gave the winner a long life. If the election compelled both the dominant parties to rethink their basic doctrines, it settled no specific issues, leaving them for settlement to Conservative policies undefined and contradictory. At this writing their evolution and doubtless further contradiction are unpredictable.

Against the facts, economic, social and military, now confronting us, the election was largely irrelevant. But as Robert Burns observed, "facts are chiels that winna ding and downa be disputed." Assuredly they will not long be disputed in Canada, among them higher taxes, deeply embedded unemployment and, for many Canadians, a reduced living standard as measured by the consumption of goods. After too much shallow quibbling and bickering the nation faces a test different in kind from those of the past.

The boy reporter on the train, a boy peculiarly ignorant and naive, foresaw none of these things at a time of flimsy boom and worldwide euphoria. Least of all could he expect to see two shattering depressions, a second world war, ten prime ministers and many foreign potentates. Even more unlikely he was to find these men denying their public legends, to hear some of their unpublished secrets and to entertain some heresies of his own.

Little could be learned by a watcher on the fringe of events now generally forgotten. Nor did the nation seem to learn much. Then how can we decipher the day's news so blurred by the practical men of government and business who have given us the most impractical age on record? While the historian may see all the facts interconnected, they do not appear to the layman in any neat progression. Life itself has a logical structure only in retrospect, and a backward glance rarely saves us from repeating our old follies.

If we are to understand Canada we should look at it from shifting tangents and angles of vision. The result here, when my perspective has somewhat widened after frequent errors and reversals, must be a rambling tale with numerous flashbacks and digressions. But as Laurence Sterne, an eminent digressor, told his skeptical publisher, "digressions, incontestably, are the sunshine of life." Rather publish the digressions, he said, and delete the book.

The present reader has been fairly warned.

First, a tentative survey of the unfinished country before we creep up on the specifics like an Indian scout of frontier days who circled the white man's stockade to gauge its strength. Thus creeping and peering, we quickly spot some curious landmarks and encounter the ultimate riddle in Canada and elsewhere. It was clearly stated by John Adams, a profound student of history and second president of the United States: "While all other sciences have advanced, government is at a stand, little better practised now than three or four thousand years ago."

If that fact winna ding, Adams's verdict raises a more fundamental question: Can the democracy and freedom taken as our inalienable rights, though of course they are not, survive an age where the familiar maps are no longer to be trusted, the compass needle zigzags in all directions, the lodestar seems to have lost its bearings and the people's faith in their systems is undermined by politicians of all parties—and by themselves? We can expect no final answers from the politicians. They have none. The answer will come, doubtless after our lifetime, from prophets yet unborn, from the people's queer, instinctive wisdom in the crunch and not from their temporary governors whose fame will pass with the dawn of a different age.

But one fact we should already know for sure. It is that mankind's dangers and hopes have no precedent in all recorded experience. The human condition will not stop changing. Instead, change will accelerate under the drive of science, technology and loss of faith in the old truths. Hence the future of Canada will be unlike its past or present. Among other things its national sovereignty will diminish with that of all nations when the world is becoming tightly interlocked, the quarrelsome parts joined, willy-nilly, or else condemned to separate havoc.

Studying the French Revolution from his limited angle of vision, Charles Dickens designated his times as the best of times, the worst of times, the age of wisdom and the age of foolishness. Our own times duplicate that cycle on a scale never equalled in the revolutionary year of 1789.

Since then a wider, deeper and many-sided revolution unknown in France has destroyed the ideologies of capitalism, communism, fascism, nazism, socialism and other pristine utopias beyond counting, has cast them aside like sucked fruit, rinds only, to leave a social vacuum, just as the falling Roman Empire left the vacuum of the Dark Ages into which flowed the revolution called feudalism, and its ensuing fall produced the floodtime of Renaissance.

Now another vacuum gapes. An empty barrel echoes with sounds numberless. The clash of theories, speeches, documents, statistics and weaponry, the threat of depression, starvation and pollution, make deafening clamour but no sense to Canadians and other peoples in the many languages of mankind.

Not sound alone rises from the void. Spectres also rise out of the past. But compared to the greatest upheaval of all times its early progenitors and their crimes appear almost insignificant. Our revolution has tortured, murdered and starved millions of men, women and children. The Terror of Paris killed a few thousands under a painless blade. In the latest sequel, Dr. Guillotin's cunning machine was replaced by instruments more brutal—the gas oven for Jews, the Gulag Archipelago for Russians, the labour and re-education camps for Chinese. In Asia and Africa the instruments are slower but just as effective. The food bins are depleted and in news photographs that bear no looking at, the children, misshaped by famine, suck their mothers' depleted breasts.

Even distant Canada hears the lamentations and entreaties of the poor in tongues diverse and incomprehensible, mixed with the tongues of the rich who, thinking themselves immune to mass misery, spare a crust now and then from their loaded tables, seldom guessing that hunger, plague and war can burst out of the barrel to engulf them, too.

Who will silence the clamour and decide the fate of our species? In the immediate future perhaps a dozen men at most, some of them undoubtedly mad, with their obedient lackeys, bureaucrats, economists and witch doctors compiling statistical projections and game plans, workable and unworkable, wondrous to behold. By miscalculation, madness or accident such men can press the decisive buttons and end all life on the planet, human, animal and vegetable. If the buttons are not pressed, new men will soon replace the old, better men or worse. But we must look elsewhere for a tolerable life. We must count on the maturing sanity of mankind whole, buying time until it learns that its fate has become indivisable under the nuclear sword.

How much time is left? What latent reserves of sanity are within our grasp? This we cannot know. All we now hear are sounds of local wars, clashes of strange foreign peoples, tumult of mind soaring beyond the pull of gravity into sidereal space roamed by vehicles more wondrous than earthly politics, human creatures inside them talking across limitless distance to other creatures who, antlike, crawl about a tiny speck in the universe. Wondrous indeed for Canadians to behold, but what meaning is carried by the ever-spreading net of communication as ideas, fantasies and lunacies speed from man to man on the instantaneous electronic grapevine?

Not yet have we truly accepted a unifying idea whose time has to come to heal the sick mind of our creaturehood. But like a new continent rising from the primordial sea, there begins at last to issue the essential, long-missing idea, the idea of oneness glimpsed in the seventeenth century by John Donne. He might have been describing the twentieth, and Canada within it, when he wrote that "we are part of the maine." Even his genius could not suspect the more dangerous idea of our time—that if the last bell tolls, it will toll for us all.

To the idea, or at least the hope, of oneness, Canada has belatedly contributed its morsel and accepted its modest though respectable place in the world family. Trudeau's peace mission may not have been much heard outside the Canadian border by the unrealistic men who misrule events in the name of realism, but it will be heard later on, unless the world's ears are stone deaf, its brain numb. In a prime minister's departing voice Canada uttered a fact so simple that it has been too little understood, shrugged off or ignored, as we ignore the daily environment surrounding us—the fact that if they fail to change their ways, humans of every kind, race and colour are likely to perish in collective suicide. Those who understand the fact often try to evade it and live their lives in quiet despair, the world presumably safe for their brief span.

His hasty methods, endless travels and brash manners aside, what did Trudeau actually say to foreign governments? Not that the Western nations should disarm before Russia is ready to do likewise; not that NATO should be weakened, or even that no American cruise missiles should be tested in Canada. All he said was that the two superpowers must cool their tempers, calm their frantic dialogue, recognize their joint peril and get down to serious bargaining which, at best, would take years.

Some Canadians who ought to know better have dismissed Trudeau's warning against self-slaughter as too obvious to require argument. Why elaborate it? Because the obvious is generally the last thing that humans are willing to acknowledge. Most of us prefer the easier, paved highway of convention and conformity leading, in our time, towards the abyss.

It is tragic that the voice of reason from Canada was followed by a different voice of sheer cynicism and patronage jobbery. Trudeau's appointment of Liberal heelers to cushy jobs discredited his political ethics within Canada but not his foreign mission of peace. Later in Washington, before a grand assembly of notables, he received the Einstein Peace Prize and responded by attacking all the NATO leaders for their repeated failure to seek a workable nuclear bargain. His previous speeches abroad had gone largely unreported in the American press; suddenly he found himself on the front pages and must have been amused. Ronald Reagan, the unnamed central target of the attack, was not.

The president, vowing that peace is the supreme objective of his second electoral term, has to struggle with his divided counsellors, the NATO allies and the Soviet Union. At this writing his Star Wars project (or fantasy) imperils all disarmament negotiations and makes the world's prospects increasingly dubious.

However the presidential career ends, in triumph or discredit, Trudeau, in his last year of office, gave Canada a constructive foreign policy, not just a native prejudice after his long wandering in limbo as he searched for reality. At last he found it. His successors have confirmed his policy and now pursue it with their less abrasive methods but with the same goal. Thus policy has been switched from Trudeau's original and Mackenzie King's enduring isolationism to the broad internationalism of Robert Borden, Louis St. Laurent and Lester Pearson. Happily a misguided detour has ended.

Where Trudeau will stand in history's arcanum, though a continuing theme of household conversation, is of small moment. What concerns us now is Canada's inevitable adjustment to the new world around it, the *realpolitik* of the future glimpsed through the frequently unreal scramble of men and parties.

The time lag and misfit between world and nation was clear enough before a royal commission noted it with comic solemnity. Still unfitted, does a Canada so economically mismanaged and politically fractured have something of importance to offer in the human quandary?

Yes, one thing above all. It offers the modest example of its working duality, of two unlike families living in peace under the same roof. In their English-French partnership, always troublesome and shadowed by old quarrel and grudge, Canada is a microcosm of humanity's overriding predicament, of races, languages, cultures and economic strife that threaten to burn down the world-house entire.

Despite the occupants' recurring mistakes, the Canadian house has been preserved without fire, terror or tyranny in modern times. To be sure, this example of compromise, trial, error and the middle way is far from perfect and can never afford much logic. The house needs constant repair. But most of the world's inhabitants, hearing of the Canadian experience, would envy it. There, in the completion of a work well begun, *only* begun, is Canada's endless task decreed by its circumstance and very nature.

Are Canadians ready for the task? Do they see that their economy, misused wealth and things more precious will be at continuing risk until they revise their comfortable habits and unlimited expectations? To judge from our floundering political system, we are not ready for a revision necessarily drastic and painful. Nonetheless, the collective national mind is thinking thoughts harder and wiser than the first flabby thoughts of boomtime, more honest than the sedative official platitudes. The unreported debate within the family circle is more important than the debates of Parliament and will finally decide everything.

When you next talk to some ordinary, inarticulate citizen—not the extraordinary, articulate persons savouring the insolence of office—you will find that the Canadian people have more sense than the mirror of politics usually reflects. But as Carlyle said, on learning that a famous lady was reconciling herself to the universe, "By God, she'd better!" So had we.

From another angle of vision we must likewise remember the vast magnitude of our possessions. Since Champlain's time Canadians have owned, expanded and mastered the second largest national land mass in the world. On a terrain of stubborn obstacles and harsh climate they have built a society distinct from any other. This is a creation without exact parallel, deserving no lament by disappointed dreamers, but rather the satisfaction of a grand success. But we should never forget its cost to the men who undertook it in their flimsy habitation beside the rock of Quebec before the terrible winter of 1608–1609. Next spring, among the starving garrison of 27 men, "only 8 remained and half ailing."

These were the nation's founders and their legacy is ours to enjoy or loot. Without knowing the words, Champlain had posed and by his lifework had begun to solve the identity crisis still absurdly fretting us today, as if Canadians ever lacked an identity that greets and usually puzzles all foreign visitors. He also began unwittingly to divide North America between Canada and an American Republic, both then inconceivable. The line drawn by his war with the Iroquois was the starting point of the double march towards the waters of the western sea and the imagined wonders of Cathay. After many wars and much political trickery, the line is now at peace, but it can never be free of neighbourly dispute. Border friction, perhaps even grave future clashes, are among the continental facts that we must always live with.

As still another angle of contemporary vision will tell us, the character, instinct and driving force of Canada are largely the product of its land. Yet here we confront a queer ambivalence, a people moulded by the land and its lonely toil who have erected a society concentrated in swarming agglomerates, at costs yet to be reckoned. The land and the splendour of it: foaming Atlantic seacoast, lush Laurentian meadows, naked Pre-Cambrian stone older than time, flaming prairie dawn and sunset, mammary swell of foothills backed by the Rockies' white teeth, dense western rain forest and winding Pacific fiords, mighty rivers surging to three oceans—such is our fair estate, deserved or undeserved. Against its setting our largest cities are daylight huddles, flickers and winks in the midnight darkness of immensity.

Mature Canadians are products, too, of childhood memories, bittersweet. The haunting cry of the loon and splash of trout on a silent lake, the springtime taste of maple syrup from boiling cauldrons, the buzz of insects and the crackle of deer hoofs in summer thicket, the autumnal incense of wood smoke, the whisper and bell-jingle of sleighs across the snow, the locomotive whistle in the mountain gorges telling Canadians that they are not alone in their loneliness when a myriad of life forms accompanies them—these memories are rooted deep in our past and will permeate the future. But they cannot be shared by the foreign traveller or immigrant who sees only the surface of the nation and wonders why it is so troubled about itself.

A boy reporter on a primitive train understood little beyond the land stretching endless outside the window. Brought up in dusty western towns and the saddle, among real cowboys and Indians, he knew the land well enough without knowing politics, his then unexpected working material. His angle of vision may be narrow and blurred even today, after three score years of experience with politicians far more sophisticated, though seldom more acute and cunning, than Honest John Oliver.

So was I to live, a spectator merely, on the avails (as lawyers say of an older trade) of politics.

Canadians never cease to talk about this fascinating subject, but not many, up to now, have bothered to examine and understand it. The wonder, unforeseen by the skeptical John Adams, is that the democratic process, in its few habitations, somehow flourishes when the voters have long neglected their common business. Still, like all peoples, they never hesitate to declare judgements on problems baffling to the best-trained minds.

Thus a plumber, expert only in his skill, might offer to perform brain surgery or a medical doctor to fix a leaky pipe. For the most part our votes flow from inherited attitudes, familial custom, visceral hunch and the passing news of the day. The unalterable verities and vital issues are often buried under the immediate avalanche of trivia.

Yet democracy, confined to a few islands in the world-ocean of authoritarian systems, does survive. It must be made of a sterner stuff than its enemies assume. That stuff, and its managing apparatus known as politics, deserve close scrutiny if we are to see through the gathering fog on the road ahead. A newer, clearer angle of vision is needed. Perhaps we can find it before the road turns again.

2

THE COCKPIT

January of the year 1925 found me in the Ottawa press gallery learning politics. But I lacked the wit to guess that I had arrived there at a fateful turning point in Canada's history. Its governors, too, had yet to suspect that they stood at the end of an era, their comfortable lifelong postulates already outworn, obsolete.

When we now stand at a second turning point of greater moment, the first must be recalled if we are to avoid its worst errors. This is asking a lot from a confused nation, perhaps too much.

Of course I was unprepared for either turning point. So, in both, were the men who supposed that they understood and controlled them. So are their counterparts today. In one sense history is repeating itself.

Less than anybody in Ottawa did a callow reporter from the remote Pacific Coast begin to grasp what was happening around him and the two political giants of the time. Like them, I was out of my depth but, unlike them, lonely and frightened. Still more frightened when Mackenzie King received me in his office (only because I worked for a Liberal newspaper, the Victoria *Times*) and put on his act not only as prime minister but as the humble servant of the people, the friend of the poor, the native Uriah Heep, the most unlikely and successful politician since John A. Macdonald.

King was comparatively young then at the age of fifty-one, short, fat, round of face and gushing of manner. His clothes were dark, old-fashioned and immaculately tailored to hide his growing paunch. His tiny hands fluttered in their long starched cuffs. Altogether the last man you might expect to see at the apex of power where he would remain, with brief interruptions, for the next quarter-century.

Having mastered power, he was pretty smug behind the public humility and looked forward to a summer election in total confidence. Once a reporter himself, he had time to begin my political education (only because I might be useful to him). Slowly my rustic angles were to be rubbed smooth, a process never completed even with his help and the help of better men.

King supposed, quite wrongly, that he knew all the angles of his trade, and one in particular. For his second election he would make no avoidable commitments. A platform, he said, gave "the other fellows" a broad, easy target to shoot at. The convention of 1919 (though he did not mention it) had chosen him as the Liberal Party's leader and framed a platform the very opposite of his radical convictions, and he had simply ignored it to win office two years later. By the same methods he would win again.

He had said nothing that could not be safely printed, but I left him with a feeling of shared secrets, just as he intended.

In the next two decades I was to see much more of this complicated, ambivalent creature. For the present I saw him only on parade in his various acts from Heep to Hampden, with his grandfather, William Lyon Mackenzie, occasionally introduced to prove his own spirit of rebellion.

The House of Commons was a curious spectacle as I observed it from my gallery seat above the prime minister's desk. Beside his diminutive figure lolled his French Canadian partner, Ernest Lapointe, a tall bear of a man with black curls and bristling mustache who had come to Parliament without a word of English. Now he spoke it with Gallic eloquence and an accent musical in two languages.

The dominant politicians of the day, the bantam prime minister and his bulky colleague, looked rather like a vaudeville team, a pair of strolling players as, indeed, they were in election campaigns and must be. It took me some time to realize that in both physical and human terms Lapointe was the larger if not the wiser of the famous partnership.

Across the aisle sat their lifelong enemy, Arthur Meighen, once a transient prime minister and now leader of a truncated opposition, his party outnumbered by the farmers of the Progressive Party. Meighen was lean, pale, motionless until ready to speak. Then he rose, straight and stiff as a ramrod, hands locked together. His chiselled sentences, apparently spontaneous, were ready for Hansard or a book with no word edited. We did not know that all his major speeches had been written, engraved on his matchless memory and recited without a single note. The House listened to the greatest orator since Laurier.

Meighen had succeeded Robert Borden, a greater man, but the successor's talents were not political. They belonged to law or business. Meighen's judgement of great affairs was notoriously flawed, though his worshippers to this day have sustained the myth of his genius as far superior to King's. In 1925, however, the real Meighen had not been divulged to the country or to King. He seemed to command the House by his rigid posture, his corrosive sarcasm, his words that fell like chunks of ice from a glacier. They froze his audience and, unfortunately, the public, too.

But they had the opposite effect on King. They heated him. When Meighen got underway the press gallery reporters watched the red blood line rising from King's white collar to envelop the bald head and descend over the round face. A shaky hand gripped the stub of a pencil and tapped it on the desk. That was the signal of his anger and his fear. Meighen alone could frighten and infuriate him. The long race between the Conservative hare and the Liberal tortoise had started and would end in the hare's destruction, the triumph of the tortoise. No one could foresee that savage contest. At the beginning both men seemed equally fitted for the race. All we knew was that their mutual loathing dated from their years together at university and could never be appeased or hidden.

In Meighen's warped view, and even in his speeches, King was a sanctimonious fraud. Outside Parliament King told me that Meighen was a man of "neat mathematical mind," small but perilous to the nation. Once, in a moment of frenzy, provoked by the wartime conscription crisis of 1944, he shook his fists and described his opponent as a neo-Fascist. This was preposterous but, in King's usually cool mind, revealing. Towards the rest of the House he showed a genial countenance while he played the instrument of politics like an organ. Only when Parliament was in session did he feel entirely safe. He thought himself embarked on a social rebellion more important and lasting than his grandfather's weird adventure at the barricades of York. For this work he needed Parliament's support.

What, after all, did the latest parliamentary foes signify in their time and ours? They hardly knew, themselves, and few Canadians know today. But, looking back, we can see that they meant more than their followers suspected. They meant a sea-change in politics and history still proceeding at accelerated speed.

Meighen was a Conservative of the original Macdonald school, of high tariffs, "brick-for-brick" against foreign competitors, of the free market (except for international trade), of classic liberalism, though Meighen would be the first to repudiate that definition. His neat mathematical mind held too much logic, too many facts, always a danger in politics.

The contrary was true of his enemy. The young King had been an orthodox Liberal like Laurier, who actually was a kind of illogical Canadian Whig, an expatriate Walpole. Then Laurier's heir, the small-town boy from Ontario encountered the real world and it appalled him, transformed his whole view of society. Appearance and reality were in violent contrast. After this shocking discovery he entered politics with a private heresy and later disclosed it in his tortured book, *Industry and Humanity*, which, luckily for his career, had few readers in King's party. Otherwise he could not have won its leadership.

The book stood the historical doctrine of Liberalism upside-down, as it stands today. Instead of supporting Adam Smith's imaginary free market as the norm of human behaviour, King denounced it as abnormal. To the disillusioned Utopian the market's brutal Law of Competing Standards was the weapon of the rich, the oppressor of the poor.

Once the Liberal Party had made him leader, unaware of his doubts, King did not mention them publicly but spoke in safe, rotund generalities, exposing no easy targets to Meighen's dying government. Besides, he was totally confused by world events that seemed to disregard all law. Enough, for the present, to know that the Canadian future belonged, or should belong, to him.

It included a multitude of useful acquaintances, few intimate friends inside or outside politics and no wife. Despite his youthful flirtations and firm decision to marry (as often recorded in his diary), King remained a lifelong bachelor and, off-stage, an instinctive Victorian snob. Meighen was already a husband, father and, on-stage, a natural autocrat. And unlike King, he had troops of genuine friends.

In a time of hollow stability both political parties ignored or did not yet grasp society's great emerging issues. Conservative and Liberal policies showed little difference aside from the tariff, the central debating point as it had been for a century. Meighen was the exponent of protection, King of worldwide free trade (even though he deplored the brutality of the market system at home). But in office neither party dared to leave the market free. The tariff was raised or lowered as political pressures, not theories, directed.

Paying necessary lip service to the free-trade ideal when he sought the western farm vote, King devised a handy, ambiguous slogan. To satisfy the protectionist vote of Ontario and Quebec, he was only for somewhat "freer" trade. Having backed Laurier on Reciprocity with the United States in 1911, he never risked that gamble again, not even when, in 1947, Washington expressed a sudden interest in it.

The tariff was, and is, a cash register proposition, a reckoning of votes, a shifting balance between the unprotected export industries that sell in the competitive world market and the noncompetitive manufacturing industries of the protected Laurentian heartland.

Something more important than the tariff debate was happening in 1921, though its importance was not then appreciated. James S. Woodsworth arrived in Parliament to make himself its conscience and perhaps the noblest public figure of our history.

This innocent Christian minister from the Winnipeg slums had been arrested in the general strike of 1919 and become a secular humanist, a champion of the poor in the visible world, here and now. But with his pointed beard and finely sculptured face he resembled some prophet on a stained-glass cathedral window. Underneath his gentle, saintly manner, Woodsworth lived a life of passionate devotion to the reform of society by methods unclear in his mind, as he candidly admitted among friends. Not yet calling himself a Socialist, and always detesting communism, he reintroduced the ideas of King's apprentice years when the mature politician had deserted them. From Woodsworth's passion much followed, including a radical Socialist party, the Co-operative Commonwealth Federation and, by its pressure, a Liberal Party that moved leftward just far enough to outflank today's New Democratic Party.

King is given credit for the present welfare state and deserves most of it. But its origins are to be found in Woodsworth and his little band of fellow reformers, such men as M. J. Coldwell, T. C. Douglas, David Lewis and Stanley Knowles, good men all, though they frequently stumbled in practical politics. On the whole the left-wing movement has been as effective in its own field, and at least as honest, as the two national parties. Today it rivals Liberalism for leadership of the opposition.

While the Parliament of 1922 had droned on, certain latent explosives undetected, the prevailing twilight sleep was suddenly broken by an occurrence in far-off Chanak, of all places. There, at the Dardanelles, Lloyd George's British government backed the Greeks against the Turks and appealed to the Dominions for military support. Travelling on party business, King heard nothing of the appeal before he read it in the newspapers. That breach of manners was not forgiven. Lloyd George had misjudged Canada, the new Commonwealth and Britain's power. King hastened to Ottawa, consulted his foreign affairs adviser, O. D. Skelton, and announced that only Parliament could decide whether Canada should participate in a war which he regarded as lunacy.

By this time Lloyd George had been defeated at Chanak and at home. The British Parliament and people were finished with Greeks and Turks. So was King, his judgement vindicated, for the time being only. But lasting consequences flowed from the apparently minor Chanak incident. King had retreated to his long spell of delusive isolationism. He had designated Parliament as the sole authority empowered to make war. And he had raised Borden's work of Canadian independence from British foreign policy to a higher, though not necessarily a wiser, level.

Strangely, in a man of his intelligence, Meighen had misconstrued the whole affair. When the Chanak war began he committed the first of his fatal blunders. As soon as he heard of Lloyd George's appeal, the opposition leader, consulting nobody, rushed into print, repeated Laurier's cry in the South African war and demanded that Canada stand by Britain's side, "ready, aye, ready."

That cry suited King precisely. It also helped to define, though vaguely, his own foreign policy, or nonpolicy. Most Canadians shared it.

To the press gallery the political parties represented no clear alternatives, but we reported their speeches in longer newspaper columns than anyone would read nowadays. Mere shadows of the nation's future choices were visible, shadows already long in the apparent Liberal dawn, growing longer in the Conservative sunset, reappearing in our time, stretching towards misty horizons across Canada and the world.

All the shadows were misleading, especially in Ottawa. A lumber village converted into a cockpit of politics by Queen Victoria, who never saw it, the nation's capital remained clustered, like the towns of the Middle Ages, around its castle and the tangled towers on Parliament Hill. The Chateau Laurier hotel, half its present size, was the haunt of politicians, the only good hotel but too expensive for me at four dollars a night.

From my mean attic room on Bank Street most of the other streets looked shabby long before today's concrete donjons soared upward to house the proliferating hosts of a government that keeps swelling despite its promises to shrink. Laurier, who had said that Ottawa was an ugly town, likely to remain so, was mistaken. With its canal, driveways, parks and blossom, Ottawa has turned into one of the world's finest capitals. And like most capitals it is a parasite, a kept woman, feeding on taxpayers from coast to coast, many of whom will never visit it. A Canadian who sees them is likely to rejoice in these outward improvements, but they are trivial compared with the changed status of Ottawa and the nation in the world community. That change is unlikely to be grasped by the present generation.

Although Canada had become, after the First World War, a sovereign state, a signatory of the Versailles peace treaty and a member of the League of Nations, strong traces of an earlier colonial spirit persisted. The British Empire had begun to dissolve, world power to be redistributed, new systems of government, economics and society to appear in strange places. If it should have been obvious that Canada must frame a new foreign policy and new world attitude for a new age, the fact was not realized, at least in the press gallery. We had yet to see the obvious and hear from Trudeau that the universe kept evolving as it should. Or even to hear his name.

Since then the evolution has also changed something else. The Liberal and Conservative governments of the King-Meighen era governed, as they supposed, in obedience to the nation's will expressed by majority vote, unthreatened by minorities. The great pressure groups of modern society had not been born, or conceived, except for the farmers' Progressive Party, and it was merely a short-lived revolt within the Liberal Party. The future organs of business, labour and ethnic voting blocs were still in embryo.

Most of the evidence accepted as truth in Ottawa was false. The road signs had been misread, even by King who seemed to know everything. Despite this sunny weather he took no chances. The bouncy prime minister was now the Liberalism of electoral politics incarnate. He rolled the word *party* deliciously off his tongue to sound like "p-a-r-t-y," a magician's spell. He knew all his minor local henchmen throughout the country, wrote personally signed notes to them, congratulated them on family births, sympathized with their griefs and maintained a network of power equalled only by Macdonald in simpler times.

Before the Commons King wallowed in flatulent ambiguity and delivered three-hour speeches to mask purposes still obscure but slowly ripening in his mind. He was soothing and reunifying the people, or so he believed, after the strains and divisions of wartime. Hardly noticed then or remembered now, this was the first installment of his lifework. As he said years later, when leading the opposition, an economically sick country needed "the hand of a physician"—his hand, of course—not "the fist of a pugilist," R. B. Bennett's fist.

Always King relied on his own intuition, not other men's facts. An insight that came to him from a region above human reasoning, from a higher authority that advised him (the public never suspecting his secret) through spiritualistic channels.

The turgid speeches came from a different source to provide a rationale for decisions already reached elsewhere and to satisfy a worldly Parliament. For this task he had discovered the perfect speech writer. Jack Pickersgill, a blunt-speaking young history professor, gathered the necessary statistics, quotations and precedents. Then he would exactly imitate King's cumbersome style and drag in every fragment of evidence, however irrelevant, to make a defence of policies however dubious. But Pickersgill, his own remarkable career then unimagined, was a strong-willed servant unique among the official establishment. While silent in public, he never hesitated in private to criticize the government's strategy and offer advice frequently accepted by his boss without thanks.

In short, King was the consummate political manager. Meighen (like Trudeau) was never a real party man. He scorned King's methods, refused to woo the voters with sweet talk and assumed that they were intelligent enough to support his sound principles. This was a grave error in an otherwise brilliant mind.

King's personal habits were regular, selfish and concealed from the voters. Over the years I saw him in his two official offices, his hide-out (with a bedroom for afternoon naps) a few yards from the Commons chamber and once for dinner in his Laurier House, only the two of us and his Irish terrier in that gloomy mansion littered with bric-a-brac.

While Parliament was hard at work he talked steadily until past midnight, joked about colleagues and enemies, his eyes twinkling, and recalled old battles. This was the supposedly dull, uninteresting little man whose posthumous biographies have expanded into a Canadian growth industry; the man who, as the Earl of Athlone, a former Governor General, explained to me in London, had "just missed being quite a decent feller."

(On an earlier occasion, in Victoria, Athlone had ruminated on Winston Churchill, then saving Britain from invasion and the world from Hitler. "Ah, Churchill," he said. "They sent the boy to me at Sandhurst to be trained for the cavalry. He went into politics and did quite well. Makes a very good speech, you know. But he'll never make a soldier! No, no, never make a soldier!")

If man and legend stand far apart, Athlone's recollection of King was pretty accurate though it overlooked one curious point—in his age King had ceased to be a rebel. He regarded himself almost as the royal family's overseas uncle, the trusted intimate of King George VI and Queen Elizabeth. This conversion to royalty had not begun in the sleepwalking days of 1925. While they were already near their end, no Canadian statesman or economist like King guessed that within four years the world economy would collapse, that within fourteen years peace would be followed by a second war more devastating than the first.

King's blindness is unbelievable in retrospect. After the Munich deal, which he ecstatically approved, lasting peace seem to him permanently ensured. A year before our evening at Laurier House he had talked to Hitler and now informed me that the German dictator was a "simple peasant" with only limited and legitimate territorial ambitions. King's third-floor sanctum had become the real centre of government but it was well insulated from simple reality. Its occupant, usually a shrewd judge of men, had been totally fooled by Hitler.

If this mistake was not only pathetic but tragic, Meighen, and most Canadians, were just as mistaken about the future. The age between the wars was a universal mistake. No one questioned King's assurance of peace less than the ignorant reporter from Victoria. Men far wiser could not imagine that the apparently timorous prime minister was to make himself the nation's greatest war leader and an unequalled social reformer in peacetime.

Still, I had learned something in Ottawa and made three friends who knew more. They, too, symbolized the era now ending, the era in its unnoticed birth. Each of them was to influence the nation's future and change mine.

A young fellow of stern look and fastidious dress occupied a desk next to mine in the press gallery workroom. His name was Arthur Irwin. After his war service he reported Parliament for the Toronto *Globe,* unaware of the notable career ahead of him in magazine journalism, motion pictures and diplomacy.

My second friend, also a war veteran, was a man of different sort. Grant Dexter had come to Ottawa from the Winnipeg *Free Press* as the eyes and ears of its great editor, J. W. Dafoe, and later succeeded him. Among Grant's contemporaries he was the ablest political analyst of his time. Our lives were to be inseparably linked in business and friendship until his ended too soon.

A third future friend strode into the workroom now and then, but I did not venture to approach him. Thomas Alexander Crerar, a tall, handsome, powerful man with a shock of red hair and sun-tanned prairie face, had led the Progressive Party whose seats, won in the election of 1921, outnumbered those of the Conservatives. Crushed by the death of a beloved daughter, he left politics, as he thought, forever. But he returned to join King's government, served throughout the second war while detesting the prime minister and finished his public life in the Senate. Like many old-fashioned Liberals, Crerar remained at heart a conservative, a free-market Adam Smith believer and, as I had good reason to know in the latter years of our intimacy, a gentleman of shining honour. Unknowingly, he was a vivid symbol of the dying era.

At last it was time for me to go home with Dorothy, my bride. Before we could build our home, a sudden political crisis disrupted the whole course of Canadian events.

3

CONSTITUTIONAL FROTH

The election of 1926, still the most controversial in our history, seemed to settle a single question, the supremacy of the prime minister. In fact, it was only the first of many questions yet to be settled, questions bequeathed by King to Trudeau who in turn bequeathed them to his heirs.

Without understanding the events of 1926 we cannot understand what is happening around us today, in politics, the courts and even private households. Although books innumerable have been written to explain the inwardness of the constitutional crisis launched by the election of 1925, all of them are outdated. But old, respected authorities like Eugene Forsey still argue their convictions and prejudices. Some men have devoted their last years to hatred of King, architect of the crisis.

He had come out of the 1925 election with a Liberal minority, staggered by Meighen's 116 Conservative members as against 101 Liberals, 25 Progressives and a few independents. Nevertheless, King promised the Governor General, Lord Byng, that he could govern with his reduced minority, supported by the Progressives as in the past.

Byng, an English general, had commanded the Canadian Army in France (the "Byng Boys" of song and legend). Ignorant of politics, he yet doubted King's promise and decided to summon Meighen. At length, however, he agreed to let King carry on for the time being. In military terms, of course, the arrangement was absurd, the stronger force yielding to the weaker. But this was war of a different sort and King was its master. Byng could not comprehend it. The quarrel between Crown and Commons had begun.

The late autumn was spent in preliminary skirmish, King creeping up to his target, Meighen watching, incredulous, from the outer lines. The ramshackle government lived through the early winter, the new Parliament restive but yet to assemble. Everything depended upon the promise extracted by Byng from his prime minister, the promise inter-preted differently by the two men. As Byng understood it, King would immediately resign in Meighen's favour if the House of Commons rejected the government. As King understood his promise, or said he did, the government would remain in office once it had won a single vote of confidence. What no man then saw was another wild card in play. The Customs Scandal would disrupt the whole game.

Parliament met early in the new year. King, who had lost his own seat (though he was returned in a February by-election), observed the House from the gallery and won his first vote of confidence with the Progressives' reluctant support. It was enough, he thought, to redeem his promise.

The session had hardly started before the scandal erupted. H. H. Stevens, a scholarly ex-grocer from Vancouver, rose to declare that the Customs Department was riddled with graft. But he had sympathy for its minister, the fat little Jacques Bureau, who had resigned in disgrace months earlier. Stevens spoke with all the charity of "one human being to another." That opening courtesy did not last long. Meighen was poised for the kill.

It came in the form of detailed charges spread day after day on the record in ugly detail—friends of the government smuggling goods across the American border in perpetual cataract, bribed officials winking at the crimes, revenues lost, taxpayers defrauded on a scale never seen before or since, the Pacific Scandal of Macdonald's time dwarfed.

Of these evils King professed to be well aware. Already he had undertaken to cure them by a scandalous appointment. Bureau had been punished with elevation to the Senate, replaced by young George Boivin in the Customs Department not long before his sudden death.

Now the grace period of human sympathy was over—committee of investigation, evidence undeniable, beyond belief, Progressives almost ready to support Meighen, Woodsworth wavering, even Liberals threatening to change sides, King in despair, the public's stomach nauseated, its nostrils revolted by the stench. Yet King hung on while Byng awaited his resignation. The previous year's promise, said King, had been fully honoured. He had won the confidence of Parliament if not of the country. He was entitled to govern until Parliament voted against him, and soon he had won several votes. But they were not enough to satisfy the House. Endless days of speeches, points of order, appeals to history, to the Constitution, to Athenian philosophers, to God—clearly this mad melodrama could not last.

It was ended in the spring on a tricky motion which, if passed, would force King's hand. He retreated to Rideau Hall, confronted Byng and asked him to dissolve Parliament, an election following. To the Governor General that advice was outrageous, unthinkable. He refused it and summoned Meighen to form a government.

King had his issue and exploited it in his finest, or at least his most triumphant, hour. As he thought, quite wrongly, Meighen had fallen unawares into a constitutional trap. By taking office, the opposition leader, out of ravenous ambition, had discredited the Crown itself, for if a British Governor General rejected the advice of a Canadian prime minister, violating all constitutional precedent, then Canada was still a colony of Britain, incapable of self-government.

King's reasoning had not yet fully matured. Later he revised it, admitting that Byng could reject prime-ministerial advice if he found a workable alternative. But for the present any argument would serve.

In truth, Meighen had seen the trap. He had consulted Borden, who also knew the risks. Neither man needed the last-minute warning of the bumbling R. B. Hanson, M.P. of New Brunswick. Alerted by Arthur Beauchesne, a zealous Conservative and supposedly nonpartisan clerk of the House, Hanson rushed to Meighen in a state of panic but was sent about his business.

Meighen saw no way to avoid the danger. If he refused office, where could Byng find an alternative prime minister? Not the Governor General alone as a man but the Crown as an institution would be discredited. Accordingly, Meighen must do his duty at whatever political cost. He took office, convinced that Parliament and people were uninterested in the niceties of the Constitution, concerned only with a government that could govern.

It was not easy for Meighen. In the House he faced a Liberal opposition still nagging day after day, month after month as spring merged into summer—the House sitting all night, Customs Scandal forgotten, overlaid by more exciting news, Mr. Speaker Rodolphe Lemieux, in knee breeches and silver-buckled shoes, now utterly spent, unable to control the disorder, many members sleeping upstairs or drinking themselves insensible, again appeals to history and God, Liberal protests of loyalty to Britain and the empire, Progressives determined to vote for the Government as the lesser of evils, the nation convulsed, the voters divided, passions flaming, Prime Minister Meighen calm and acidulous in his finest hour. But in this shambles he forgot King's second astounding somersault in actually advising Byng to consult London and thus act as the governor of a colony.

Meighen's difficulties were only beginning to appear. He had thrown together an "acting" cabinet of sorts, its members unsalaried and therefore entitled to sit in the House without individual re-election. Meighen, the only salaried minister, must seek the voters' approval in a by-election as required by an old law soon to be repealed. He resigned his seat, remained in office but out of the House and governed from behind the curtain, scrawling notes to his colleagues on the front bench. These hasty instructions were often misunderstood, worsening the makeshift government's dilemma, comforting the opposition.

The crisis was still unresolved. Resolution was to come at two o'clock in the morning of 2 July. Now King's whole career was on the line. Failure must instantly destroy him. His leadership would pass to Charles Dunning, a Conservative masquerading as a Liberal, a handsome, tough, able man and ex-premier of Saskatchewan, who awaited the verdict, his elevation already guaranteed by the party's magnates in the West.

King, knowing these arrangements, defied them. Meighen's government, he shouted through the clamour, was unconstitutional, had seized power in defiance of all tradition, governed illegally, imperilled the Crown. But even in the guise of his rebel grandfather or, alternatively, of Hampden and Heep, he was careful to respect Byng, a gentleman of unquestioned honour wrongly advised by Meighen who must take responsibility for all the actions of the Crown.

With this tortured logic, King worked himself into high passion, fists waving, sweat pouring from his bald head, tears from his eyes. But he had finally constructed his issue. On the one hand he had trapped

Byng and, on the other, he had explained his devotion to the Crown, to those "islands of freedom in the North Sea" where a sitting prime minister's request for a parliamentary dissolution had always been accepted by the monarch for the last two centuries. This was a misreading of history, unnoted in Ottawa's bedlam.

No wonder Meighen was baffled. Contempt had warped his political judgement as it always had and would. He even missed King's second lapse, the admission that Byng could have refused his advice if Meighen were able to govern.

But King was still at the mercy of the final vote and of the Progressives' support. On the eve of decision Meighen was sure of winning it and slept well, King badly. Then luck, luck beyond credence, beyond reason, came to the opposition's rescue.

Most of the Progressives voted for Meighen, despite his right-wing policies, but two of them, J. W. Bird and D. M. Kennedy, were "paired" by the customary gentlemen's agreement and could not vote. At the last minute Bird stumbled into the House and cast his vote. In vain he protested that he had meant to vote the opposite way, had voted absent-mindedly with King and defeated the government. A single vote stood to decide everything.

Not quite everything. Meighen still had a prime minister's whip in hand. He repaired at once to Rideau Hall and advised dissolution. The government would appeal to the people. Byng agreed, certain now that King had betrayed the promise, never to be forgiven. So the nation plunged into the second election within a year, the constitutional election whose overtones echo and haunt us today.

For King the issue was clear. As prime minister he had been refused a dissolution. The nation must decide whether it was indeed a colony. Liberalism and Conservatism were outweighed by nationhood. All else was irrelevant. To Meighen the issue was phony, fraudulent, mere "constitutional froth" whipped up by a charlatan, "a lobster with the lock jaw" who sought only office and revenge. Both leaders had reached the pinnacle of their powers.

On his private railway car King raced from coast to coast with a precious box of notes under his bed. He spoke nightly to huge audiences and was now convinced that the nation had grasped the issue, jealous of its nationhood. He even achieved eloquence without his notes, vindicating his grandfather, reviving memories of 1837, obviously winning votes.

One major Conservative foresaw a Liberal victory. R. B. Bennett (only four years away from his own prime ministership) had been absent in Calgary during the parliamentary wrangle. Afterward he always insisted that Meighen should have refused office as he would have done in the same circumstances. He was ignored by Meighen, his old enemy, who spoke in public better than he had spoken in Parliament. He followed King across the continent to the point of physical exhaustion. But he had misconstrued politics even if he understood the Constitution.

So the voters decided at the polls on 14 September. King had 116 seats, Meighen 91, the rest won by a variety of independents. Apparently the issue had been settled for all time, the prime minister's power of dissolution confirmed, the nation autonomous, King its master for unnumbered years ahead.

Meighen, to all appearances, was finished, but he did not yet suspect it. On his advice he had been replaced in office by King and now planned to replace King in turn, the race of hare and tortoise resumed. It was not to be.

Byng, abhorring King, had invited him to form a new Liberal government and soon retired to England, his mission to Canada a tragedy, as the British government saw it. A large Canadian minority did not agree. To constitutionalists like Eugene Forsey the Liberal victory of 1926 had been theft, pure and simple, had burlesqued history, broken all precedent. As Forsey wrote, the Crown in Britain and the Dominions had often refused a prime minister's advice. Byng was right, King wrong.

To Forsey's argument in journalism and books the reply came from J. W. Dafoe. Contemptuous of King, he nevertheless had supported him with all the influence of the Winnipeg *Free Press,* with full pages of furious editorial argument, denigration of Forsey, Meighen and the colonial Butler Mind. The controversy of issues and men raged for years and is unsettled to this day. Many Liberals, Thomas Crerar among them, had decided that Forsey had been right, Dafoe wrong.

What, then, of the future Constitution? Was it firmly fixed by the vote of 1926? No, it was not. It was unfixed when Trudeau, the modern constitutionalist, came to power in 1968 and by slow degrees wrote a new Constitution. Like the original British North America Act, it established Canada as a state of the British model, under a Canadian monarch resident in London, with a cabinet responsible to the Commons, a prime minister who alone could advise the Crown and a Charter of Rights and Freedoms that gave the Supreme Court unprecedented authority. Before then Trudeau had used the Crown as the instrument of a partisan strategy that misfired.

In Macdonald's time a Governor General, always from Britain, was appointed by Queen Victoria on the advice of her British and Canadian prime ministers. In St. Laurent's time the first native Canadian, Vincent Massey, was appointed on the sole advice of a prime minister who said it would be disrespectful to Canada and Queen alike if no Canadian were thought fit to represent her. Only a bold, though gracious, leader could have got away with that change of tradition.

Trudeau, a nationalist and a Socialist in his youth, had different ideas. He was a monarchist when he reached office. He respected Queen Elizabeth even while sliding down the banister of her palace or executing an impromptu pirouette behind her back for the press photographers. But the monarchist and constitutionalist had become a politician in later years and was desperate for western votes.

At first Trudeau chose George Ignatieff, a nonpolitician, experienced diplomat and, in youth, an exiled White Russian, for the governor generalship. His wife had been schooled for Rideau Hall as a lady-in-waiting to the Queen. This excellent choice was to be announced at a ceremonious banquet in Toronto. Shortly before the notables convened, Ignatieff learned from Ottawa's emissaries that he would not be appointed. Changing his mind, Trudeau had done few rougher jobs in his career.

What were his motives? He had received bad news from the West, knew he was winning no votes there and decided to throw a crumb to the voters in the person of Edward Schreyer. Certainly Schreyer would make a respectable Governor General, but he was the ex-premier of Manitoba and now the bitterly partisan leader of the New Democratic opposition in that province.

If the bid for western votes was peculiarly rough, Schreyer had nothing to do with it and was just as surprised as the nation by his appointment. The responsibility was Trudeau's alone and the deal a failure. Schreyer came to Rideau Hall but no western votes came with him. The Crown had been given a political tinge without helping the Liberal Party or Trudeau's prospects in the least. Schreyer deepened the tinge when, finishing his term and taking a diplomatic post, he said he might return later to politics. At this announcement Forsey, the erudite monarchist, again flew into passion and print.

In 1983 Trudeau looked around for Schreyer's successor and chose Jeanne Sauvé, a woman of admirable qualifications who bravely fought a long illness before she could take office. Like Schreyer, she had been an active politician, a minister in the Trudeau government and a vigorous Liberal campaigner before she became Speaker of the Commons. But only nit-pickers, certainly no opposition spokesmen, objected to her appointment, even if it suggested a reward for party service. The nation seemed happy to find a woman, a very able woman, as head of the state.

The new Constitution raised questions far more complex. Its Charter of Rights and Freedoms had introduced principles and consequences little understood except by lawyers, and some of them recognized it mainly as the assurance of endless litigation, a meal ticket. From now on the Supreme Court of Canada, like its counterpart in the United States, must render judgements on ultimately political issues. By interpreting the Charter as it affects federal and provincial laws, the Court will decide what the law makers intended and whether their intentions can be accepted in a "free and democratic society." However freedom and democracy are redefined in Canadian terms, an awesome, open-ended responsibility is transferred, in many vital areas, from elected legislatures to a judiciary appointed by the Crown (in fact by the prime minister).

Here is an organic change in the whole governing system. Trudeau, himself an eminent constitutional lawyer, knew that lawyers of equal learning were opposed to his reform. They held that freedom already was as safe in Canada as in any nation. Moreover, they believed that it would be diminished rather than protected in the attempt to enforce it by a process which will not be clarified without many years of legal argument, the Supreme Court's judgements meanwhile left in doubt.

For example, John Owen Wilson, the most respected of British Columbia's modern chief justices, a man who had always vigorously defended freedom in his court, could see no need for any bill of rights. On the contrary, he saw it as a grave danger to those rights. With him the absolute separation of political and judicial authority, now threatened, was sacred, freedom's very bedrock.

Other judges held the same view. While they agreed, of course, that law should evolve to meet society's evolving needs, this was the business of the legislatures, not the courts. But the Charter, with its imported American principles, enjoyed overwhelming, almost unanimous, public support. It is a fixed element in our society, recognized as a final guarantee of individual liberty, an unalterable fact of politics, its full meaning yet to be explored and interpreted.

Long before the constitutional debate began, a new institution was quietly changing the nation's political machinery. The federal system invented by the Founders of the American Republic and reproduced, with native amendments, in Macdonald's Confederation must be a system of checks and balances, never static. No system less flexible could govern a sprawling country of five distinct regions, each with its own demands, interests and hopes.

National and provincial power operate like an accordion. In times of emergency, like war or depression, Ottawa's power expands. In easier times it flows outward to the provinces, the movement centripetal and centrifugal by turns. In recent times the provinces have acquired power far exceeding Macdonald's design. They exercise it nowadays through the mechanism of the federal-provincial conference which would amaze and alarm the first protector of central government. The conferences, obeying political need regardless of precedent, have often made or unmade the basic decisions of national policy. And always the provinces seek extra money from Ottawa as if the same taxpayers throughout the nation did not pay the bill.

Lately they have sought an additional organ of power in the Senate. At the time of Confederation the Senate, with the right of veto over all legislation, was supposed to be a chamber of unhurried second thought where the errors of the hasty Commons were corrected. That hope perished overnight. King revived it in his first election by promising to reform the Senate and then continued, like Macdonald and all his successors, to appoint unreformed senators who deserved reward for party service. As a pasture for the worn-out horses of politics, the Senate remains a bizarre anachronism, though it has not used its veto in modern times. But under the impetus of a reforming age, doubtless it, too, will change some day.

At one point Brian Mulroney proposed to abolish the Senate, as always urged by the NDP, if the Liberal Party would support him. This was a spur-of-the-moment political ploy—far short of an elected second chamber—too obvious to fool anyone. Mulroney then sought the backing of the provincial governments for constitutional limits on the Senate's right to delay or veto bills passed by the Commons. When the provinces, with their varied notions of reform, seem a long way from agreement, the Senate is in no immediate danger. As an imported and debased form of the American original, which is elected, not appointed, it remains safe in its haven probably for years ahead, even if its powers are reduced.

After the constitutional progress of a century and more, a gaping lacuna remained. While the Constitution was home at last, Quebec had not accepted it. And suddenly, in the spring of 1985, Premier René Lévesque proposed to join the nine other provinces on his own terms. They included, as "the essential prerequisite," the recognition of the Quebec people's distinct character and society; their almost complete exclusion from the national Charter of Rights and Freedoms; their power to contract out of constitutional amendments touching their vital interests, and many additional powers to guarantee their control of their unique business.

Most Canadians outside Quebec regarded Lévesque's demands as an attempt to revive the separatist doctrine of "sovereignty association," defeated in the referendum of 1980, to smuggle it into the Constitution by the back door under a new label. Lévesque indignantly denied these ulterior motives, but he surely knew that at least some of his terms were not negotiable. No Canadian Parliament would exclude any province from the Charter, which must apply to all of them or become a piecemeal, worthless safeguard of freedom, a mere sham.

What, the nine other provinces asked, was Lévesque trying to accomplish? Did he seriously expect the Constitution to be revised on his terms? Was he engaged in a preliminary bargaining gambit? Or was he contriving a popular strategy for the next provincial election after his retirement in the autumn of 1985.

Such as yet unanswered questions posed a nagging dilemma for Mulroney because he was pledged to bring Quebec into the constitutional accord on honourable terms not yet clarified in public or, one supposes, in his own mind. Like all his predecessors, he will do what the art of the possible allows as events unfold. Whatever he does, the Constitution, though doubtless amended in detail, cannot be fundamentally overhauled to abrogate the evolution of a century.

Its full results, since the watershed of 1926, have yet to come. So have the results of Canada's failure to advance far and fast enough in economic management.

4

THE
LEPER'S
BELL

Among all sciences of the Western world, economics has
long been judged the most dismal. Not only dismal but everywhere
(notably in Canada) the most discredited and least understood. In
moments of despair a layman is inclined to think that the economist,
if he has a conscience, should carry a leper's bell when he lectures the
ignorant public. Even the science of politics, however denigrated,
claims more respect than economics. This may be unfair, since most
economists are men of integrity. But their professional reputation is
now at its nadir.

In my own trade I have encountered dozens of economists, such
men as John Kenneth Galbraith (whose heresies distress his fellows);
Paul Samuelson (who holds very different views); advisers to the
American president (who always defend his policies even when they
disagree with them); professors in the London School of Economics
(who quarrel over their beer); savants of Paris and Rome (who quarrel
more passionately over long gourmet lunches); German experts (who,
also eating well, had performed a postwar miracle), and other lively
denizens of the same dismal environment.

None of us can escape the osmotic influence of such men. Right or
wrong, they command the respect of governments and frame policies

touching everybody. Still less do we escape the humdrum economic imperatives of daily life, however boring and uncomfortable we find them.

If humans cannot live by bread alone, assuredly they cannot live without it, preferably with some jam as well. Every household in the land, from the richest to the poorest, is an economic organism of sorts. And fortunately, the average household budget is better managed than that of any government. Otherwise the nation would have collapsed in bankruptcy long ago.

Why mention this melancholy record? Because it haunts us today and threatens much worse damage tomorrow. Our ignorance of economics, in government and household alike, is dangerous to our living standard and the whole democratic process, for politics and economics are Siamese twins—they can never be separated, as we have good reason to know in Canada where we have so grossly botched them both.

The original question always returns to fret and perplex us: Where do we actually stand? The answer is depressing.

True enough, Canada ranks among the seven major industrial nations in the Western world despite its small population. It stands with them at the Economic Summit. But as reckoned in per capita consumption, its living standard, once the second highest, exceeded only by that of the United States, now ranks below those of some smaller nations like Switzerland, Denmark, Sweden and the oil-rich sheikdoms of the Middle East. And the Canadian standard is likely to fall during the next few years unless the nation's business methods are improved and the Third World's poverty is relieved.

Concerning tomorrow's prospects, the economists quarrel and the politicians outpromise one another, but life cannot be measured in their terms. It involves much more than consumption of bread and butter. Or, as Pierre Trudeau put it in a speech never repeated, the worship of the Great God Gross National Product is a religion sterile and nonproductive. Nonetheless, its worshippers are more numerous than those of any other religion, and it gains new acolytes year by year in a secular age, an age of countless economic theories, none of them working satisfactorily.

Still, all factors considered—consumption, physical environment, safety of person, individual liberty and our native pursuit of happiness—Canada probably enjoys as high a real living standard as any on earth. Few of its inhabitants would choose to live anywhere else, not even in the supposedly richer Republic beside them.

But their economy does not operate as it should, and would if well managed. Admirably built for a vanished world, it no longer serves in the new world of technology, and it must be rebuilt from top to bottom. In the jargon and code words of the dismal science, we need a new "industrial strategy" which, on examination, usually turns out to be the old strategy with added semantic trimmings.

Most of the computers, flow charts, diagrams and statistical projections that enchanted the young Trudeau (and produced only laughter in the supposedly ignorant Mike Pearson) have been wrong, compounding the blunders of the past.

To quote again the economically illiterate but pawky Robert Burns, "The best laid schemes o' mice an' men gang aft a-gley." All of them are subject to an iron law of politics, what may be called the Law of Inevitable Contradiction. On taking office governments will commonly do the opposite of their promises and honest intentions, for they have to live with circumstances foreseen by no computer, no economist, no prophet. Economics is allowed no immunity to this and other laws. Like politics, it keeps changing as it reflects changing human demands, buying or saving habits, fashions and fads.

Learned scholars write books to describe various economic systems, past and present. But what is a system? Nothing more than the way people have earned a livelihood since they emerged from the first system of hunting animals and gathering wild food. Systems, so-called, change fast, human nature slowly.

In any serious study of the present North American system, the first fact to be noted is that the continent lives too much on its depleted capital, like a man who drinks champagne while his house burns down. This precious capital of nature cannot be reckoned in known figures. It includes the productive soil, the potable water, the breathable air, life's essentials, as well as forests and nonrenewable supplies of oil, gas and minerals. The collective capital known as the infrastructure, built by man, has not yet been reckoned either and it, too, is depleted. The cost of repairing neglected and weak bridges, inadequate railways and highways, broken sewers, polluted waterworks and decaying city cores undoubtedly will run into billions or trillions of dollars.

The private structure of many great industries is in need of similar basic repair. More jobs could be created in this work than in the booming military-industrial complex and the armaments race. But governments the world over have not yet found a way of switching from weapons of destruction to usable goods of peace.

No government ventures to make a total reckoning of social necessities. The immediate money deficits are enough to require all the skill of politics and economics without considering the future balance sheet. Its true deficits are too frightening for public acknowledgement.

Behind the figures, known and unknown, lurks a blazing fallacy. Thus we are told by the influential London *Economist* that our tiny, overcrowded planet contains ample resources for every human need and no real deficit. If necessary, science can manufacture food out of stone for an unlimited population. Even if this were mathematically true, the fallacy remains. The fair, or tolerable, distribution of food and other necessities to the poor peoples is a task that baffles all governments however generous their intentions. A political more than an economic problem, it is belatedly attracting some of the world's best minds. In Canada it attracted the spacious Trudeau mind but with no visible results when the United States and other rich nations were unwilling to share enough of their wealth with the needy. The North-South dialogue attempted by Trudeau was soon muted.

At least Canada tried to play a modest part in a task which cannot be safely postponed much longer. It will fail altogether if the rich keep refusing to buy the products of the poor who, lacking sufficient exports, cannot pay their astronomical foreign debts and live a tolerable and peaceful life.

Of more immediate domestic concern to Canadians was Trudeau's egregious neglect of practical affairs. With all his sympathy for the unfortunate, his policies, or nonpolicies, his deficits and taxes, bedevilled the business of his own people by some fifteen years of erratic experiment, advances, retreats and futile gestures. In retrospect we can see that his brilliant mind could not master the dismal science, and it repelled him.

Trudeau's first steps as prime minister had been sober and responsible. To win the 1968 election, he offered no financial bait to the voters, promised the central bank to offer none and kept his promise. But in the following year he took fright. Raging inflation, he discovered, had endangered the whole economy and somehow must be contained. Deflationary measures were then imposed and a commission appointed to enforce them. It barely outlasted the year. Now the government was terrified by unemployment. The brakes were eased again. The inflationary fever chart rose to a new high but it did not terrify the government, for the Canadian boom also kept rising, and the solemn warnings of previous years were forgotten.

By 1971 the government seemed to regard inflation as a normal though regrettable fact of life in a sophisticated society. No Canadian would be seriously injured by galloping prices because all wages and pensions would be increased to keep pace with them. The magic Index had been immaculately conceived and painlessly born.

The discovery that inflation, a dangerous threat in 1969, was relatively harmless two years later oddly came from men who had studied economics at prestigious Canadian and foreign universities. Some noneconomists were unconvinced. The men of power admitted only that if Canada priced itself out of the world market, the international results would be serious. And they soon were.

What Trudeau did not yet grasp was that the results already had become serious in Canadian politics at a critical moment. But he must face them in his second election, scheduled for the summer or autumn of 1972 on the inane slogan of "The Land Is Strong." Unwisely, he postponed it until the end of October, and meanwhile the Conservative leader, Robert Stanfield, was rapidly gaining on him. Even without the delay, the outcome probably would have been bad for the government. By autumn it was disastrous. A prime minister who, only four years earlier, had swept the country in a spasm of Trudeaumania, lost his majority in Parliament.

Although amazed, shaken and no doubt incredulous, Trudeau took his defeat with a brave smile on television, explaining that the universe always evolved as it should. His colleagues found no solace in his cosmic vision. What, then, had deceived him? Above all, inflation. His Index was a political flop and an economic absurdity.

Now the government must govern with a Liberal minority paying Danegeld to the astute David Lewis and his New Democratic splinter. That price was paid in full with higher expenditures, inadequate taxes, resulting deficits and a new outburst of inflation. The fever chart spurted upward again.

Still, Trudeau told his cabinet that he relished the experience, the adventure. Doubtless he did. Had he not written, in the first paragraph of his first youthful book, that he was always happiest when opposing the opinions of others? His colleagues were not made of such stern stuff. They found no happiness in a minority government. Only Trudeau seemed to enjoy an interval of masochism.

All this time the central problem of inflation remained unsolved, hardly considered by the government while its Socialist allies tightened their grip to punish what Lewis had joyfully described as "the corporate welfare bums" of Big Business whom today's government regards as the essential architects of prosperity.

It was a time of continuing inflationary boom that could not last and already had begun to convince the voters of their mistake in defeating Stanfield. This modest, quiet man from Halifax, a far better economist than Trudeau, a sardonic wit in private but no television actor, would have made an excellent prime minister, much foolery avoided.

The media had not begun to appreciate his true worth. With peculiar brutality they exaggerated his lack of synthetic stagecraft, as if it mattered. But it made him the ideal butt for cartoonists and columnists. To this end the camera was a wonderful help, eagerly picturing him when he failed to catch a football. That fumble, however irrelevant, was damaging in the age of sport and politics as theatre. It was also a bleak commentary on the intelligence of the press and the public.

What came from Trudeau's hairline survival had not satisfied the nation or even the NDP splinter, despite its lavish Danegeld. By May 1974 Lewis, as a man of principle, tired of the parliamentary charade and, voting with the Conservatives, defeated John Turner's budget. The resulting election was one of the most confused and spurious on record.

Stanfield proposed temporary state control of wages, prices and profits. With searing and shameless ridicule, Trudeau denounced the Conservative policy as unworkable, absurd. "Zap, you're frozen!" he jeered from coast to coast, and by this bogus hue and cry managed to restore some shreds of his lost glamour.

He won his third mandate but, it soon appeared, on false pretences, for now prices were rising beyond public tolerance, and Trudeau realized that something, anything, must be done to curb them. In sudden desperation he then performed the grand somersault of his career. On national television he announced that zap, wages, prices and profits would be frozen after all as Stanfield had proposed, though the Conservative formula was slightly altered to make it look different in Liberal custody.

It was not different. It was the same except for rhetorical flourishes and Trudeau's promise to "wrestle inflation to the ground." In the next few years, however, the government seemed to be unzapped, the political universe again evolving as it should.

This is a weary tale, largely forgotten, but it must be remembered before we can understand what is happening around us now. And only half the tale has yet been told here.

5

THE
BIG
DRUNK

While the politicians of every label continued to strike their customary attitudes and play their genial games, the nation as a whole took leave of its economic senses. Few Canadians yet saw that the Big Boom of nearly four decades was an aberration, unnaturally long, and could not be sustained. It had fooled the public in Canada and all the rich nations as they had often been fooled before, apparently learning little or nothing from past experience.

There seemed to be no end to the boom when the presiding economists of government and business had mastered the new art of fine tuning, had broken the secret of perpetual motion. Statistics, computers and the best professional judgement showed only rising prosperity ahead, with minor, healthy adjustments unless, of course, the stupid politicians aborted the Good Life.

Some obscure economists had not been fooled. They doubted the mass wisdom but, lacking mass influence, went unheard. Humbler folk, with no intellectual barriers or economic learning to stand in the way of common sense, also doubted the fine tune played in Ottawa.

Along the rustic lane where I live, for instance, the neighbours were skeptical of governments and economists, but they could not altogether escape the prevailing ambience of euphoria. It was reasonable for them, they agreed, to buy a second automobile and, if possible, a speed boat, to travel in the adjacent American states and plan tours in Europe or Asia. Not only were these plans within their reach, or soon would be, they were sound economics. They stimulated business. Prosperity was Canada's birthright.

Few if any governments the world over accepted a truth too simple for the comprehension of the expert mind that prosperity never ceases to wax and wane at the mercy of climate, crops, war, disease and human error. Canada refused to admit, if it even suspected, that it had been on a Big Drunk ever since war, not government, had ended the Great Depression.

Now a Big Hangover must soon face a country whose habits had become un-Canadian as it fled from sobriety, from its natural roots. And of this unnatural transformation politics was an accurate mirror.

Trudeau had done nothing to arrest the flight, though he occasionally muttered vague warnings and then fell silent. Perhaps his mind was secretly troubled but not enough to make him discipline his spendthrift government and adoring Liberal Party. Himself personally sober, he tolerated the national spree, heedless of the morning after. He no longer enjoyed the old pleasure of defying the majority will.

The morning after had been coming since the Pearson government took office. Its rapturous Sixty Days of Action produced Walter Gordon's first budget with its tax experiments, the masterpiece of his whiz kids from Toronto. That was an honest mistake, but for a politician it looked shattering.

Despite such a bitter lesson, the making of budgets has not changed. As in 1963 so today the budget, pivot of economic management and election victory, offers the strangest exhibit of cabinet solidarity. The full cabinet, never leakproof, is seldom allowed to see the work of the finance minister and his advisers until no change can be made. By the time the budget reaches cabinet, texts have usually been sent, under seal and release date, to the branches of the central banks in Canada and foreign capitals.

In 1963 Paul Hellyer and others vainly protested that Gordon's new taxes would not work. The prime minister, busy with larger problems, hoped they would. When the budget immediately turned into a fiasco, Gordon tendered his resignation. Pearson would not accept it and part with his closest friend, but he had grown wary.

The gulf of basic principle between the two men—an internationalist prime minister and a nationalist colleague—was so obvious that I brashly mentioned it to Pearson. For the first and last time in our long association he flushed in anger and told me to mind my own business. Later he realized that the gulf could not be spanned. The ruptured friendship of Pearson and Gordon was mended only in Pearson's final days of life.

After the fiasco, Gordon withdrew his budget and revised it, partially satisfying his cabinet and business critics. Governments often have to make some revisions of detail, even of substance, while always explaining that they had meant something quite different from the start. Gordon, however, had never meant something different. Shorn of direct (though not of indirect) power, he remains at this writing a sincere, unreconstructed nationalist and protectionist, trained in Big Business but still the social reformer on the left wing of Liberalism. The craft of politics is hard on personal friendships.

Bernard Shaw well described this clash of ideological faiths. The New Left, he said, was simply the Old Right with the nonsense knocked out of it. But enough nonsense survived for both in our time. Believers and nonbelievers on both sides are equally skewed, politicians, economists and citizens equally at sea.

Here we encounter a curious quirk in typical right-wing corporate thinking. Managers of big or small business preach the virtue of private enterprise and the abuses of government when it invades the economic system. Simultaneously they demand, and often get, the aid of government. What else is the tariff? What else are loans, guarantees and subsidies of various kinds to ailing corporations?

Extolled in luncheon speeches, unlimited competition is admirable but, the speakers warn, it can be unfair and destructive in the market. These rites would hardly surprise Adam Smith, the market's father. Had he not said that whenever two or more businessmen assembled they instinctively conspired against the public? On the other hand, he knew, as events would prove after his time, that only private enterprise could ensure adequate growth. It was and remains the vital engine of prosperity.

And Karl Marx. What would he say now? Would he admit the manifest failure of his dream system wherever it has been imposed? In honesty he could not pretend otherwise. But he could claim a moral victory of sorts over his anti-Communist enemies. Like him, many business executives and labour leaders are unconscious economic determinists, though many others have learned social responsibility. The less responsible type disparage noneconomic values as true and important only in the unreal world of theory and politics. Such men fail to see that business and government, no matter how honest, often have basically dissimilar motives, purposes and necessities. The difference between them was well described by Dean Acheson with his long experience in both.

When a successful businessman enters government, Acheson wrote, he finds that the rules and customs of the private sector are virtually useless to him. He is not free to buy and sell, to hire and fire, for the sake of efficiency and profit. He is governed by laws he did not make and may consider insane. He is forced to deal not with figures on a balance sheet but with living, incalculable humanity, and in the end with votes. While he can draw flawless blueprints to show how things should be done, he lacks the power to implement his plans unless the law makers agree with him. Thus the money-making art is no apprenticeship for an art much more complex.

Among the latest business generation, thoughtful men and women of business have learned to understand why government cannot always imitate their methods even if, in money terms, it is the largest business of the Western world. They realize, too, that their system, like government, must change with the changing times. Some ideas once regarded as ruinous have proved to be successful and are here to stay. Others have failed, but the business system, naturally tough, resilient and durable, must live with them until they can be improved through the political process, with more changes to come.

In short, government and business are groping through the new age towards ends seen by neither. For neither will the task be easy or pleasant, but it is inescapable and unnecessarily hard if the two powers cannot learn to understand each other more clearly than they do now.

The search for a fairer process is one of the cardinal imperatives in all free societies and one of the most painful, baffling and dubious in its result, still a long way off.

Whatever the result, whatever the economic system of the future may be, the market will remain in some form. The harsh adversarial bargaining process, with all its flaws, has endured as supposedly the best that flawed human nature can provide. But the flaws cannot be permanently endured without correction because the quarrels of the adversaries in government, business and the labour unions too often mutilate the helpless community at large. A less disruptive process must be devised and is now beginning to evolve in slow, clumsy experiments varying from nation to nation.

Perhaps the most successful American experimenter is Lee Iacocca who, with state underwriting, rescued the Chrysler Corporation on the verge of ruin and became an instant folk hero. More clearly than his competitors, he recognized that no economy can isolate itself from government, that there never has been real isolation. The practical concern, as he sees it, is the wisdom, method and degree of integration, not in vague theory but in each specific case like his own. Some failing private enterprises can be rescued by their managers, labour unions and government working together. Some cannot and will die, slow or fast.

Whatever else, Iacocca's method means continued state intervention, always assuming that it is wisely used and only where the state's presence is needed. Wise corporate management seems willing to accept all the resulting risks, and he overcame them in his business. No doubt he knows that many industries have been as foolish as governments in their affairs and exist on the taxpayers' subsidies direct or, like the tariff, indirect.

Once he had written a book to explain his rationale, the message travelled far, reaching even distant British Columbia. There a right-wing Social Credit government read the book with others like it and thought furiously. Having long resisted intervention (with the usual contradictions of policy) it changed course overnight and sought new co-operation between the three natural economic partners in a province noted for their quarrels.

The British Columbia experiment, the effort to revive local industries by tax incentives, cheap electricity or other benefits, at the cost of budgetary deficits, will be worth national attention and already is getting it. Consciously or unconsciously, Premier William Bennett has undertaken a kind of Hegelian synthesis, merging the thesis of private enterprise and the antithesis of the expanding state. He thus sponsors "tripartism," which the unions have long opposed as an employer's threat to their interests. The results in British Columbia and other provinces are not yet measurable.

Canada had enforced a primitive Iacoccaism ever since French pioneers settled here. Nothing else could have built the CPR, spanned a continent and built our modern society. From the beginning the Canadian economy was more "mixed" than its American competitor. So it had to be and so it remains now as Canadian government has stood relatively left of centre. That either economy can be unmixed is a notion dear to the hearts of some business executives but not to bold thinkers like Iacocca and his counterparts in Canada.

Other notions are also out of date. It is widely supposed, for example, that Canadian expenditures on social services exceed those of most industrial nations. In fact, Canada ranks sixth among them, according to a recent survey by the Organization for Economic Co-operation and Development (OECD). It is supposed that Canada's tax rates are comparatively high, but they rank fourteenth among the twenty-three OECD members. Again, it is supposed that the Mulroney government has reduced the public payroll when, including the armed services, it has been increasing, though its future reduction is promised.

The confusion of our political parties Conservatism becoming more internationalist, Liberalism more nationalist is interesting but not surprising. It reflects the same confusion in the public mind. What matters is the clear breach between politicians of all parties who think that our economic problems can be solved by increased governmental spending and those who, like Mulroney, insist that the existing budgetary deficit must somehow be reduced before the economy can hope to prosper.

However this dispute is compromised, nothing alters the fact that the economy does not fit the present, much less the future, world. (Whether it should fit itself into the economy of the United States is a question of daunting magnitude for later consideration here.) Another certainty should not be forgotten—unemployment on the existing scale cannot forever be safely tolerated under any system. Idleness, especially among the young, even if its victims are supported by the state, is no substitute for useful work. Nor are mere hobbies and enforced leisure. While robots may eventually replace countless human workers, they are no substitute, either. Men and women need to feel that they are doing a useful job of some kind; as the great Justice Wendell Holmes put it, they must "function."

They cannot function on doles however generous, and they will always disagree, bargain and try to get maximum personal rewards from an always unjust society. Greed is an inherent part of human nature. So is the charity that moves them to sacrifice, suffering and triumphs of the spirit unknown in other species. We are all creatures of erratic contrasts and conflicts, never reckonable. And that is the central fact, or platitude, of politics and economics everywhere.

As a rule the Left, even when it extolls socialism, is economically determinist like the Right. The labour unions, operating in the market, seek an increased portion of the total pie. Having grasped it from their employers or from the unorganized majority of workers, they wrangle among themselves over the individual shares. Within the craft the reward is subdivided between the older, more skilled members and the younger, less skilled.

This is normal as equality is not. In every aspect of society, economic or intellectual, some kind of hierarchal ranking order prevails. On both sides of the bargaining table the same mixed morality also prevails. Each side has much of right and wrong to teach the other. Neither can long resist the market. Nor can any power on earth. Even OPEC, after deranging oil prices, was itself deranged by the law of supply and demand that may grind slowly, like the gods' mill, but grinds exceeding fine.

No alternative to the law, however amended, can long maintain and nourish employers or workers in a private enterprise system. At some point the market, domestic or international, will have its way. Before that point is reached the sharp edge of a domestic market under a nation's control may be dulled in the public interest, its social damage minimized. To temper the law of supply and demand and restrain its abuses is a major concern of any respectable society and constantly frustrates its good intentions. But the international market rises and falls like the ocean tides, benefiting some groups, damaging others.

Samuel Gompers, chief architect of the present American union, well understood the domestic market and tried to use it for the advantage of the workers. Labour, he said, should punish its enemies and reward its friends. Like his capitalistic enemies (or friends in disguise), he was a natural free enterpriser. He knew that the all-powerful state, under any name, had no place for unions with any power of their own. So it turned out in the rigid Marxist state of Russia, though Marx could not recognize his illegitimate offspring.

To the first great economist of my acquaintance the wild gyrations of the marketplace look obsolete and unnecessarily cruel. When I met

John Kenneth Galbraith in the middle of the Second World War, this immigrant from Ontario was administering a loose, selective, flimsy price control law for the United States government. He warned me that Canada, having just frozen its whole economy, must fail altogether. Its scheme, he said, was unworkable. On the contrary, as he confessed a year later, it became a spectacular success; the United States soon imitated it.

Galbraith was young then, a modest fellow distinguished only by his height of nearly seven feet and his gift of sardonic language. The discovery of his genius had not yet occurred and, with it, the soaring flight of his ego. When we last met at Harvard, he could claim to be perhaps the most celebrated economist in the Western world after Keynes, his earlier idol.

Has Galbraith been right in his belief that capital and labour live in good times as unacknowledged blood brothers maximizing their profits and wages in sham-battle negotiations at the cost of the consumer, the ultimate victim, who pays the price of their gains? Was he right when he gradually perfected the Galbraithian thesis, improved on Keynes and declared that the consumer must be permanently safeguarded by direct controls of profits, wages and prices in the giant industries operating outside the market, while their small competitors operated within it? On all such questions the answers will vary from economist to economist. The layman must consult his own oracle, his prejudice or, perhaps better, his hunch.

Certainly Galbraith was right in arguing that the economic system of our time is as different from its schoolbook model as a mummy is different from a living man. But Galbraith went too far in asserting that business corporations, if large and powerful enough, can always dominate their own markets, defy their less powerful competitors and operate as they please. There Galbraith was wrong.

The huge American steel, automotive, forest, textile and other industries argue that they cannot meet what they call unfair foreign competition and must be protected against it. They are not as invulnerable as Galbraith assumed. But the recession of the 1980s confirmed his rather obvious prediction that high interest rates, used to control inflation, would depress the economy and gravely injure the poor, at least for the time being.

This, of course, was foreseen by the Federal Reserve Board when it deliberately increased the rates in spite of the political and economic fallout. What else could it (and the Bank of Canada) do? Since governments refused to keep their budgets in reasonable order, there was no available brake on inflation except harsh monetary policies. Thus left to make the unpopular decisions, the money managers in Washington and Ottawa took the blame for the immediate results while most politicians tried to dodge or blur them. But the harsh anti-inflation remedy succeeded.

After my last talk with Galbraith at Harvard University, I met his world-famous neighbour and friend, Paul Samuelson, whose work had earned a Nobel Prize. He did not share Galbraith's faith in state control of prices levied by the few hundred corporations supposedly immune to the free market. Prices, Samuelson told me, could not be directly controlled for long in a private enterprise system. They were workable only in times of acute emergency like war. Later he candidly admitted in print that he knew no way, in a free society, to guarantee unbroken prosperity and eliminate the familiar cycles of inflation and deflation, economic growth and shrinkage. Samuelson lacked Galbraith's omniscience.

Private enterprisers generally insist that the state is mostly to blame for society's sea of troubles, as witness the gross blunders of government. But the blunders are sometimes no worse than those of the market, as witness the reckless loans issued by the private banks, including those of Canada, to foreign borrowers who can never repay their debts, let alone, in some cases, the interest charges.

If, clearly, the errors of government and business are mutual, so are the talents when concentrated in the right places. If the state is a bad manager of business, the businessman, as demonstrated by Herbert Hoover, Neville Chamberlain and R. B. Bennett, among others, is typically a bad manager of the state.

Nonetheless, every government needs a few businessmen like Clifford Sifton and C. D. Howe, men who, in the right places, cut red tape, discard outworn methods, flout convention and get things done. Without them the Canadian wartime economy could not have been built. Without them any government will mismanage its massive growing share of the peacetime economy. The lack of such men in the Trudeau government was one of its major weaknesses.

The efficiency of government and private enterprise often tends to shrink with growth. Giantism has the theoretical economies and advantages of scale, but bigness is not always efficient nor socially responsible. Sometimes, as Louis Brandeis asserted in his memorable dictum, bigness can be a curse, inherited from the early, primitive days of industrialism. Even so wise a Supreme Court justice could not imagine the modern American industries bigger than some nations, their internal politics as ruthless as that of any government, their efficiency outcompeted by foreign newcomers to the market.

Hence the puzzle of an economy that we call "mixed," a convenient but meaningless label. Of course the economy is mixed and always has been since the first exchange of food and women between wandering tribes of cave dwellers. Mixed, yes, but what is the present and what is the desirable mixture? What will it be in the new world of technology? Around that question our society revolves and will keep revolving, the question never finally answered, the mixture always changing.

At the moment it is said that the private sector advances, the state withdraws, conservatism triumphs, liberalism wanes. But this may have been said too quickly by nostalgists like President Reagan, whose knowledge of history was too limited. Preaching the return of the good old days, his government vastly expanded the total state apparatus. It curbed expenditures on social welfare while increasing those of the defence establishment which, directly and indirectly, is the largest American industry.

The good old days, as Reagan remembered them, were not returning after all. Good or bad, they were gone forever. In preindustrial societies a messenger of such unwelcome news would have been killed or hurled over the rim of the economic abyss as if he had created it. Today he gets the softer treatment of mere contempt. Anyone who mentions today's plain facts is widely impeached by private enterprisers as a champion of the state, even if it horrifies him. In Reagan and his Canadian counterparts, nostalgia aches like a decaying tooth. The hope of recovering things unrecoverable is a pain not to be soon, or possibly ever, alleviated.

Long and varied Canadian experience had preceded it. Into the mixed economy between the world wars, the Keynesian revolution was brought to Ottawa from London by an unlikely messenger, the youthful Robert Bryce. He had heard the message from the original source and on it rose to the highest ranks of the civil service. The flaming arrow shot across the Atlantic still burns in Ottawa, though dimly, under the politicians' neglect.

What Maynard Keynes recommended is generally forgotten or misconstrued nowadays when other economic theories are in fashion. His proposition simply (perhaps too simply) stated is as old in essence as Pharaonic Egypt where Joseph filled the granaries in good crop years to feed the people in bad ones. So, too, the Iroquois stored corn against the cold North American winter. In a modern society, of course, the process is infinitely more complicated but the objective is the same.

Observing the economic lunacy of the 1930s, young Keynes saw that a lack of public purchasing power, even in the richest countries, had made the Great Depression inevitable. Therefore the medium of exchange should be more widely distributed by higher governmental expenditures and lower taxes, at the cost of budgetary deficits and debt. Then the economy would prosper. Or, to use President John Kennedy's favourite campaign metaphor, a rising tide lifts all boats just as an ebb tide strands them.

At first glance, Keynes seemed to be reviving the crude inflation practised by Roman and Chinese emperors and later by such English kings as Henry VIII. In fact, Keynes was proposing something entirely different, something so new and drastic that the world's contemporary leaders needed several years to grasp (or misunderstand) it.

Only in depressed times, Keynes wrote, should the money supply, for the most part in the form of credit or figures on the balance sheets of the central banking system, be expanded. Once prosperity returned, the money supply must be curtailed, the extra public debt repaid out of higher taxes, lower expenditures and resulting budgetary surpluses. For laymen's understanding, Keynes called his remedy the "cyclical budget," balanced or unbalanced over a period of several years, to counteract the age-old business cycle.

Like all remedies, medical or economic, the Keynesian proposal was subject to dangerous abuse when administered by the amateur physicians of politics. Oddly enough, the sophisticated British economist did not foresee how they would exploit and derange his system by running deficits in good times as in bad. The cyclical became a political budget, taxes reduced on the eve of an election but seldom, or never, raised adequately when the election had been won.

Unless that cycle is broken, the result must be perpetual inflation, governments paying off their debts to honest citizens with devalued money. In the skill of legal counterfeiting the modern governments of Canada proved to be especially adept. Before elections they reheated an already hot economy until the treasury's boiler neared the bursting point. The citizen's bond and the worker's pay cheque were worth less than half of their earlier value.

But when the Keynesian experiment was brought to Ottawa, all went well. The pioneers of the new system understood exactly what they were doing and, more important, what they must not do. After the war they obeyed the master's instructions, replacing the economic accelerator with the brake. The budget was not only balanced but moved into surplus by a courageous prime minister, Louis St. Laurent, and his quick-learning finance minister, Douglas Abbott. Just as Keynes had prescribed, the swollen war debt was reduced and inflation curbed until the Korean War rekindled it everywhere.

In economic principle the government had been right, in politics wrong. Fighting the 1957 election, John Diefenbaker enjoyed a sudden revelation and denounced surplus budgets as "over-taxation," the cause of rising prices. If the revelation was mere drivel, it helped to ensure his victory. The burden of its age, complacency and mistakes broke the Liberal regime even though its total vote was higher than that of its successor. A minority Conservative government seemed likely to hold office for a long time. As usual, prophecy erred.

How all this experience affects Canada will be told here from a later angle of vision. Meanwhile Keynes's theory had become a travesty wherever it was invoked and distorted. The master himself had begun to lose faith in politicians. As early as 1933, after meeting Franklin Roosevelt, Keynes said to Frances Perkins, secretary of labor, that he had "supposed that the president was more literate, economically speaking."

The irony did not end there. Roosevelt had entered the White House as a budget balancer, assailing Herbert Hoover's wild extravagance, and soon launched a New Deal of deficits, unaware of its consequences and unable to comprehend Keynes's "rigmarole of figures." Then the new president torpedoed the London economic conference and doomed any immediate hope of worldwide business recovery.

Caricatured and farced, the British prophet needed more time to realize the enormity of his betrayal, to see that the betrayers had finally turned his benign hatchling into a cockatrice. Not until his last years did Keynes clearly understand how far politics and economics had moved in opposite directions. Then, too late, he wrote a book to explain what had gone wrong and died before he could finish his work.

All this time King had watched from Ottawa the spectacle in Washington. After one of his meetings with Roosevelt, he informed me that the president was economically illiterate but a very great man. Not yet for King a Canadian New Deal. Although now wavering back to his youthful radicalism, he still remained, in misty principle, a laissez faire Liberal. Re-elected in 1935, he warned Parliament that it was impossible to spend the country out of depression into prosperity. He was learning all the same.

Bennett had learned, or unlearned, faster, thanks to his brother-in-law, W. D. Herridge. As Canadian ambassador to Washington, Herridge had drunk deep at Roosevelt's magic fountain and carried a trickle from it posthaste to Ottawa. Reluctantly, and only because his government was near the end of its term and tether, Bennett reversed his lifelong economic creed and announced his own New Deal in 1935. Even Trudeau could not match such a somersault.

King condemned Bennett's apostasy as senseless and mostly unconstitutional. That was a mistake equal to King's worst previous lapse when, in office, he had refused to give "a single five-cent piece" to any bankrupt province governed by Conservatives. It was not only a mistake but it blinded him to the need of his own subsequent apostasy.

Already the depression should have taught both political parties at least enough to question the old givens and to cultivate a new field of experiment. In terms of human misery, failure on both sides of politics was tragic beyond possible exaggeration.

The thirties are now remembered as a tale told by official idiots— food supplies abundant, thousands of Canadians hungry, drought searing the prairies, unemployed youngsters riding freight trains in search of work and finding none, herded into government camps, parading, striking, rioting, social morality abandoned under Bennett and then King, each a pious Christian, their budgets sacred, human beings expendable.

Canada no longer seemed Canadian. It was indeed a time to try men's souls and overwhelm their intelligence, a time never to be forgotten by those who lived through it. And the depression could have been cured, or even forestalled, if the great nations had followed Keynes's advice instead of clinging to the old classic rules of a time now past. But the advice had been planted deeper than the politicians guessed. Henceforth it must change the dismal science forever.

Before then King was lucky, as always, in losing the election of

1930. He pretended afterward that he had wanted to lose it. Not so. He desperately tried to win and expected to win.

Bennett, with invariable Conservative ill luck, won power at the worst of times, and they destroyed him. His Pyrrhic victory had defeated King but not the depression. His morning glory lasted little more than a year, though his bold adventure of 1932 apparently crowned it. At Ottawa he assembled a grand assize of the Commonwealth to promote its interdependence and expand its profitable trade, and retaliate against sky-high United States tariffs. Bennett was resolved to "blast" his way into prosperity or "perish in the attempt."

The original thinking behind a doomed enterprise had come from the fertile mind of Lord Beaverbrook, who was Bennett's oldest, closest friend. Neville Chamberlain, Britain's peerless economic thinker, welcomed these plans with public enthusiasm and some private misgivings. None of the eminent trio suspected that the whole idea was hopeless, a formula for deepening depression. The Commonwealth was too small and too poor a *Zollverein* to live prosperously hived off from the world market and, besides, foreign nations were sure to retaliate against the Commonwealth's protective tariffs.

Even if the scheme had been sound, as it certainly was not, the Ottawa conference botched it by increasing these tariffs without significantly reducing the barriers already erected between the Commonwealth members themselves. The theory of autarchy, self-containment and bootstrap economics quickly perished. So did its Canadian author, Bennett, when he was belatedly seeking freer trade with the United States.

A silent spectator in the gallery of Parliament had not been surprised by the performance on the floor. Himself bemused, King still clung to his faith in trade, then at a discount. With the guidance of the Invisible Hand, he would fade out the Ottawa agreements. But he still had much more to learn about modern economics, and about Bennett. His future lessons were taught in the agony of war.

6

THE MAGIC
OF MONEY

Depression had spawned more than Bennett's New Deal, King's slow turnabout and the new thinking in Ottawa. It had spawned everywhere, but mainly in the western provinces, local variants and local prophets of the Keynesian school. Above all, it spawned an almost mystical faith in money as the sovereign remedy for every ill that the economic system was heir to. Spread enough public purchasing power today and tomorrow will take care of itself. That notion is not yet dead.

At Regina a conventicle of 135 farmers, churchmen, labour unionists and radicals of many faiths wrote, in 1933, the Co-operative Commonwealth Federation's original Manifesto. Its plans for social reform did not depend on the magic of money alone. Newly organized Canadian socialism went far beyond such a simple remedy and the doctrines of the two established political parties.

The CCF seemed to swallow the Marxian thesis entire. According to the Manifesto, all means of production were to be taken over by the state or by co-operative industries, capitalism "eradicated," the workers emancipated, the Just Society created long before Trudeau invented his alluring catchword. The Manifesto's life was short. Like Marx's imaginary state, it soon withered away under the impact of political forces too stubborn for theory, too deeply set in an unjust society for quick removal.

Although the West, an always pregnant womb of reform and counterreform, had produced in J. S. Woodsworth a Canadian immortal, it had produced in the CCF no coherent social design. Neither had King nor Bennett, and Trudeau was to produce none. But in M. J. Coldwell, who succeeded Woodsworth during the war, the CCF found another man of noble character with a sense of practical politics.

This Saskatchewan schoolteacher and native of Devon, who never lost his religious faith during a private life of sorrow, had all the needed qualities of a prime minister. Or so I judged him. At one point, in 1943, the opinion polls seemed to place him near the highest office when I was too young and ignorant to appreciate his character. We became close friends later on, and now I deeply regret some mean articles I wrote about him in my careless salad days.

For his part, Coldwell regretted the early mistakes of the CCF, knowing that its Manifesto was unworkable. He also regretted some of his own speeches, uttered in moments of righteous anger. Coldwell's instincts were those of an English country gentleman, as I once told him, and he only grinned at my impudence without rebuke or denial. But nothing ever changed his passionate protest against the injustice he saw around him.

King had recognized Coldwell's talents from the beginning and invited him to join the government since clearly he was a Liberal at heart, standing only a little left of centre. But James Gardiner, the party boss in the West, made sure that no rival would threaten his power base. Coldwell remained in the CCF and was soon recognized as Woodsworth's natural heir.

Meanwhile a new economic alternative had been wafted like a spark across the Atlantic to land in Calgary, of all places. There an otherwise undistinguished schoolteacher, William Aberhart, set it aflame and anointed it with his fundamentalist religion.

How the Social Credit theory, a British invention, had defied geography, or how it could work anywhere, was not clear to anyone. Nor did Aberhart attempt to understand his own evangel, though he was quite sincere and, in a crude fashion, understood politics. Carried to the Alberta premier's office on a wave of public desperation and hope, he ruled at Edmonton like a portly, benign Buddha modelled in glistening white porcelain. Even for a wandering reporter he kindly stayed late in his office, granted an interview, extolled Social Credit but confessed that its details were beyond him.

Accordingly, he had imported English experts, and they would work out the grand strategy. When I ventured to suggest that the money system was under exclusive federal jurisdiction, his reply astounded me. Yes, he said, money was federal but credit was not. The fact that credit was another name for money had escaped him. It had not escaped his advisers. So they undertook to rewrite the Canadian Constitution and give the provinces the necessary control of the exchange medium within their boundaries, while Aberhart proposed to censor the critical newspapers.

Of these plans and their miscarriage I was soon to hear. On a liner bound for England my wife and I were placed, by odd chance, at a table with a charming and talkative Englishman who had been one of the Alberta government's hired experts. His description of it was hilarious. At every cabinet meeting, he said, the premier's wife sat beside him like the matrons of the French Revolution beside the guillotine. Whenever Aberhart grew testy she would admonish him— "Now, now, William!" Then he subsided and listened to the experts, obviously without comprehending their figures and charts.

My fellow passenger had gone too far among his friends by calling the premier "a stranded whale." Accused before the cabinet of this utterance, the offender readily admitted it and was fired on the spot.

Aberhart, his promises and the provincial debt payments defaulted, his press law annulled by the Supreme Court, held office until his death. E. C. Manning, a gradually disillusioned Social Creditor and typical Alberta Conservative, succeeded him and enjoyed a long, successful reign before entering the Senate.

In neighbouring British Columbia money magic took an even gaudier form. There a prophet of eloquence, charisma and mighty voice had arisen in the ruling Liberal Party of Premier Thomas Dufferin Pattullo. Excluded from the cabinet, Gerald ("Gerry Himself") McGeer broke with his leader to pursue his own financial mysticism. McGeer was born for the politics of demagoguery and perfected it at an early age. By providential inspiration, as he always believed, he stumbled on money which could be the final solution of all economic problems. His bulky figure and empurpled nose, complemented by oratory of the same hue and a hoarse mimicry of Roosevelt's Harvard accent, soon became familiar to the whole nation.

In his own province he was not only a member of the legislature and its unofficial opposition leader but also mayor of Vancouver, a local hero. As such, he persuaded his fellow legislators to approve his monetary system, though none of them understood it.

What McGeer had actually proposed was nothing less than governmental management of the economy with fixed wages, prices and interest rates. The nation's purchasing power would be vastly expanded, dangerous inflation somehow avoided and free enterprise preserved but under necessary central discipline. All this could be achieved with the wise use of the money mechanism and its supplementary instruments of control.

By now McGeer had elevated money above politics to the supernatural summit of religion. Abraham Lincoln, he discovered, was like himself a monetary reformer but not the first. Jesus Christ, the first, had driven the money changers and primitive bankers from the temple. Thus inspired, McGeer, a humble Christian, went far, and I often accompanied him on his travels as a reporter, confidant and unwitting press agent. At Calgary he ignored the folly of Alberta's Social Credit and mounted a Church of England pulpit dressed in a long frock coat and flowing white tie, contrasting vividly with the florid face, to preach Eternal Truth.

This was only the beginning of McGeer's adventures. He had yet to reach Ottawa. But he reached it in R. B. Bennett's time and testified as *amicus curiae* before a committee of Parliament. Cross-examining the managers of Canada's private banks, he quickly made them look like schoolboys or fools. They did not seem to know even their own mean business and had no understanding of money as McGeer understood it.

The youngest of the bankers was no fool. In his field he was the best brain of those times. Graham Towers, still in his thirties, had been appointed governor of the central Bank of Canada when Bennett established it in 1934. Bank and governor were Bennett's enduring gifts to the nation.

Both bank and governor had yet to reveal their permanent impact on society. But under questioning, Towers easily overcame McGeer with clipped answers. He seemed to me then a living ledger of facts and nothing more, a creature without humanity, a mechanical man. His tall, lean figure and handsome angular face gave no hint of humour or compassion. He understood central banking and nothing else.

My original impression was entirely wrong. When I came to know Towers intimately, I found him a sparking wit, a raconteur of endless jokes, a mischievous mimic, the darling of Ottawa's Rockcliffe supper parties.

McGeer must have discovered these qualities after their first confrontation. Drinking martinis and lunching together, the strangely assorted pair bandied their wits, Towers always victorious. He, too, had made a discovery long unsuspected by McGeer's friends. The western evangelist of money was preaching, with undoubted sincerity, a system of massive state controls modelled on the Nazi system invented by Hjalmar Schacht, which McGeer frequently praised without endorsing its abuses, not yet fully disclosed.

Condemned for advocating rubber money, McGeer replied that the prewar German army was not made of rubber. Sound monetary management was working in Hitler's Germany and would work here if we only had the sense to adopt it, together with peaceful Christian ethics. Towers was unconvinced. He had his central bank free of politics and was now Ottawa's second most powerful man, but he never exaggerated his power, never supposed, as did McGeer, that money was magical. It had its limits—limits often unrecognized to our day by governments eager to slough their responsibilities off on the bank, force it to print money.

McGeer was all in favour of creating more money, which the new bank could do by a stroke of the governor's pen. No printing press, like that of the latter Bourbon kings, was now required, only the wisdom and will of government. To strengthen them in his work of national salvation, McGeer decided to reach Ottawa not as a witness but as a legislator who never doubted his mission.

When I informed King, now in office again, that McGeer would run for Parliament, the blood faded from the prime minister's cheeks. "Oh, tell him," he cried, "that his place is in British Columbia!" King's warnings were futile. A single province was no longer big enough for the local hero.

In any case, King had an odd notion of politicians on the West Coast. Even the able Pattullo had shocked him. "That man," he once said to me, "thinks every household should have an electrical washing machine!" Such thoughts and men were dangerous and must be resisted. But McGeer was not easily dismissed from his seat in the House of Commons where, though calling himself a Liberal, he attacked the government until King promoted and muted him in the Senate. McGeer's labours had undermined his robust health. A career once so promising and, in some ways, useful to the nation was finished.

After Towers resigned and died too young, he was succeeded by James Coyne, the deputy governor then too blunt for his own good. Friends warned him against the risk of publicly criticizing the government's policies, but nothing could stop Coyne, nothing extinguish his torch. He delivered a series of speeches to picture the approaching disaster of inflation, to advocate tariff protection and to explain the truth of Conservatism as he saw it. Prime Minister Diefenbaker saw it differently and the two men quarrelled.

That quarrel would have destroyed Coyne if Diefenbaker had not begun his own destruction by accusing the governor of personal rapacity in seeking an excessive future pension. Diefenbaker controlled the Commons but not the Liberal Senate which vindicated Coyne, the philosophical Conservative. Well satisfied, Coyne promptly resigned with the admiration of the public.

Something much more important than personalities had been settled by the quarrel. Unlike a Federal Reserve Board legally independent of the United States executive and Congress (because Woodrow Wilson, the great Democrat, distrusted them with money), the Bank of Canada was not autonomous. No one was sure where its power began and ended.

After the Coyne affair, the government waffled on the question. In one breath it proclaimed its control of the bank's monetary policy. In the next it held the bank responsible for the policy's mistakes and resulting economic damage. Coyne's quiet, discreet successor, Louis Rasminsky, rescued the government from its confusion. He interpreted the law to mean that in a case of serious dispute the government could overrule the bank. A governor thus overruled had only the option to resign, as Rasminsky would have done if his money management had been repudiated.

Thereafter no government repudiated the central bank. Yet successive governments, running large budgetary deficits, counted on it to bail them out by creating the required money at the risk, or certainty, of inflation. Since he could not let a government go broke, Rasminsky had to buy some of its bonds and automatically increase the exchange medium through the increased lending power of the private banks.

He was too wise a man to cross the line from banking to governmental policy as Coyne had done. That issue did not arise in Rasminsky's time.

It recurred in the time of the next governor, Gerald Bouey, a deceptively calm man of unbending honesty and iron spine. Politicians and much of the press chose him for their easy target, a sitting duck. In the recession of the early 1980s he was made to look like a sadist resolved to impoverish the nation and grind the faces of the poor, though his aim was the exact opposite. Endlessly questioned by the cabinet and parliamentary committees, he responded, like Towers, in polite, clipped sentences and never yielded an inch.

When Bouey limited the Bank of Canada's purchase of the government's bonds to contain the inflated money supply, Trudeau dared not overrule him at the cost of his resignation and political damage too great to be risked. The Liberal Party was prepared to do many strange things but not to repeat the Coyne affair and the first installment of Diefenbaker's *Götterdämmerung*. The bank thus controlled the volume of the exchange medium, but no monetary policy, however tight, could fully counteract the government's loose fiscal policy and mountainous deficit.

In theory, the bank also controlled interest rates and, according to its critics in Parliament and press, kept them too high when they should have been reduced to stimulate economic growth. In fact, they could not be significantly or safely reduced until the Federal Reserve Board relaxed the monetary policy of the United States, for if the Canadian dropped below the American rate, capital would flee Canada and devastate its economy. So, perforce, Bouey tried to protect the devalued Canadian currency from further devaluation and grimly awaited events in Washington.

They moved fast in 1984, a year of worldwide change with results yet to be reckoned. American business emerged from its slump. Inflation fell to a tolerable rate under the impact of the Feds' tight money (the White House naturally taking credit for this success). Then, as economic growth slowed, the money supply was expanded and interest rates subsided but threatened to rise again under the impact of the government's huge borrowings. These changes across the border automatically reduced Canada's interest rates, though its unemployment rate was little changed. But Canada's recovery, obstructed by the bungles of a decade or more, lagged behind that of its neighbour.

At this writing, nobody can know whether the supply-side experiment in the United States, with its instantaneous effects on Canada, will be a temporary success or an ultimate failure. Many things will happen to warp the most expert prophecy, but always we come back to a fundamental question: Is Canada ready to face the many-sided test, political and psychological, now looming inexorably before it? And the time for some of the hardest choices in the nation's experience already is running out.

A student of history, Brian Mulroney knows, of course, that Canada is less immune than any foreign nation to the shock waves moving from Washington. In his early days of power he studied the American supply-side exercise and imitated bits and pieces, among them tax incentives to stimulate the western oil industry despite heavy revenue losses. Like Reagan, he also believed that the state's distended apparatus could be permanently deflated. But Mulroney and his finance minister, Michael Wilson, rejected Washington's cardinal premise that economic growth of itself would swell revenues enough to cut deficits and eventually balance the budget. If the Canadian government had promised much, too much, it had never duplicated Reagan's promise of a balance in his first term, when he produced a record deficit.

Canada's problem was worse than that of its neighbour because its deficit was proportionately far higher and must be reduced this side of disaster, even if total expenditures kept rising. Most Canadians seemed to agree on a reduction but complained bitterly when any expenditure was cut.

Mulroney was further embarrassed by his pledge to create abundant jobs, to avoid any significant tax increase or any impairment of the safety net protecting the poor. Apparently, Wilson's colleagues expected the minister to pull from his conjurer's hat a rabbit larger than the gigantic invisible Harvey of stage and movie fame.

On 23 May 1985, a date of some historical importance, Wilson introduced his first budget and called it a "fundamental break with the past . . . rewarding success, not subsidizing effort." The Mulroney government was beginning, only beginning, to clear away the rubble left by its predecessors who, out of office, denounced a policy that enriched the rich and further impoverished the poor.

Substantial income and sales taxes broke the opposite pledge given by the Conservative Party to win office, but various tax incentives were applied to business investment. The government relied on risk-taking private enterprise and the "entrepreneurial spirit," not the state, for durable prosperity. The budgetary deficit, which had long failed to create the jobs expected by Liberal governments, was reduced, though very slightly.

How far Canada has actually broken with the past, how far and how soon the state can withdraw from the economy, and when durable prosperity will be achieved, events to come will show, and many of them are at the hazard of a world economy where the nation earns a major, essential part of its livelihood.

Wilson, the first treasurer in recent times to grapple even marginally with the ruinous deficit, was too candid to promise quick results. His projections over the next five years assumed a continuing huge gap between increased total expenditure and revenue; high unemployment; mounting debt but possibly falling interest rates, and inflation of a 3 to 4 per cent range. These are bold assumptions and they assume something still bolder—that Canadians will accept increasing future sacrifices for their own good.

In a labyrinth of figures where typical taxpayers are lost, they can discern the central question posed by the budget: Will the economy grow fast enough, and yield enough revenue, without higher taxes or more spending cuts, to support the state apparatus even if the government manages to shrink it? Can our society indefinitely maintain the living standard to which it is accustomed and demands?

That question raises some others. Has Wilson been too tough or too soft on the taxpayers? Has he persuaded them, and a reluctant cabinet, that the rest of this decade cannot be soft for an economy distorted by the false hopes and promises of all the political parties? Have he, the government and all of us underestimated or overestimated the rebounding strength of free enterprise if the state widens its freedom? There indeed is a vast imponderable now before Canada and yet to be tested.

In the United States, meanwhile, the president dismissed such problems as temporary and for the most part already solved. Deficits in foreign trade and domestic budgets, overpriced American dollars, upward pressure on interest rates and the risk of a future business slump did not alarm him. Reaganomics, his people were told, would overcome all obstacles. Men of superior knowledge, like Paul Volcker, chairman of the Federal Reserve Board, and some White House insiders, thought differently. None could daunt the Great Communicator, but his economic program must daunt the Canadian government whatever it says in public.

Nevertheless, there are similarities in the thinking of the two governments. Both share the hope that a flood tide in world business will lift all boats. Reagan's critics reply that the boats of the American rich have been lifted but those of the poor remain stranded.

However that may be, the Canadian economy has special need of a rising tide since it thrives, as a huge foreign trader, only in a thriving world market. How long can it wait until world forces lift it? And has it yet realized what strong competition the exports of its resource industries, once easily sold, now face when new suppliers have entered the market with products as good as Canada's, and cheaper? These questions lie at the heart of the nation's economic dilemma, and the political debate surrounding it offers varied options, all troublesome, none yet embraced.

While Mulroney wooed American investors with neighbourly rhetoric and talked about freer trade in safe generalities, he must have known that the United States, though rich, was not an economic model for Canada's precise duplication. The two economies are similar, almost identical, in many ways. In others they are very different.

The United States possesses the world's largest market. Only some twenty-five million Canadians, roughly a tenth of the American population, are thinly spread over half a continent, a small market. Canada is therefore much more dependent than its neighbour on exports, more indeed than any other leading industrial nation. Also, because of its sprawling human settlement, distinct regions, harsh climate and resulting political strains, Canada has always been highly dependent on state intervention in business, and millions of Canadians, rich or poor, receive monthly cheques from the public treasury. These are taken for granted, almost as a natural right.

Hence comes a difference not only in the economic but in the psychological and social attitudes of the two North American peoples. That difference, subtle and hard to define, poses, as we shall see, the supreme unanswered question of Canada's immediate future.

Canada's past was coloured by nostalgic illusion. As late as the depression years Canada had not fully emerged from its colonial thoughtways and assumed that the highest economic wisdom resided in London. It did not. Britain's economic management was a tragicomedy of errors between the world wars, though disguised by a superior front of manners, pomp and circumstance. Now the true record, disclosed in books like Francis Williams's *A Pattern of Rulers,* must warn Canadians that they should expect London to offer no sure guidance. Where, then, can they find it?

In Japan, their second trading partner, they will learn, and unlearn, some useful lessons. Any foreigner who has seen the Japanese factories, assembly lines and robots is amazed by a miracle, as it is called without exaggeration. The world's third largest economy, risen from the debris of war, has no parallel. And in the new Hiroshima, built on the nuclear ruins of the old, the foreigner sees the definitive symbol of war's madness and yet of human survival.

No figures and official explanations convey the secret of the miracle. Although lavishly nourished by American money and wise foresight, it is essentially the product of a native character which, with its traditions, achievements and crimes, still remains a mystery to all foreigners. Here, no attempt will be made to explain it.

At least the Canadian sees that the miracle differs from any system in the Western world. The Japanese business executive tells you that he stands for unrestricted competition, the free market ideal and a minimum of government interference. In truth, government penetrates the whole economy through its intimate familial relationship with the corporate elite. This, one supposes, is the contemporary version of the ancient native hierarchy and the paternalism accepted by its beneficiaries.

Whatever else it may be, Japan—in denial of its American-made constitution and, so far, relatively small military power—has become the Western world's vital defence bastion in the Far East. But it is not merely an imitator of foreign business methods as it was in the first days of industrialism. It is now a daring innovator, a pioneer of the technological age so successful that the earlier pioneers, like the United States, often try to imitate its methods.

On another plane these methods have a special interest for Canada. They seem to resemble, in basic premise or necessity, the Canadian method in spite of a diverse experience and more diverse mentality. Both countries erect their policies on the same foundation not of theory but of pragmatic and flexible compromise.

What Canada may learn from Japan is not social attitudes and lifeways. In those regions the twain will never meet when apparent Japanese candour seldom, if ever, reveals the real thinking and instincts behind it. But assuredly Canadians should learn, import and use some of Japan's latest economic breakthroughs.

Its technology in many areas is far ahead of Canada's or even that of the United States, once the world's unchallenged leader. On the other hand, the eclectic Japanese have much to learn, and are rapidly learning, from Western societies. So-called Americanization—usually deplored by old folk as vulgarization—is likely to be a mixture of the socially good and bad. This is Japan's problem. Another looms on the horizon. When competitors like the United States overtake the present Japanese miracle, as undoubtedly they will, can further miracles be performed? And will Canada catch up with the innovators?

Belatedly realizing that their economic future will depend more on the Pacific Rim than on the Atlantic, Canadian businessmen and politicians flock to Japan in search of technological secrets as well as markets and investment capital. The search is only beginning and has yet a long way to go.

China has been a large market for Canadian wheat while selling little here, but its future imports from Canada will depend mainly on its success in rebuilding a failed Communist system. And some useful lessons can be learned even in Taiwan, a mere speck of geography, where Chiang Kai-shek, after flight from his debacle in China, founded a successful economy, or allowed better men to found it while he presided on his gaudy throne like a bogus Sun King and informed every visitor that he would soon reconquer the mainland. Such was the megalomania of a wizened little figure once admired and massively subsidized by an American government in one of Roosevelt's worst blunders. Since then Taiwan has shown that a minute island can prosper if its people, expecting no miracles, work hard enough in field and factory. Canada, an immense country, has not yet fully learned this lesson and has nothing to learn from Taiwan's oppressive authoritarian society.

Newly aware of opportunities—and low-wage competition—on the Pacific, Canadians should not neglect the lessons still to be found across the Atlantic, notably in West Germany. The presiding genius of its miracle was Ludwig Erhard, a stout, red-faced, cheerful man who drank gallons of soda water and smoked innumerable cigars as he explained his methods to the foreigner. They boiled down to unrestricted competition and bold entrepreneurship—the ostensible American system with German improvements. But Erhard and Chancellor Konrad Adenauer did not repeal the system of social benefits inaugurated by the realistic, cold-blooded Bismarck. Instead, they expanded it and proved that only a well-managed economy can afford a generous welfare state.

There is another lesson yet to be learned in Canada. Although Erhard failed as chancellor, he had given Germany, with American backing, its first chance to recover from Hitler's war. Like Japan, it profited from the lessons of defeat. Recently, however, its *nouveau riche* entrepreneurial class has begun to abuse its wealth and the miracle has lost some of its early glamour.

If Canada has many economic lessons to learn from competitors like Germany and Japan, they teach it little about the politics of a free society. In this area the newcomers lack the necessary experience, and even the old democracies often stumble in the management of their own affairs. The ultimate lesson must be learned at home. Our true Canadian future lies, as always, within ourselves.

7

THE TUG
OF WAR

As Canada plunges deeper into the new world, the immediate question is whether it has a foreign policy to take with it; indeed, whether any nation has a workable policy when all of them behave more erratically and less morally than their individual citizens.

In Canada the question is partially but not wholly answered. For most of its life Canada had no foreign policy of its own, not even the pretence of a policy under some governments. Until modern times what policy it had was framed in Britain, whose military power defended Canada as an appendage of its empire. With that defence lost, Canadians were forced to frame a policy of some sort, and they are still working on it, with frequent changes, today.

In this field I have only such secondhand knowledge as experts could give me, and they rarely agreed about the facts of record, much less about their current meaning. Too often I weakly accepted the prevailing conventional wisdom and later found it to be wrong.

However debated, rationalized and enforced, foreign policy can never be easily framed in Canada. A peculiar native ambivalence complicates and obstructs it, as shrewdly observed by Arthur Irwin after his three embassies abroad and a distinguished career in journalism. The typical Canadian, he says, has always been tugged on the one hand by history back to the old world, on the other by geography and rugged experience into the new. Mainly from these opposite tugs came, and must come, what policy we can devise.

Other tugs should be noted but usually are not.

Before a policy is articulated by the government it is examined, written and rewritten in the unseen depths of the bureaucracy. Then it is tested in the caucus of the ruling party which is supposed to represent the composite view of the nation (a dubious proposition at best). Only when a prime minister has sounded out his followers, the voters and the climate of public opinion does he announce a policy, and it is subject to sudden amendment, or even reversal, described as merely a shift of emphasis.

This method serves well enough in normal times. In times of crisis few men are consulted because instant action is required. A strong prime minister will act on his own if a quick decision is necessary and sometimes, as we shall see, when it is not necessary.

Whatever its origins, a policy contains many elements. It is heavily weighted by commercial interest as, for example, Canada's overwhelming economic dependence on the market of the United States. It is swayed by native prejudice, old friendships, old enmities and blind spots like Canada's neglect of Latin America. It is also influenced by a dwindling indigenous Canadian population and massive immigration with results not yet forseeable but sure to be profound; by the more subtle element loosely known as culture; by the information media, books, speeches, international seminars; countless groups of obscure local thinkers, and even athletic contests between the home teams and the foreigners.

Thus people pressure (for lack of a better word) is a yeast ceaselessly working to leaven the loaf of policy in a kind of osmotic process without definition.

The roots of policy are long. They can be traced all the way to Champlain's battle with the Iroquois beside his lake. There began, though nobody could suspect it, the bisection of North America, the boundary changed only in detail from then on by war and diplomacy. Frontenac's bloody massacres in the New England colonies, his defence of Quebec against British raiders, Talon's expansion of New France to the Gulf of Mexico, Radisson's penetration of Hudson Bay, La Vérendrye's march across the prairies and the Battle of the Plains of Abraham were all aspects of a coherent but doomed policy made in Paris.

After the British military (though never the civilian) conquest of

Canada, everything changed. Through its governors Britain controlled, or thought it controlled, the future of merely another permanent
colony. But everything changed again with the American Revolution,
which was necessarily postponed until the menace of a French and
Catholic enemy to the north had been removed.

Now the time came for the rudimentary American Republic to
possess Canada. Montgomery's siege of Quebec, Carleton's defence,
fierce midnight fighting in the shambles of a narrow cul-de-sac on
New Year's Eve, 1775, American retreat, Burgoyne's bungled expedition southward, surrender at Saratoga, again at Yorktown, and Britain's recognition of an upstart rival—all delineated a British foreign
policy, self-defeating as it was. But would Canada ever have a policy of
its own?

From the start the Republic had such a policy. After the Revolution
it expected to grasp the northern half of the continent and nearly
succeeded in the peace treaty. Britain had suffered enough defeat in
America. It wanted an end to the empire's civil war and was tempted
to let the rebels have most of the continent as the price of peace. At
the last minute the cunning American negotiators in Paris were
thwarted. Britain decided to keep Canada after all. But what was
Canada? A few acres of snow, as Voltaire sneered? A peltry of dubious
profit? A millstone too heavy for imperial ambition to bear? No, it was
something unexpected, unique—a second child of that prolific
mother, the American Revolution.

Once the United Empire Loyalists had settled in Canada, its destiny
was fixed as a dual colony, English and French, far short of nationhood. What Washington and London failed to understand was that
the Loyalists, themselves North Americans, would found a second
North American nation if any nation could be founded.

In 1812 the Republic lunged north, the lesson of 1775 forgotten, the
wine of Manifest Destiny turning the usually sober heads of the invaders. Queenston Heights, Lundy's Lane, Beaver Dams, Chateauguay,
inland sea battles on the Lakes—all this struggle for the border proved
that Canada, its first sense of nationhood aroused, would survive as an
entity in one form or another. Unwittingly, the United States had
been one of its most effective creators.

Even in 1837, when William Lyon Mackenzie, in red wig and three
overcoats, stormed the shabby town of York, the Americans (now
claiming that name as exclusively their own) had not quite learned

their lesson. They covertly supported Mackenzie's rebellion, giving him refuge in their territory. Next year they eagerly hoped that Von Schoultz's crazy Battle of the Windmill at Prescott would succeed. No one observed his single defender in court, a young, bibulous Kingston lawyer named Macdonald, the unlikely maker of a nation yet unimaginable either in London or Washington. Von Schoultz was executed. Macdonald's career had begun.

On the Pacific Coast, Manifest Destiny had taken on a more alarming guise. President James Polk was promising to annex all land between Oregon Territory and Alaska with the war cry of "Fifty-four-forty or fight." But he had plenty of Mexican conquests to absorb in the Southwest and California. When the British Navy patrolled the Strait of Juan de Fuca, the Queen's writ running even there, he desisted. With the Oregon Treaty of 1846, the boundary was anchored.

The frail infant Canadian union of 1867 was again largely a response to Manifest Destiny. Already the Fenian raids of 1866 and the Battle of Limestone Ridge had confirmed Canada's fear of more American attacks. Macdonald now had a domestic policy but no independent foreign policy. None, apparently, was needed. Britain would look after its colonial children.

Fortunately, by this time, the neighbouring Republic with the largest armies the world had ever known was tired of its civil war. Lincoln had refused to move northward in revenge for the South's raid on Vermont out of Canada. One war at a time was enough for him. As president, Gen. U. S. Grant also refused to move. Confederation seemed to have a chance of survival if it could reach the Pacific—a dubious chance.

The chance was not improved by Britain, sole maker of Canadian foreign policy. On the contrary, Britain sold out Canada at the Washington conference of 1871 to placate the Americans by giving them full access to the Canadian fisheries. Macdonald never forgot or forgave that betrayal, though he still vowed to live and die a British subject. But a British subject could vaguely meditate an independent policy, and Macdonald was meditating it.

His Liberal successor, Wilfrid Laurier, expanded it with bolder thoughts even when he had been sedulously wooed by the British government and the duchesses of London, once declaring his hope that Canadians would someday sit in an imperial parliament—a slip of the tongue instantly regretted.

Yet again Manifest Destiny strengthened Canada's growing mood of independence by the tug of geography in the Alaska boundary dispute of 1903. With his famous Big Stick waving, his voice no longer soft, President Theodore Roosevelt was determined to grasp the Panhandle and bar a huge Canadian territory from the Pacific. A supposedly judicial commission representing the United States, Britain and Canada had been well instructed in advance and duly awarded the Panhandle to the United States. As Laurier saw it, London had sold out Canada for the second time—and this after he had sent a Canadian contingent to the South African war against the bitter opposition of his own Quebec people.

Now that power politics was nakedly revealed, nothing short of a Canadian foreign policy, or at least its rudiments, would serve. It made an initial but politically disastrous appearance in 1911. The Laurier government negotiated a Reciprocity, or almost free-trade, deal with President Howard Taft, who was in need of a winning issue for the American election of 1912. Then, to Laurier's amazement and alarm, Taft aborted his scheme by publicly hinting that it ensured the future annexation of Canada by the United States, "a parting of the ways."

When Laurier, still confident of the outcome, took Reciprocity to the voters, they rejected it as a threat to their nationhood and thrust their former idol into the wilderness and the heartbreak common to his profession. For him there could be no escape.

He was succeeded by Robert Laird Borden, the underestimated Conservative Party leader, a Nova Scotia lawyer whose dull speeches, modest manner and stern look under a double ruff of grey hair had failed to impress the electorate until he met the Reciprocity issue head-on. From his unexpected success in that fight he had learned much, more than he yet realized.

Although Borden, like Macdonald, considered himself a loyal subject of the King and led Canada into a European war at Britain's side, he quarrelled with the British government because it was treating Canadians as colonists and "automata" instead of essential allies who deserved to know the truth about the war, then going badly. Startled by this blunt warning, the London authorities hastily sent bags of top-secret military documents to Ottawa, all weighted to sink in case of shipwreck.

Already Borden's honesty and common sense had surprised his critics at home, despite some nauseating scandals of wartime profiteering.

With the Allied victory came his real test, and he faced it boldly to make himself a great prime minister. At the Versailles conference, against the objections of Woodrow Wilson and Lloyd George, who could never understand Canada, he demanded a separate Canadian signature on the peace treaty. This demand won grudging approval.

A former colony, matured by war and bloodshed, was becoming a truly autonomous state and a signatory of the League of Nations Covenant. Borden, too, had matured. He was now a nationalist but, at the same time, an internationalist, a vigorous defender of the league. That apparent contradiction was, and still is, the necessary equipment of successful Canadian leadership, but foreigners are unlikely to understand it, while few of his contemporaries understood or appreciated Borden.

His health had been undermined by the war years, the conscription crisis of 1917, the task of managing a Conservative-Liberal coalition government, above all by his horror of committing the nation's young manhood to the mismanaged battles of Europe. Borden's release from public duty was well earned and, his health recovered, he was a respected elder statesman on both sides of politics.

The partisan truce achieved in wartime collapsed immediately afterward. Arthur Meighen, the new prime minister, was the last man who could hope to maintain or to want it, and his career was to prove tragically unlike Borden's, despite a promising start.

Meighen (politically doomed in Quebec as the chief architect of conscription) rallied to the support of postwar Britain and seemed to favour, at least in broad principle, the centralized empire foreign policy then advocated by the leading statesmen of London. But he would not be their obedient servant as they vainly expected. After all, he was a North American and mainly under his pressure Britain cancelled its alliance with Japan to satisfy the United States. In Meighen the opposite tugs of history and geography were especially visible and painful.

If his foreign policy was ambivalent in a brief term of office, William Lyon Mackenzie King, his Liberal successor, had no policy and would have none for a long time ahead. Nevertheless, his thinking had advanced further than his friends and enemies suspected. The first semblance of a policy emerged in a 1923 treaty with the United States to preserve the depleted Pacific halibut fisheries, an odd vehicle of growing autonomy. Ernest Lapointe thrust aside the British ambassador at Washington and applied Canada's signature. After that episode, policy was thrust aside, too. King reverted to his instinctive isolationism which, despite much public equivocation and private soul-searching, dogged him to the end of his life.

King's attempt to escape the world was based on a premise smugly uttered by his representative in the League of Nations, Raoul Dandurand, who explained that Canada lived in a "fireproof house," though the world already had started to burn.

The fire erupted in Ethiopia when King had just returned to power in 1935. Walter Riddell, the Canadian delegate to the league, awaited instructions from the new government. Should he cast a vote in favour of sanctions against Italy, the invader of a helpless little African country? In hindsight it can be argued that sanctions would have stopped and probably ruined Mussolini, even forestalled the Second World War. If Riddell so believed, he waited in vain.

King was holidaying in the United States, his latest cabinet not yet chosen; Lapointe remained in charge at Ottawa. Lacking definite authority but assuming that the government would back him, Riddell cast Canada's vote for sanction. The government promptly repudiated the vote and, in J. W. Dafoe's phrase, "politely conducted the league to limbo with sentiments of distinguished admiration."

When King returned to Ottawa I questioned him about his cabinet appointments, but something else was on his mind, and maybe his conscience. He had just begun to explain and excuse the repudiation of Riddell when Lapointe strode into the room, his bulky form weighed down by trouble. He told me, King nodding approval, that the sanctions against Italy could not have worked. They had been unhinged by Britain, not Canada, in the cynical Hoare-Laval agreement with France. Yes, said King, in a fine show of moral indignation, the deal had proved Canada's wisdom.

The few Canadians who questioned that explanation did not include me. And yet even then I suspected misgivings in the honest Lapointe, misgivings that increased to the point of tears, his friends said, when he later realized how badly the government had treated Riddell and that a second world war might have been prevented by the league's sanctions.

Thenceforth Canada lurched towards war still without a foreign policy. As world events flowed in cataract, all King would say was that only Parliament could decide Canada's action. He added, in sincere anguish, that the quarrels of Europe were nightmare and madness.

This evasion, though it could not last, well suited most Canadians, including me, but it was not a policy since the government must advise Parliament and take the responsibility for its advice. The same unreality also seemed to suit most Britons in the time of Stanley Baldwin and Ramsay MacDonald.

Parliament received no advice from King. Once the Munich deal was contrived to appease Germany, he applauded it with gushing cables of congratulation to its inventor, Neville Chamberlain. Dafoe's voice was raised against futile appeasement, but he stood almost alone, deserted by many friends.

Not until 1939 did King announce a policy or, more accurately, a reaction to the inevitable. He advised Parliament to declare war when, already, it was underway across the plains of Poland. That advice was wrung out of his misery in one of his worst speeches, larded with irrelevant poetic quotations after he had quarrelled with his still more isolationist adviser, O. D. Skelton. King's mind was clear at last, his interval of delusion ended.

A man of peace, he became a man of war overnight. No one imagined that a man so timid, so shifty, so ignorant of the world could lead Canada to victory. He fooled everybody, perhaps himself. Settling down for a war of several years or longer, guarding his health like a precious national asset, his daily life as regular as a grandfather clock, he made himself the ablest war leader in the nation's history, and his cabinet has had no equal since those days.

But victory did not end his isolationism, which soon returned. At its founding conference in San Francisco he wrote off the United Nations as a certain failure. Or course he made the required public gestures and, so he claimed, invented the role of a Middle Power for Canada, a role sufficiently vague to disguise his lack of faith while he spent his time writing speeches for a summer election with the aid of Jack Pickersgill.

It was not easy for the indispensable ghostwriter; he had just learned that the Germans had tortured and executed his gallant brother as an Allied spy in France. But the speeches were written, the election scheduled, the public deceived by King's ostensible support of the United Nations. Now lean, haggard, hardly recognizable to young voters, he won a final term of office to beat Walpole's record.

This internationalist pose had not fooled the two most important men around the prime minister at San Francisco. His chief lieutenant,

Louis St. Laurent, the modest Quebec lawyer, was learning about world affairs for the first time with mental and moral equipment superior to King's and becoming an outright internationalist. Their basic disagreement had begun, though neither yet realized it.

Lester Pearson, then ambassador to Washington, was still less deceived, and he revealed his growing doubts to me and my senior Winnipeg *Free Press* colleague, Grant Dexter. Having watched the stone face of Old Stone Bottom Molotov (whose orders were so strict that it was said he dare not sneeze until he consulted his government), Pearson already feared that the world was being split between the United States and Russia. From these same fears came the future partnership of St. Laurent and Pearson with results momentous for Canada.

How did their nation fit into the latest world schism? Such had been Canada's dilemma since the days when power was divided between the British Empire and the American Empire-To-Be. Canadian governments were accustomed to that ambiguous position and reacted, as best they could, to varying external pressures. But after San Francisco, Canada had the makings of a coherent policy based on collective security and enforced by the United Nations, if possible, or on some alternative system, if necessary.

The policy was actively pursued. Canadian peace-keeping forces were soon spread around the world, and the nation's repute reached an all-time peak. Canada could not be suspected of seeking military power or selfish interest. Through moral power alone it was everybody's friend, the international darling or fortune's fool. Those heady days could not long continue since they were the product of brief circumstance—a thriving nation in a devastated world hungry for Canada's resources. But it had a foreign policy that might outlast the boom.

The only serious dissenter at the peak was King, the man in whose name the policy was pursued. His mind had not changed. And the only man able to change it—or at least to maintain the policy—was his new external affairs minister, St. Laurent. Their inevitable clash resulted from the United Nations' attempt to pacify Korea. During King's absence overseas, St. Laurent pledged Canada to join a commission that would seek the union of the two Koreas, north and south. On his return to Ottawa, King was outraged. Through his spiritualistic mediums he had conferred with the dead Roosevelt who had warned him that the Third World War would start in the Asiatic country of which Canada knew little. Why, King demanded, had St. Laurent plunged Canada into such a cauldron?

At the breaking point, St. Laurent refused to budge. Instead, he offered his resignation. King was terrified: he could not part with his lieutenant and heir as he had parted with lesser men. Faced by a tormenting choice, he backed down. St. Laurent's decision on Korea was accepted, his resignation withdrawn. The next prime minister had surely arrived, the total internationalist.

Before his arrival many things had happened to change the world if not King's mind. Notable among them was the Titan Theory advocated on behalf of the British government by Lord Halifax, one of the leading appeasers at Munich. In the final spasm of empire he proposed—an old idea in a new generation—that all the Commonwealth nations should unite on a single, centralized foreign policy and become a titan like the United States and Russia. King instantly shot the theory down. Canada, he said, would follow its own independent policy.

This answer to Halifax might be construed as King's unchanging isolationism. But St. Laurent construed it differently. While he favoured Canadian independence so far as an interdependent world allowed, he knew that no nation could ever safely isolate itself again from its friends and allies. Pearson had always held the same view.

On taking over the highest office, St. Laurent persuaded Pearson, until then a nonpartisan civil servant, to become a politician and minister of external affairs, the offer Pearson had refused from King whom he never trusted. Now Canada had both a policy and a team fit to implement it. Did the policy fit the world of two superpowers? Convinced that the United Nations, as idealized at San Francisco, was incapable of keeping the peace, St. Laurent and Pearson meditated an unused section of the charter. It allowed member states to combine in their own defence.

Some Americans, like Dean Acheson, were thinking along the same lines. From this spontaneous union of minds came NATO, Canada one of its original architects. Against the objection of Acheson, who doubted the wisdom of mixing military and economic power, the NATO treaty included the "Canadian" clause, pledging the allies to co-operate in seeking joint prosperity. Not that Acheson doubted the importance of economic power when, almost single-handed, he had devised the Marshall Plan; he only wanted a treaty concentrated on military power lest both be diluted. Not without a long, secret struggle, Canada's view prevailed.

Suez, of all places, was to test the unity of the West; also Canada's ties with Britain. When British, French and Israeli forces attacked Egypt without a word of advance notice to Canada, St. Laurent was infuriated. He wrote a message to London so brutal that Pearson had to tone it down. But St. Laurent's anger was not cooled as he soon demonstrated in the worst political mistake of his career.

Without definite instructions, because the crisis was too fluid for planning, Pearson flew to the United Nations at New York. There he was met by the heartsick British delegates who asked him to contrive some face-saving formula and rescue Anthony Eden's government from its fiasco.

Canadian history had come to a decisive turning point. Pearson was alone at New York, in touch with St. Laurent only by telephone. Nevertheless, he contrived a formula of United Nations intervention, persuaded a reluctant U.S. Secretary of State John Foster Dulles to accept it, saved Britain's face, ended the Suez crisis and incidentally won a Nobel Peace Prize. This, at any rate, is the Canadian version of a mysterious affair still being re-argued in many books.

Eden, of course, was ruined.

Returning to Ottawa, Pearson could not fully explain to Parliament what he had done lest he worsen Britain's humiliation, its loss of rank as a great power. Silenced by the old transatlantic friendship, he heard his Conservative friend Howard Green denounce him for knifing Britain in the back—a false charge, the exact opposite of the truth even if the honest Green believed it. But St. Laurent was not to be silenced for long.

On the eve of his speech to Parliament, the prime minister telephoned Walter Harris, the wise and cautious minister of finance. What should the speech contain? Harris replied that it should contain anything St. Laurent wished to say but no attack on Britain. This advice seemed to worry St. Laurent so deeply that he telephoned Harris twice again and received the same warning. Harris went to bed satisfied that his chief would do nothing to aggravate the transatlantic breach.

Next day, his Irish temper bursting out of control, St. Laurent delivered the speech which, even more decisively than the earlier and notorious pipeline brawl, would defeat his government in the following year. It was time, he said, that the "supermen" of Europe (apparently meaning the British) ceased to bully the smaller nations. At this sudden outburst the faces of Harris and the rest of the cabinet ministers could not mask their panic. They instantly suspected that the government was doomed by its leader's passionate candour.

Afterward, out of office, St. Laurent confessed his mistake on television. He had simply "got mad," he said, and this was the simple truth. The fact that by "supermen" he had meant not Britain but the white world in general could never be explained to the voters of the 1957 election. In politics the Suez slip was irreparable.

The government, battered by pipeline, supermen and a declining economy, floundered into an election already lost before it started. Despite his failing health and a family grief, St. Laurent agreed, against his better judgement, to fight his last campaign as the only leader who might win it. But now he was too old, tired and sick for the game of politics. He struggled through the campaign with dignity and unseen courage but no longer with the familiar charm and panache of the nation's Uncle Louis.

Back in Quebec, private life and good health again, he told me that he should have resisted the pressure of his well-meaning colleagues, resigned before the election and left his party's leadership to a younger man. It was too late for regrets, though St. Laurent never ceased to blame himself for the mistakes of others.

In the 1957 election the government won a slight edge in the popular vote, but the Conservative opposition had the largest group of parliamentary seats, far short of a majority. King, as in 1925, probably would have hung on, governing with a minority, trusting to the CCF group and the blunders of his enemies. Not so St. Laurent.

On election night, in his Quebec home, he rejected any such expedient. The government had been morally defeated and must resign at once with no whimper of complaint. From the opposition benches the Liberal Party, under a new leader, could live to fight another day, preferably not on foreign policy.

The new prime minister, John George Diefenbaker, knows little of foreign policy. For the most part he acts on a visceral anti-Americanism which, deepening into something like mania, is to wreck all his hopes. Until his quarrel with President Kennedy,

Diefenbaker apparently has nothing to fear, even in the prevailing ugly climate of the border. After his landslide victory of 1958, his government controls Parliament with the largest majority on record.

As Diefenbaker has yet to realize, the majority lacks durable substance. He comes out of the 1962 election with a minority of seats and staggers through another year. Then the Liberal Party, now led by Pearson and supported by the minor opposition groups, defeats the government in a House of Commons vote and in the subsequent election. But the Pearson government, too, lacks a majority.

Having ended the Diefenbaker-Kennedy quarrel (only to earn the later fury of President Johnson by urging a pause in the American bombing of North Vietnam), Pearson has found other problems to think about, among them China and Taiwan. While he favours the membership of the Communist Chinese government in the United Nations, he is unwilling to abandon Taiwan. Its people, he thinks, deserve the right of self-determination according to the doctrine enunciated by Woodrow Wilson at Versailles. But the diplomatic future of the huge mainland territory and the little offshore island is unresolved when Trudeau succeeds Pearson in 1968 and reverses Canadian policy. The government at Peking is recognized by Ottawa, Taiwan downgraded, its status left unclear.

Now the fat is in the fire at Washington. Canada has defied the anti-Communist policy of the United States. One of the highest officials of the State Department takes me aside after a diplomatic dinner party, as if I were personally responsible for Ottawa's new policy, and declares that Canada has "crawled on its belly" to the Chinese Communists, strained the border friendship and lost the respect of all decent Americans. The official is beside himself in sputtering rage. I, of course, have nothing to say, knowing nothing. What the official does not know, what only one other official in the State Department yet knows, is that Henry Kissinger, on President Nixon's orders, has landed already in Peking and launched detente with China. Has the United States, imitating Canada, also crawled on its belly? And is the State Department to be kept ignorant of the presidential policy that it is supposed to execute?

These are among the publicly unasked questions facing Trudeau throughout his long term of office. In the meantime he has been vindicated by Nixon on China, but his foreign policy is formless, experimental and erratic. In fact, he has no policy that native or foreigner can understand. Like his predecessors, he is torn between the old tugs of history and geography. Somehow they must be reconciled or compromised.

Immediately after his victory in the 1968 election, a brief spasm of Trudeaumania, he orders a deep study of Canada's contribution to NATO's defence posture in Europe. It is said, even now, that he has planned to withdraw the small Canadian forces altogether, and such thoughts may have crossed his mind. But if he attempts a withdrawal, the resignations of at least two powerful colleagues will follow.

After some confused wrangling in secret, they are satisfied that Trudeau does not actually propose to go that far. Instead, with no warning to Canada's allies, the NATO overseas contingent is cut in half because its existing cost is too heavy for the national budget which, in those days, is managed with a thrift soon abandoned. But the United States government, given no advance notice of Canada's decision, is angry, fearing that it may have set an example for other allies to follow. This, at any rate, is the truth of a curious incident as remembered, or misremembered, by some of its chief participants.

Whatever the truth may be, Trudeau still has no real grasp of foreign policy. His ignorance, confusion and lack of common fairness are demonstrated in a ghostwritten speech which describes the Pearson government as too much dominated by its military advisers. After that careless and outrageous rebuke to his former friend, Trudeau's mind begins to clear. His isolationism is gradually discarded. While he learns the facts of international life, a man always pragmatic and willing to experiment moves in zigzag course.

Thus his opinion of the United States often varies from friendship to hostility and fear. The same inconstancy marks his domestic policies. As a youthful Socialist he had urged Quebec to end its economic isolationism, to trade freely at home and abroad in contradiction of Socialist dogma. Now he contradicts himself by erecting new barriers against competitive imports.

The Foreign Investment Review Agency (FIRA), his instrument of a reviving nationalism, is instructed to examine, limit or prohibit foreign, mainly American, penetration of the Canadian economy. But Trudeau's nationalism is mercurial and remains so to the end—FIRA strengthened and then weakened under American pressure, defence budget raised or lowered, aid to the poor nations increased but their vital exports to Canada restricted. The Third Option, intended to divert more of Canada's trade from the United States to other markets (an unadmitted imitation of Diefenbaker's futile attempt), again fails to work. The commitment to the market closest at hand, and incomparably rich, does not decline. It grows, mandated by the laws of geography and economics. But as we shall see, the old political issues never separable from the economic are returning in new form today.

Meanwhile Trudeau has been thinking hard on foreign policy with the help of better-informed experts. In the resulting windy document he announces that Canada will cease to act as a broker and fixer of diverse international interests, its customary role. This detachment is short-lived. Soon he becomes the chief broker of the Commonwealth and, as he believes, has prevented its rupture by conciliating its divided white and nonwhite peoples. In the 1980s he is a respected veteran among world statesmen, more respected abroad than at home.

Not on sudden impulse, but after wide travel and long thought, he launches the peace initiative of late 1983. His critics say that he is merely seeking Liberal votes for a last election. His confidants, who often disagree with him on other questions, know that in this venture his sincerity, often questioned in the past, is beyond doubt. The father of three young sons is haunted and tortured by the threat of nuclear war, partisan politics now a secondary concern.

At first the Conservative opposition is skeptical, having long suffered from Trudeau's wiles and insults. But Mulroney, warned by more experienced colleagues, grasps the point and hurries to the prime minister's support lest the Conservative Party be suspected of opposition to peace when it is just as sincere as the government. So, too, is the New Democratic Party.

Trudeau has a unanimous House of Commons behind him when he sets out again on his travels to seventeen countries and meetings with more than fifty government leaders. What is he taking with him? Very little, say the men of practical affairs in Washington. President Reagan gives Trudeau a faint Godspeed and apparently still thinks of Russia as an Evil Empire, though already his mind, or at least his rhetoric, has begun to change.

The peace initiative is only a "metaphor," harmless but futile, says one of the State Department's most experienced diplomats. It is useless for a Canadian to argue that Trudeau is taking with him not only a metaphor but his nation's revised and at last coherent foreign policy; also a simple idea long rejected by official Washington but long advocated by Americans like George Kennan who have lived in Russia, studied its people at first hand and speak their language.

The idea is that while the Russian governing apparatus is primitive, ruthless and as expansionist as any czarist dictatorship, the very opposite of Marx's Communist dream, it is not insane. It knows the outcome of a war against capitalism. Given patience and adequate armed strength at the bargaining table, negotiations with the Kremlin can succeed step by step by step over many years, perhaps a whole generation. The process will be slow, frustrating and often bitterly disappointing, but its alternative is a world under permanent siege or the end of humankind.

Opposed to this view are the so-called hawks of the deeply divided Reagan government who hold that, given time and American patience, the stumbling, inefficient Russian economy will collapse under its own insupportable weight, military power with it. No such view is shared by men like Kennan. They hold, on the contrary, that if the Russians are driven into deeper isolation, they will rally around their government, accept still greater hardships and become more dangerous.

Reagan, torn by conflicting advice and preparing for the election of 1984, tones down his belligerent speeches and says peace was always his highest priorty, though relations between Washington and Moscow are now at a nadir, the superpowers hardly on speaking terms.

It is thus in a bleak world environment that Trudeau carries to Europe, Britain, China, Russia and lesser states his message of hope, mixed with desperation; above all, the belief that peace is still negotiable and that Russian society, despite its government, is as human as others elsewhere. But at no point does Trudeau propose unilateral disarmament by the West. Against strong opposition outside and inside his cabinet he is ready to allow the test of unarmed American cruise missiles over Canadian territory.

Nobody can yet reckon Trudeau's influence on world events when they move at accelerating speed, but at this writing the superpowers have resumed their long-stalemated disarmament negotiations. A leading Canadian diplomat is probably right in saying that the Canadian initiative has been a useful tributary, swelling the weak mainstream of peace.

History's verdict on Trudeau as an international broker cannot be foreseen as he announces his resignation after a term of office longer than Laurier's. But his work, however it may be judged in the future, is not yet finished even in the present.

Out of office, and with the Liberal Party demoralized largely by his economic record, Trudeau goes to Washington again in November 1984 and accepts the Albert Einstein Peace Prize of $50,000. Before an audience of the official elite, television cameras grinding, he reveals for the first time publicly his opinion of the Western world's leaders. Having met them at many summits, he says they assemble "only to go through tedious speeches, drafted by others with the principal objective of not rocking the boat. . . . Is it any wonder that the value of NATO as a political alliance is increasingly questioned?"

Then, in a quiet voice, he adds an explosive sentence: "The politicians who once stated that war was too important to be left to the generals now act as though peace were too complex to be left to themselves," but "it is the politicians who will be held accountable for the success or failure of efforts to turn back Armageddon."

To me, as a Canadian listener, this is one of Trudeau's finest public utterances, unlike his many foolish ones. It has been aimed far beyond the immediate gathering to the worldwide audience in language at once eloquent but, in diplomatic manners, brutally offensive. It comes from the heart, out of an experience unique to himself. It sums up his final conclusions on his time and on a human species living close to the brink of total catastrophe.

In the past the American newspapers have dismissed his peace initiative with brief or no coverage. Suddenly, his speech is spread on the front pages of the Washington and New York press under big headlines. Although he has not mentioned the president's name, every reporter knows that Reagan is the central target of Trudeau's searing criticism. These two men have never been compatible, have never understood each other and never will. Trudeau shows no regret for his speech and already is planning to warn Mulroney against "kowtowing" before his compatible new friend, the president. Instead, the prime minister must tell Reagan "the truth" in "the crunch" or "Canadians will soon turn against him."

Reagan is firmly installed in his second term, the world crisis at some kind of crossroads and the superpowers again at the Geneva bargaining table, while Trudeau is a private citizen in Montreal.

His work of success and failure has been handed on to a successor about as different from him as any man can be. Will Mulroney and his already divided government carry on where Trudeau left off, given Canada's limited power? They promise to maintain his direction with the changed and less spectacular methods required in a changing world climate. The traditional Canadian method of "quiet diplomacy," of private talks between old friends in the "special relationship" of the continent, has returned. The Pearson foreign policy in its essentials has become the accepted doctrine and it cuts straight across party lines. But does it serve the new times? Apparently, External Affairs Minister Joe Clark is not sure.

His Green Paper of spring 1985 adds little or nothing to the foreign policy debate. It merely outlines, in safe generalities, the issues facing the nation and invites public comment on them. Whatever he may think of it privately, Clark indicates no decision by the government on the greatest immediate issue—whether Canada, having approved American research into antimissile space weapons, should actively join this dubious undertaking.

When Clark's paper is published, a committee of Parliament has begun the most extensive review of all the available policy options since Trudeau's first years, intending to report in two years. But it is given no adequate time to study the Star Wars issue which the government plans to settle one way or the other by the fall of 1985. What use, then, is the study? Opposition members of the committee see none. What they and the public see in the paper is for the most part a rambling discussion of foreign affairs as a supplement to more important economic policy, the nation's daily bread and butter.

While the government refuses to commit itself on the vital issue, what tantalizes it is obvious. If Canada fully participates in Star Wars research and if antimissile missiles are invented—a very large if—can their deployment be avoided with unknown consequences for the world's peace? If research goes ahead, at vast unknown financial cost, and against eminent scientific advice, will it drive the Soviet Union into equal or greater efforts and destroy any chance of disarmament? Already, Washington believes, Russia has its own research well underway, though denying it. Meanwhile nuclear weaponry threatens to proliferate among some nations unfit to be trusted with it, and the superpowers have not halted a spread endangering the entire world.

That horror aside, will Canada's participation in research create many new jobs at home? Such a chance is hard to resist in times of high unemployment, and Mulroney cautiously dangles it in front of the public without saying whether he favours it or not. Warned by Galbraith, the American economist, that money spent on peaceful investments will create the most jobs, Mulroney remains silent.

His search for national consensus may be a kite-flying exercise. If he chooses participation, Canada's foreign policy will enter a new and unlimited experiment, reaching far beyond earth's atmosphere and the law of gravity to build a sidereal Maginot Line; it will involve the future of all planetary life. Few harder choices have faced any prime minister.

There are some additional facts of history that should not be overlooked. Among them is Bismarck's shrewd insight when he considered the future of a German Empire which he had founded at Versailles. The greatest of all facts in the world of *realpolitik,* he said, was the common language of Britain, its overseas kindred and the American people—a conclusion as valid now as it ever was. Churchill, a greater and better man, saw in this curious fraternity a natural place for Canada. He once called it the "linchpin of peace and world progress." If his words seem to be only genial hyperbole, they contain some truth and hope, even when the world's power balance has shifted drastically since Churchill's young days.

Will the Mulroney government be wise and strong enough to keep the linchpin, such as it now is, firmly fixed? Despite their urgent domestic problems, no larger question faces Canadians today. And central to that question, as always, is their often misunderstood and often mismanaged friendship with the superpower beside them.

8

ELEPHANT
AND MOUSE

The past, present and future of Canada's foreign policy are fixed by its history, geography, wealth and lack of military power. Ottawa reacts daily to the shock waves of the world, above all to the shifting policies of the United States. So it must, for Canada is a North American nation. It has vital interests elsewhere and its more distant friendships should always be fostered as counterweights to the adjoining superpower. But the close neighbourhood can never be escaped.

What, Canadians must ask, is the real foreign policy framed by Washington? Long ago, when that capital city was a squalid village in a steaming marsh, the French traveller and author Jean de Crèvecoeur asked a larger question: "What, then, is an American, this new man?" If he were alive today, Crèvecoeur would get no sure answer. The new man and woman defy analysis. They become increasingly diverse in habit, thought and ambition. Policy changes as they do, but the preponderance of American power remains unchanged on the continent though not in the world.

Trudeau once gave the continental relationship a vivid metaphor. The Canadian mouse, he said, lives perforce beside the American elephant, and when the heavier beast twitches even slightly, with no evil intention, the smaller is pinched and could be crushed. So, for that matter, could all Western nations. The elephant's twitches spread worldwide. Canada feels them soonest with the greatest risk of injury. On the other hand, when the elephant is awake and friendly, no nation benefits as much as Canada. Nowadays the benefits far outweigh occasional danger.

It was not always so. At the beginning, New France, then the elephant, was stronger than New England, though less populous, and enfiladed it along the Appalachians to the Gulf of Mexico. The English mouse was hived on the Atlantic coast and constantly harassed from the north. The foreign policies of both had the same origin, in the wilderness. Both struggled against the same obstacles, nourished the same ambitions and had no policies beyond the will to live. But already their attitudes differed and would remain different.

The English colonies, from the landfall of the Pilgrims onward, lived amid frequent violence until it became a lasting element of their society. They fought the Indians and fought among themselves. The French colony, under Champlain's management, allied itself with the Indians, paid them to fight the white enemy and used them to carry the power of Old France across the continent. A mental as well as a physical boundary line was drawn by men who, like their successors, seldom knew their enemy's intentions.

Not until Britain conquered and ended New France were those opposing attitudes clarified. Even then the border was still undefined before the American Revolution. Thenceforth the sovereign question for Canada, as Trudeau was to learn by hard experience, has been, and is today, how much leverage the mouse can exert against the elephant. Inevitably, the leverage grew weaker as the new Republic found new strength and exerted it not only against an English parent but against a Canadian neighbour.

George Washington, in a farewell address written by Alexander Hamilton, warned his countrymen to reject entangling alliances with any foreign state, though he had already won the Revolution by alliance with France and could not have won it otherwise. Nothing went, or could go, as he or his successors planned.

It was all very well for the Republic's Founders to declare Self-Evident Truths and the equality of man while Jefferson, author of the Declaration of Independence, and his fellows owned a multitude of slaves. It was all very well to choose the Pursuit of Happiness as the highest value of life, but the Founders had no intention of pursuing democracy as we know it.

To many of the delegates at the secret constitutional convention in Philadelphia, the mob seemed more dangerous than foreign enemies. Washington, the presiding officer, kept silent, meditating his own political creed. It would have surprised the men of genius around him. When his country still lacked a constitution, and the convention was deadlocked, the Virginian aristocrat and future president wrote to the Marquis de Lafayette in Paris that "democratical States must always *feel* before they *see*. It is this that makes their Governments slow but the people will be right at last."

Had Washington been too hopeful? Two centuries after his departure, are his people now right at last? And what are they doing to Canada and the world's peace? The superquestion awaits its answer in our time. All Washington could know was that democracy had appeared even in his time of office and could not be repressed, along with other hopes or perils.

Of such things the northern neighbours thought vaguely if at all. When they united in 1867 no Declaration of Self-Evident Truths, no Pursuit of Happiness, no Bill of Rights was mentioned in their Constitution. Enough for them if the union survived by any available means. Noble sentiments would be left to the Americans and their mistakes avoided. Canada must live on toil and experiment, not words. It would declare itself in action, not written documents. Pragmatism, then as now, was the internal, unwritten governing fact of the state.

Beyond the internal fact loomed the larger fact of the American presence, and it was growing. Monroe's doctrine forbidding European colonization in the Western hemisphere; State Secretary Olney's warning, in the Venezuela boundary dispute of 1895, that the United States "is practically sovereign on this continent and its fiat is law"; McKinley's war with Spain, his conquest of Cuba and the Philippines; Theodore Roosevelt's arrival with plans, soon abandoned, to provoke another war with Britain and conquer Canada; his arbitration of the Russian-Japanese War and his Big Stick in Alaska—these were the first probes of American imperialism contradicting Washington's policy, announcing a new great power in the world. But imperialism did not last long.

After Taft had failed to secure Reciprocity with Canada, in suspected preparation for its peaceful annexation, Wilson reinterpreted Manifest Destiny to mean American friendship throughout a world made safe for democracy. That moral experiment did not last long, either. In November 1920 the League of Nations, Wilson's shattered dream, and all entangling alliances were rejected by the voters, isolationism restored. A young Canadian reporter, standing in crowded, rainy Times Square that election night, soaked to the skin, could not imagine the dimensions of the tragedy. Nor could the American voters and the world at large. Alike, they accepted President Warren Harding's "normalcy" as normal.

A second Roosevelt did not accept it. He had run for the vice-presidency in 1920, sure of defeat, on a League of Nations platform, was stricken with polio and emerged, with useless legs, to make himself governor of New York and then president. Like Wilson, he saw that the world was one, or should be, but unlike Wilson, he also saw that his people were not ready for such a world.

In its place he watched the fall of France, agony visible on his haggard face as he sat in the hot Oval Office without a jacket, shirt sweat-drenched, and confessed to the reporters that the United States was powerless to aid its ancient European ally. There were no "clouds" of American planes to answer the French government's dying appeal, no American support for a war in Europe, no break in isolationism. Roosevelt's 1937 speech proposing the "quarantine" of aggressors had failed. It could not be repeated.

Having seen him regnant in the first days of the New Deal and in 1937 when he descended a gangplank from his destroyer, to the Victoria wharf, his hands on the railings, legs dragging, face covered with sweat, to be lifted bodily into a limousine, I was shocked by his look of helplessness. In the spring of 1940, he seemed broken in spirit as in body.

His recovery was rapid and instantly involved Canada. King, summoned to Ogdensburg, New York, on 17 August 1940, met the president in his private railway car. There a defence agreement between the neighbours was quickly signed, though neither president nor prime minister had the authority to sign it.

If Britain fell, as seemed likely, the neighbours would survive together, the border eliminated for all practical purposes. The United

States had embraced its first modern entangling alliance. Naturally, it was with Canada. The symbiotic continental tie could not be severed. War only strengthened it.

King was always lucky in politics. Meighen denounced the Ogdensburg pact as "twilight twitterings," his third fatal mistake to rank with Chanak and the contradictory Hamilton speech of 1925 proposing that Canada must never go to war without the people's affirmative vote. King had no need to answer Meighen's twitterings. Among Canadians they answered themselves.

There was more to Ogdensburg than the defence of North America, more than King then dared to reveal. Roosevelt, he had found, was bickering with Churchill over the United States' proposed gift to Britain of a destroyer fleet in exchange for bases in the Western hemisphere.

Transatlantic relations, King told me, were "very bad." But as a master of brokerage, he had soothed the feelings of the two giants and saved the deal. Or so he always claimed, rightly or wrongly, and to prove it would pull out of his wallet a tattered cable from Churchill supposedly thanking him for his help. Although reporters were not allowed to read the secret message, they saw that King's isolationism was temporarily discarded. Ogdensburg had erected a mountainous milestone in Canadian history.

By autumn, however, isolationism still gripped the United States. Running for an unprecedented third term against Wendell Willkie, a formidable Republican opponent, Roosevelt promised "again and again and again" that no American boys would be sent overseas to fight a foreign war. On Willkie's campaign train I listened to him make the same promise, three or four times a day until his voice was hoarse, almost inaudible. The candidates were outpromising each other. Whose neutrality was the more reliable? That was the chief issue of the election which, in retrospect, shamed both of them. Or, as a blushing Willkie put it when questioned by the Congress after he had circled the world and become a total internationalist, his promise had been mere "campaign oratory."

On this conversion to his One World, I thought he would have made an excellent successor to Roosevelt. And so did Roosevelt. But Willkie died before he was given the chance.

All this time Canada was expanding its war plans on a scale that must eventually stretch its resources past their limit. While Britain had survived the blitz and the threat of German invasion, it could not hope to dislodge Hitler from Western Europe by itself. Only the added power of the United States could defeat his mighty war machine, now idling in preparation for advance eastward. Nevertheless, the United States still maintained legal neutrality despite Roosevelt's increasing breaches of it.

King refused comment on the ambiguous American posture, half in and half out of the war. But some Americans did not hesitate to comment on Canadian aid to Britain. Col. Charles Lindbergh, a national hero, warned his countrymen that Canada was dragging the new world into the brawls of the old. Jerome Frank, one of Roosevelt's original brain trusters, used to tell me that my country had entered the war only to rescue its "papa," King George, and he wrote a book entitled *Save America First* which he bitterly regretted later on, admitting that he had been wrong from the start.

Fully understanding Roosevelt's dilemma, King kept in touch with him but remained silent in public and ordered his cabinet to do likewise. All he would allow, and then reluctantly, was a tour of military camps and industries by leading American journalists, not to influence them, of course, but only to show what Canada was doing and why. A luxurious train, replete with food and drink, carried the visitors through Ontario, Quebec and the Maritimes while their hosts plied them with facts, careful to avoid overt pressure. The guests saw through this clumsy disguise but wrote approvingly of Canada and the reasons for its war.

The experiment was so successful that a group of newspapers, ostensibly distant from the government, undertook a more daring venture. I was loaded on Willkie's campaign train, with $5,000 in my pocket for expenses, and instructed to report the American election. My infrequent dispatches were a flimsy cover for my real job. It was to drop in casually on editors from coast to coast and, pretending to seek political information, explain my country's purposes. Some of the editors received me sympathetically, even ran interviews or printed hasty articles from my typewriter. In other offices my reception was suspicious, hostile and brief.

I soon realized, especially in the Middle West, that isolationism was still a powerful force, the American people divided, the president's dilemma unsolved. Whether my absurd mission did any good I never knew. But I had spent all the $5,000 and, after sleeping on Willkie's train for a month, limped off it in New York, exhausted, depressed and more confused than ever.

King was depressed, too, but not exhausted or confused. He saw Roosevelt frequently in those days, their friendship ripening to the point where, he said, the president shared with him secrets never revealed to the American cabinet. On the strength of this confidence the two men scribbled on a slip of paper the agreement of Hyde Park, New York, which, according to King, Roosevelt did not fully understand. It pledged the United States to buy Canadian war materials for manufacture and shipment to Britain and thus enabled Canada to finance a foreign exchange deficit already close to wrecking its war effort.

After a visit to Hyde Park in the autumn of 1941, King returned to Ottawa and informed me that the war would soon spread to the Pacific. This news was hardly surprising. My odd friend, Adolph Berle, pixy and certified genius of the State Department, had been even freer with secrets. "We're just waiting," he said, "for the other shoe to drop." It dropped at Pearl Harbor on 7 December 1941.

Now that the United States was at war with Japan and Germany, King had no doubt of its outcome. But an old domestic problem had suddenly re-emerged to terrify him. Meighen, without benefit of a convention, had become leader of the Conservative Party again, on a platform of overseas military conscription. That news threw King into panic when a powerful wing of his own cabinet also favoured conscription which, he believed, would shatter Canada and disrupt its war plans.

Pacing up and down his office, waving his tiny fists, sputtering, incoherent, he told me that Meighen's bid for election in South York was the beginning of "Canadian fascism." He paused only to add, "The people will have their rights!"

This was only passing hysteria. But how to crush Meighen? He already had three strikes against him in the Chanak affair, the Hamilton speech and the Ogdensburg twitterings. Surely he had struck out at last? No, he seemed likely to win a seat in Parliament and there pursue his mischief. At all costs he must be defeated and finally expunged.

So he was by a pretty rough trick. The Liberals of South York were instructed not to name a candidate and split the anti-Meighen vote but to support the candidate of the CCF. That finally expunged Meighen. For King, however, the conscription debate had only begun and, in 1944, it nearly destroyed him.

The cabinet split, Defence Minister J. L. Ralston fired and replaced by the ambitious Gen. A. G. L. McNaughton, Air Minister C. G. Power resigning, the Army command frustrated and seething, anti-conscriptionist Quebec sullen and hostile—this crisis seemed likely to wreck the government and, King believed, to demoralize the nation. At the last moment he agreed to limited overseas conscription. The danger passed and the American people heard little or nothing of it.

In 1945 civilization's history of five thousand years was forever changed by the atomic bomb dropped on Hiroshima. As the only possessor of the new weapon, the United States found itself with invulnerable power, an empire in fact though not in name. How long could it last? Not long. But then, few empires lasted long, an average of some two centuries, and the British Empire even less, counting from the Seven Years War. Once Russia had the bomb, too, the empire that the Americans did not want or acknowledge lasted a bare twenty-five years from Hiroshima to defeat in Vietnam.

Where did Canada fit into it? That had always been a paramount question of foreign policy. Now, as Pearson had foreseen, it was more complex than ever. Canada remained the blind spot in the American vision of the world. In prosperous times a Canadian visitor felt embarrassed to find his country grossly, almost comically, overestimated by Americans. In bad times it was equally underestimated. The blind spot prevented any fair judgement and still does today.

Now and then the blind spot clears briefly if Canada makes sufficient fuss. When, for example, the United States applied special taxes against foreign goods, Canada was not exempted until it persuaded the American government that the taxes would injure both partners and diminish the world's largest trade volume. In a later dispute no exemption was granted.

To the Canadian in Washington the ignorance of his country among members of the Senate was unbelievable. Even its good friends, and mine, men like Mike Mansfield and Henry Jackson, did not know that in continental trade Canada was then running a huge deficit, beyond its means. Always the genial elephant twitched without any notion of its effects on the mouse.

Still, the American conscience could be aroused from time to time, a conscience peculiarly sensitive and self-accusing, contrary to foreign notions. Canada, in fact, was the primary test of that conscience, for if the United States did not fairly treat its neighbour, ally and essential partner, how could it expect the trust and support of distant nations?

By and large, the test of the border has been met, with infrequent lapses unavoidable in such a partnership, but the blind spot remained. As Kennedy had blundered in his Ottawa mission by pressing Canada too hard to join the Organization of American States, so Richard Nixon announced, contrary to the indisputable figures, that Japan was the largest trade partner of the United States.

Even when the mistake was corrected, Ronald Reagan repeated it in his time—this while the State Department's files contained more information about Canada than most Canadians ever read, editorials in their smallest newspapers meticulously classified for presidential use. But presidents are too busy to read the files, and the American people worry little about Canada. A dull, quiet, well-governed little northern country can be taken for granted. To the south, the hot-tempered Latins hit the front pages every day.

After the record, good and bad, of almost four centuries, Reagan arrived to survey, in passing moments, the latest frictions of the border and, with them, a prime minister whom neither he nor anyone else could understand. An exceedingly odd couple bestrode the border. That Trudeau was more intellectually gifted than Reagan, more educated and with a better knowledge of the world, no one could doubt on either side of the border. But the president was a nice guy who did not come last, while Trudeau was not a nice guy and seemed unlikely to come first again.

What had Reagan inherited from the experience of the centuries? And how did his heritage affect Canada? Clearly, he had inherited more than he could grasp or digest. He had taken a worldwide conservative tide and ridden it to fortune. Was the tide merely an aberration sure to land his country in shallows and in miseries? Did it mean that government would continue to retreat from the economy, as he hoped?

At best, that surmise was questionable when government rescued weak industries and desperate farmers, massively increased its defence expenditures and made its weapons industry the largest in the world—that vast military-industrial complex feared by Eisenhower, the disillusioned soldier. To suppose that the state, as an overriding, top-heavy apparatus and guarantor of peace and prosperity, would or could permanently retreat, after brief pauses, was simple nostalgia, fretting Reagan more than his people.

Besides, Reagan was haunted by the abiding presence of Roosevelt whom he had once idolized and now tried to reinterpret as a natural conservative. All presidents, since the New Deal years, had been haunted by the same towering ghost, all afraid to be bracketed with Hoover, a presence too unpopular in the American memory to be borne. Reagan's attempt to reinterpret the one and escape the other was awkward and unconvincing, but it worked in politics. And to interpret Trudeau or Canada was impossible.

Anyhow, Reagan was not concerned with Canada when he accepted the theory of supply-side economics from his whiz kids and, against all conservative tradition, piled up the deficits of a budget that he had promised to balance in his first term. For the time being, however, the new system appeared to work.

The Canadian deficits and unemployment rates were much higher than the American in Trudeau's last years of office, and they baffled him to the end as he concentrated on world affairs. He had even mused aloud that the free market no longer worked. This heresy was recanted overnight. Marc Lalonde, former Socialist and now minister of finance, became the sudden darling of corporate board rooms. The market was again the changeless Liberal credo. On it the state would count for prosperity at home and strength in the world. So would a future Conservative government.

For any Canadian government Reagan's foreign policy was as puzzling as his supply-side budgetary experiment. That policy, if it could be called a policy and not a series of hasty expedients, led to the invasion of Grenada, a Commonwealth island, without advance warning to Britain, strained the transatlantic friendship and united Trudeau and Prime Minister Margaret Thatcher who seldom agreed on anything. But the American people warmly approved the invader's easy conquest.

Reagan's adventures in the Middle East and Central America worsened the chaos there, divided his party and scared even the friendly Canadian government. Then the Star Wars controversy produced new strains in Canada and Europe and disclosed anew the North American neighbours' ignorance of each other which the experience of centuries has not fully clarified.

To be sure, Canadians know more about the United States than Americans know about Canada. But ignorance is mutual, and most Canadians today still fail to understand that the two nations are governed under systems apparently similar, basically different. As a result, Washington's policies are often viewed from Canada through a blurred or distorted magnifying glass.

Thus, for one example among many, the long-trained Canadian politician judged by the heirarchs of his party to be the best fitted for supreme office becomes its leader and may become prime minister. Without any training in elected office, Mulroney alone has broken that rule. In the United States the best-qualified man has rarely become president. Sometimes an obviously inferior man was nominated to break a convention deadlock or because he represented an area of decisive votes. In a few cases like Washington, Jackson, Grant and Eisenhower, a candidate was chosen as a war hero, with mixed results.

If the nation is lucky, the Washingtons, Lincolns and Roosevelts sometimes appear but at widely spaced intervals. The wonder in Canadian eyes is that such a chancy system of leadership works at all. Occasionally, as in the presidency of Harry Truman, it works beyond reasonable expectation. More often it does not. And the more orderly Canadian system is not without its grievous failures.

Again, many Canadians accustomed to government by a committee of Parliament, and always responsible to it, do not fully appreciate the constitutional authority of a president. He is responsible to no one but the voters on election day. His unelected cabinet officers have no power unless he delegates it to them. He can, and often does, ignore their advice, preferring that of lesser officials and nameless personal cronies. He alone enforces foreign policy, and while the Congress alone can declare war, his actions may leave no alternative. Or war may be fought without a formal declaration, as in Vietnam. But the Congress may sometimes limit the scope and purpose of foreign policy, as in Central America, by limiting the money needed to enforce them.

On the other hand, the Congress, unlike the Canadian Parliament, has no power to remove a president who loses its confidence, except by impeachment for high crimes. No president has thus been removed, though Nixon resigned in the Watergate scandal.

Presidential powers are wide, theoretically much wider than those of a prime minister, but if they lack congressional support they will become narrower in fact if not in law. For example, a president, unlike

a prime minister with a loyal caucus behind him, has no legal authority over the budget and the taxes that underwrite foreign policy. They
are the business of a Congress frequently dominated by the opposition
party and jealously guarding its power against the thrust of an executive whose term of office cannot exceed eight years. A prime minister's
term is limited only by voluntary retirement or electoral defeat.

Financial authority is supposed to be under the control of the Canadian Parliament, too, but long ago it virtually surrendered the ancient
power of the purse to the cabinet. Only twice in modern times was a
government's budget rejected by the Commons, to provoke the election of 1974 when the Liberal Party regained its majority, and the
election of 1980 when it recaptured office from the brief government
of Joe Clark.

For another example of the difference between the two governing
systems, a prime minister can be questioned daily in the House of
Commons. A president is immune to questions in the Congress. At
his occasional press conferences he answers, or refuses to answer, as he
pleases.

With all these arrangements, constitutional or reinterpreted from
time to time, the United States, fulfilling or distorting the plans of its
original architects, is governed by checks and balances that a strong
president may stretch out of joint in his favour or a strong Congress
may stretch in the opposite direction, the two powers in constant
tension.

Canada's tension is outwardly confined to the opposition's struggle
with the government. The real struggle is waged in the cabinet while
it maintains the useful fiction of solidarity. But checks and balances
exist under the Canadian system, and tension is never absent from any
system. The whip of final authority is in the prime minister's hand. He
alone can dissolve Parliament and call an election whether his followers are prepared for it or not. The president, elected for a fixed term,
has no such whip.

It follows that party discipline is much stricter in Canada than in
the United States. The American legislators—"loose fish," as Macdonald described his unreliable supporters—often defy their own president and party to join their enemies, thinking of their own local
voters. Consequently, a president must seek congressional votes where
he can, disregarding party labels and his followers' vagaries.
Roosevelt's grand coalition was composed of northern liberals and

southern conservatives who went along, more or less willingly, with the indispensable man.

A ruling Canadian coalition does the same but publicly admits no split in its own ranks. The split is always public in the United States, the party leaders powerless to hide it. From the days of the Founders, who neither foresaw nor wanted parties, regarding them as mischievous "factions," parties have overbrimmed the Constitution to dominate politics, nowadays with almost unlimited campaign funds supplied by the state itself and by interest groups on the make.

When all is said and done and the difference between two governing systems understood, Canada will never be free of a president's success and failure. How, then, will Reagan's policies affect the Canadian future, political, economic and military? Where is the personal Reagan-Mulroney friendship leading us? Perhaps some answers may be found if we re-examine the impersonal friendship of the continent from some often neglected vision points.

9

THE OLD
SPECTRE

In Ottawa, after the Mulroney government took office, I
met two old friends. Both were retired diplomats of the highest rank
and both were newly troubled by Canada's prospects. One of them said
that the prime minister had thrown away his trump cards in pending
negotiations with the United States by publicly giving it "the benefit
of the doubt." The second man declared that Mulroney was a "con-
tinentalist" who would sell Canada, piece after piece, to the greedy
Americans.

When I had just flown in from a Washington always ignorant of
Canada, these alarms seemed to me preposterous. Surely no Canadian
leader, I said, would sell Canada to any foreign nation. But the veter-
ans of many an international bargaining table had a point even if they
exaggerated it. For already, unknown to us then (and perhaps to
Mulroney), a decisive issue of Canada's life—an issue older than the
nation itself—was re-emerging in politics and another great debate. To
us old-timers it had the dreamlike quality of déjà vu, a familiar movie
seen in our youth and long forgotten.

The issue has worn various labels, or disguises, since pre-
Confederation days. In its latest installment it is called free trade with
the United States, but that label, as we shall see, can be variously

interpreted to mean much, little, or nothing. If we are to understand what our government is planning—if indeed it has any clear plan, which seems highly dubious—we must look back more than a century.

In 1849 the depressed merchants of Montreal published their notorious manifesto in favour of Canada's annexation to the United States, but they soon repented their folly. Such a cry of despair had ceased to be practical politics and today is less practical than ever on both sides of the border. Nonetheless, some distinguished Canadian minds are still haunted by Manifest Destiny, the threat nowadays styled "continentalism," the fear that the elephant will turn carnivorous and devour all territory north to the Arctic.

While the same fear existed from the earliest times, it did not prevent the colony of Canada (the present Ontario and Quebec) from seeking and enjoying a ten-year almost free-trade deal with the United States. Then the Congress, angered by Canada's supposed aid to the rebellious South in the Civil War, abrogated the deal, and the primitive Canadian economy suffered an immediate slump. On becoming his nation's first prime minister, Macdonald sought to revive the deal in some form and so did his successor, Mackenzie, but in vain.

Only when the United States had finally rejected it did Macdonald introduce his opposite National Policy of Protection (that unpopular word carefully avoided) on which the Canadian economy was built. And only once was Macdonald's design seriously challenged. In 1911 the voters defeated Laurier's Reciprocity agreement, something like free trade, because they feared it would lead to Canada's eventual absorption by its neighbour—the last thing that the great French Canadian nationalist desired.

No doubt all this history has been well studied by the current prime minister. But it is not remembered by most of the current generation of voters, and the choices now facing them are generally misunderstood or deliberately fudged. No clarity need be expected in the visible future.

What, in fact, is the meaning of the convenient omnibus phrase, *free trade?* Does it mean the elimination of all commercial barriers on the border, the partial elimination or something else not yet explained on either side? Whatever it means, we had better grasp the options before us, the chances of increased wealth and the possible threat to Canada's sovereignty. For always sovereignty, not economic gain, has decided the old issue. So, I believe, it will again.

These matters are far more complex than they look in fragmentary news items or the brief flashes of television. They are complex enough to require a book, or library, of explanation, and they baffle and divide the best minds in our politics. Here only a rough, inadequate summary can be attempted.

At the start certain dull, obvious and undisputed facts must be seen as limiting national policy under any government. Among them:

Canada, with its small population, is one of the Big Seven industrial nations and attends their annual summits. It is also one of the world's largest traders but, unlike all its leading competitors, it lacks a large domestic market.

More than any of them it depends for prosperity on external markets, sells about three-quarters of its exports to the United States and there buys about the same fraction of its imports. The movement of goods, services and capital between these two nations has no equivalent elsewhere.

Any serious drop in Canada's exports may be temporarily offset by foreign borrowing, but this is a short-run measure and piles up debt for future repayment in currencies of unpredictable value. As a rule of thumb, Canada's prosperity will rise or fall with the volume of its trade, and without massive volume its living standard would collapse. The present massive volume is not enough to raise the standard, perhaps even to maintain it, and certainly not enough to solve the unemployment problem.

For all its economic problems combined, Canada's economy is precariously balanced and ill prepared.

Up to now its great resource industries of forest, farm, mine and fishery were efficient and competitive, but they have suddenly met new, unexpected and strong competitors in the world market.

During the long postwar boom it was taken for granted, almost as a law of nature, that the world would always need and buy the Canadian resource industries' products. Now other countries, once economically primitive, can produce similar goods at lower prices based mainly on lower wages. Facing this challenge, the Canadian industries must further increase their efficiency.

Canada's competitive strength as a whole is said to have lately risen to seventh place among the industrial nations. Although all such unofficial figures are questionable, there is no doubt about the status of the manufacturing industries of Ontario and Quebec, the Laurentian heartland with its millions of workers. These industries have long been subsidized by tariffs and other forms of protection. Some have become soft and noncompetitive outside Canada; many survive on sales to the home market at artificially high prices and the willingness of the consumers to pay them. While most consumers pay reluctantly, it is in the thickly populated heartland that national elections are decided.

Aside from ordinary compassion, no political party seeking votes will allow single-industry towns to die for lack of protection. But so long as the soft industries are sure of it they will not feel compelled to harden their methods. They will find reasons or excuses for delaying their costly improvement which, over time, is unavoidable. Already some of them, unable to meet even the present test, have died along with the jobs of their workers.

If their destruction is sound economics, it is neither practical politics nor, in depressed times, tolerable human behaviour. If the problem is to be solved the solution must proceed step by step, on a definite schedule, as protection is reduced while the victims of unemployment are retrained for new jobs in new industries or, in the case of elderly workers, given a pensioned livelihood. So far, all governments have talked about effective remedies but never devised them.

The General Agreement on Tariffs and Trade (GATT), of which Canada was a major architect, stands behind these problems, the signatory nations obligated to obey a code of fair multilateral commerce. For example, if Nation A negotiates a tariff reduction with Nation B, the same advantage must be extended to all the GATT members. Or if the rules are infringed by any nation, the others are permitted to retaliate and sometimes do. Trade under this worldwide international contract has steadily expanded over nearly four decades. Average tariffs have reached an all-time low and the world's total wealth an all-time high, though it is unevenly distributed.

In recent times the spirit if not always the strict letter of GATT has been infringed by most or all of its signatories, including Canada. For agreed, overt tariffs they substituted different trade barriers like import quotas, customs regulations, harassment of importers and preference for local supplies in governmental purchasing. In Canada, moreover, the ten provinces enforce unacknowledged barriers against one another.

Wild swings in the value of national currencies often proved more effective than alternative devices in changing the patterns of trade, once the hopeful postwar Bretton Woods international monetary agreement broke down. Thus the Canadian dollar, cheap in present American terms, acts as a tariff of about 25 per cent against imports from the United States and subsidizes exporters to that market. At the same time the dollar, strong overseas, damages the nation's sales there.

All facts considered, the basic GATT principle of multilateralism is endangered by threats peculiarly dangerous to Canada. The Trudeau government was mistaken about many things, but it fully explored those threats and framed specific trade policies that often violated or reversed the original policy of the Liberal Party.

A prolonged, deep study, masterminded by Mitchell Sharp, the cabinet's ubiquitous handyman, concluded that Canada had only three options. They were increased protectionism, free trade with the United States or the expansion of markets in other countries.

More protectionism was rejected in theory but maintained in some soft industries and even applied, on overseas imports, to the formerly competitive automobile industry while in America alone automotive goods were freed of all tariffs. But apart from this special arrangement, an overall, exclusive continental free-trade bargain was rejected as likely to diminish or imperil the nation's sovereignty when Canadians gradually accustomed themselves to American economic dominance. That left the famous Third Option, and the government adopted it. Canada would seek increased markets all over the world to reduce its dependence on the United States.

Laurier's heirs, even King, after toying with Liberal Reciprocity in the postwar years, had quickly dropped it. Trudeau, King's latest heir, invested his hopes in the Third Option, a variant of the Diefenbaker government's attempt to divert a substantial fraction of Canada's exports from the United States to Britain and the Commonwealth members. That attempt failed. Against Diefenbaker's angry protests, Britain joined the European Common Market (which he called a "rich men's club"), basing its economic future largely on business with its closest neighbours.

The Liberal Third Option also failed in its primary objective. A thriving Canadian economy became more, not less, dependent on the American market. When the Mulroney government took office it showed no fear of this trend. Instead, it proposed to seek an "accord" of some undisclosed sort with the United States in direct reversal of the Conservative Party's economic doctrine since Macdonald's time.

The old issue was cutting straight across partisan lines. But something much more important than the divisions in the Conservative government and the Liberal opposition was now underway and posed for Canada a new quandary that most of the public had yet to grasp.

After the Second World War Canadian policy was fully committed to the multilateral doctrine of GATT and against the growth of bilateral trading blocs, lest Canada be squeezed between them. In recent years, all the same, such blocs were growing, and GATT permitted them—providing they did not become zones of increased protectionism to carve up the world market and limit its total wealth. Nevertheless, the European Common Market moved in that direction, its members trading freely among themselves while protecting some of their own industries and discriminating against outsiders.

In response, the emergence of competing zones could easily be foreseen and some of a minor sort already existed. To Canada's long-term disadvantage, the multilateralism of GATT was gravely threatened while the Mulroney government began to consider a free-trade deal with the United States without committing itself to any specific plan.

Thence came a momentous double question: If indeed multilateralism was dying, would Canada be forced to join a bilateral North American bloc on the best terms it could wring from its rich neighbour? And would such a deal actually threaten sovereignty? There, under the customary doubletalk and fudge and politics, stands the old and ever new Canadian conundrum.

It raises several subquestions: If North America forms the world's largest bilateral trade bloc, will it compel outsiders to form their own blocs and further carve up the world market, all nations losing in the end and, still worse, aggravating their political and military divisions?

In this divisive process who would be the most injured victims, if not the Third World peoples against whom the rich nations already are discriminating by import restrictions and largely ignoring the chemicals of future explosion among the poor that could involve the superpowers with fateful consequences? Have the rich foolishly neglected the opportunities of a growing Third World market now, according to the nonpartisan North-South Institute, potentially more valuable than Europe to Canada's export industries?

To these questions the answer is clear: Growing bilateralism would impoverish the world economy. Given such a risk, no sensible Canadian government will voluntarily surrender, though it may abuse, the multilateralism of GATT—freer trade by all means, exclusive discriminatory deals never.

For Canada the deepening quandary does not end there. Much more serious is the threat, real or imagined, to its independent nationhood.

Today some of the nation's wisest minds deliver opposite judgements. It was no wonder that the Mulroney government, beset by immediate economic and financial problems at home and within its caucus, hesitated to embrace anything more than the safe, amorphous notion of a continental "accord," thus echoing Reagan's original vague offer in Washington. Later, the government issued a discussion paper which sketched a series of options much like those submitted by its predecessor but committed itself to none. In the lingo of politics, all options were left open. In plain English, the government had not made up its mind. It probably had until autumn 1985 to negotiate a bargain of some kind with the United States. "You can be absolutely sure," Mulroney said, "that Canada will cut a deal."

If so, it will not embrace exclusive bilateral free trade, Mulroney added. Given the climate surrounding the two dealers and their overseas partners, such a deal is out of the question. But at some future time the climate may change for the better or the worse. That is why bilateralism remains a possible option with all its unknown consequences.

The shattered Liberal opposition, beset like the government by divisions in its ranks, nevertheless opted for a clear stand against free trade and confirmed the policy of the Trudeau government. Canada, said John Turner, should be ready to do increased business with the United States but was "not for sale" while Mulroney had become too subservient to his friend, Reagan.

Thus Turner hoped to devise a winning issue for the next election. By then, however, all the current issues may be outdated by different ones, now unpredictable. In the meantime the American government, beset by growing protectionism in the Congress, said that any trade initiative must come from Canada. Reagan's options, too, were left open.

The first Canadian initiative, or personal reaction, came from

Donald Macdonald, a distinguished Liberal politician and thinker, who had narrowly missed the prime minister's office in 1979. In 1985, pre-empting the report of his royal commission on Canada's economy, he boldly advocated free trade and advised the country to embrace it as "a leap of faith," a return to the Laurier policy of 1911.

Since Macdonald had the support of his commission, many old-fashioned Liberals and some leaders among the business community, the split in the opposition's thinking was nakedly exposed. The split in the Conservative Party was better concealed by safe generalities for the time being, but assuming that Mulroney's talk of an accord was more than a political ploy, concealment could not be indefinitely maintained.

From the same assumption, on both sides of politics, will come the key issue far more vital in the end than any damage inflicted by real free trade on the soft industries of the heartland and elsewhere. And this issue demands far more thought than Canadians have yet given it.

The obvious factors aside, would exclusive continental free trade really damage Canada's political independence? The Trudeau government thought it would. As an ordinary citizen, schooled in an opposite faith, I now think so, too, but rather long experience with politicians convinces me that the issue will not be settled by economic argument. It will be settled by different considerations because the nation is more than an economy. It was born and lives on factors intangible, instinctive, inexpressible. Those mindways and clustered memories are well understood, or felt, and shared by most Canadians whatever their political views may be. If that spirit is lacking, if the original idea of Canada is dead, the nation will die also, whatever economic policies are enforced to save its life.

Hard times always tempt Canadians to envy their rich neighbours, even to join them in continental prosperity, despite the risk. But there is no guarantee that real free trade would make Canadians richer. The effect could be the opposite if existing American-owned industries in Canada, now dependent on the protective system, moved home to the United States. While the benefits and losses cannot be estimated in advance, the lure of full continental economic union has always been rejected in the past and is likely to be rejected again if the chance is offered.

The total independent sovereignty of Canada, the United States or any nation, we should remember, is not permanently guaranteed by providence and the laws of the universe. It is manmade and therefore perishable. Many nations, once strong, rich and proud, have lost it.

Unrestricted, bilateral free trade would surely impinge on existing Canadian sovereignty, I believe, and this view is shared by some Americans who understand their neighbours. The best-known example is George Ball, once the undersecretary of state. He was slapped down by his Canadian friends after writing in a controversial book that even without free trade Canada might not win its struggle against ultimate continental integration and that free trade would hasten a natural process.

Some ten years later, in a second book—one of the wisest written by a contemporary American statesman—Ball withdrew his earlier judgement. It had been reached, he said, in a "daydreaming way" before he had realized Canada's "fierce sense of national identity" which he admired and which was steadily increasing. Nor did he advocate union which, anyhow, was becoming more and more improbable with the passage of time.

Then, all of a sudden in May 1985, Mulroney appeared to end the debate on free trade as those words are usually understood. At Calgary he spoke to a group of Japanese businessmen and, according to the reliable Canadian Press, said: "We do not seek an exclusive or exclusionary relationship with the United States. Whatever we do will be compatible with our multilateral obligations."

Evidently, he had thought his way past the meaningless slogans and showbiz of his March conference with Reagan at Quebec. He must have realized, then or later, that if Canada and the United States erected a joint tariff against the world, the senior partner in Washington, not the junior in Ottawa, would fix their joint import barriers. Canada would thus surrender a crucial element of its sovereignty and ensure fierce retaliation from its valuable customers outside North America.

So any deal cut in 1985 will not mean bilateralism after all. It will mean something else of a multilateral kind yet unspecified. Donald Macdonald's leap of faith in the dark is rejected by the three political parties as a danger too great to be risked.

It has been argued, in favour of the leap, that the nations of the European Common Market frame a joint tariff without surrendering a whit of their sovereignty. Why should Canada fear to do the same? Because the parallel is misleading.

The nations of Europe have a long record of independence, separate languages, cultures, folkways (and frequent wars) behind them. Besides, the leading members of the Common Market have roughly equal populations and political weight, but they are far from ready to surrender their separate political powers. The noble dream of a federated Europe, with a single supreme legislature, remains only a dream.

Canada's experience has not repeated that of Europe. It speaks the same language as its neighbours, governs by roughly the same federal system and shares much of the American people's culture flowing hourly across the border. But even with these influences to support it, the dream of voluntary political union in North America seems no more realistic than the faded dream in Europe.

Nobody can know, of course, how Canada's real sovereignty would be affected by an exclusive free-trade deal with the United States. If Macdonald's leap is too dangerous, what is the alternative? Certainly not the unaltered status quo which ill suits the future needs of the Canadian economy. The true alternative is the steady expansion of multilateral trade under the GATT principles even if they are sometimes bent or broken.

Robert Browning's couplet, though now a shopworn cliché, is the safest rule of all public and private behaviour: "Ah, but a man's reach should exceed his grasp or what's a heaven for?"

If a large part of our species is condemned to something more like hell, increased trade, worldwide, does not necessarily exceed the reach of human intelligence, and for Canada is a consummation devoutly to be wished. Nonetheless, if the world moves in the contrary direction of bilateralism, if GATT's multilateralism is destroyed by quarrelling blocs, then Canada may be forced to leap in the dark with consequences unforeseeable.

Considering them, even the most ardent Canadian nationalists must recognize that the sovereignty of all nations has been drastically limited in our time by a process outside their control. The richest and strongest of them may pretend otherwise but the world becomes more interdependent every day like a spreading and fragile spiderweb. And the menace of its weaponry speeds the process.

E. B. White, the American philosopher best known as a writer of unique style, put this truth in one of his superbly simple essays. It was written in 1956 when few statesmen had yet fully discerned the human condition. After the release of atomic energy, he wrote, a nation alone possessing nuclear weapons was a secure nation but its strength could not last long. Once many nations had them, or the means of creating them, they became unusable, short of mutual annihilation. While no nation liked to admit its dependence on others, and all were weaker than they pretended, there was no machinery to govern the age of interdependence and none had been devised, as the United Nations so tragically proved.

These failures may seem to have little to do with Canada's trade policy, but all things in the world of politics are interlocked, though a Canadian government, grappling with the day's minutiae, has little time to think beyond them. Long-term thinking, for the most part, is left to the government's advisers who know (or are expected to know) more than their bosses.

In a silly regulation the Mulroney government forbade its officials to talk to journalists, even off the record, without specific permission in each case. This prohibition will not work, and fortunately it cannot be applied to the senior officials, known as mandarins, who have retired. Some of them, their names long household words throughout the country, are old friends of mine, and recently I Gallup-polled them in a crude amateurish fashion.

Only one among half a dozen refused to worry about free trade as dangerous to sovereignty. An economist of highest credentials and worldwide experience, he said that the loss of sovereignty might be all for the best. If some Canadian industries shrank or died, why shouldn't their workers move to the American Sunbelt States where climate, life styles and job opportunities had no equal in Canada? If its population dwindled to, say, fifteen million, the grand scheme of things would not be disturbed. Thus spoke the pristine Economic Man, a man of absolute honesty. But his fellows all disagreed with him.

Only nontariff barriers like import quotas now restrict most North American trade but effectively shelter some major industries on both sides of the border. Even this dike against competition does not satisfy them. Once hard, they have become relatively soft and demand still stronger protection; Parliament and Congress alike are asked to increase it. Definite decisions cannot be postponed much longer.

Canada runs a large surplus in "visible" merchandise trade with its neighbour. The United States runs a corresponding deficit with Canada, second only to its deficit with Japan. The total deficit incurred abroad is more than even the rich American economy can afford and distorts the world's entire trade system. No wonder, then, that protectionism grows in congressional politics, despite Reagan's resistance. Is the world facing a general trade war, a return to the storm cellar of the disastrous 1930s, the era of Hoover, Smoot and Hawley in Washington, of Bennett in Ottawa? If this sounds like a mere bogey today, it could be a real possibility tomorrow unless the present drift is arrested. Must each generation learn anew for itself that there is no safety in the cellar, no profit in dog-eat-dog economics?

For all its continental problems, Canada will never lack advice from abroad, assuredly not from the London *Economist*. That prestigious oracle, regarding human life as an economic process, urges Canada to join the United States and build the new and ever-prosperous country of "Namerica" (though it admits with regret that the work of construction will not be soon completed).

This benevolent counsel brought a quick response from Richard Gwyn, one of Ottawa's most perceptive journalists. His native land of Britain, he wrote, is down on Canada these days, one London newspaper calling it "the great white waste of time." Europe, as Gwyn finds it in his travels, now suffers from "an acute case of Atlantic-envy" when "the Old World is going down not just economically but in terms of population which, psychologically, is probably the most important decline of all. The New World is coming up, including, confound it, that ex-colony on the top half."

Without understanding Canada, the *Economist* and other informed authorities fully understand what damage increased protectionism would inflict on the complex, indivisible world economy of our time. They know, too, that Canadian and American business systems grew out of the same protectionist roots, cultivated by Alexander Hamilton in the United States and John A. Macdonald in Canada.

The growth was different in speed and wore different labels. By the necessity of their life and small numbers, Canadians always relied more than their neighbours on government. Or as the familiar cliché puts it, Canada stood, and stands, to the left of the ideological centre. But the contemporary governments in both nations are relying on the same economic theory expressed in John Kennedy's metaphor of a rising tide sure to lift all boats and benefit all classes. In Canada the tide has not yet risen far enough to satisfy one class or the other. The Kennedy-Reagan theory is still not fully tested.

However that may be, a tide lifting free, or even much freer, trade up to the level of practical politics would force Canada to make one of the most critical decisions in its history.

The present century faced it with three apparent threats to its nationhood: the conscription crisis of 1917, the Quebec election of 1939, when Premier Maurice Duplessis proposed to take his province out of the world war, and, most dangerous of all threats, the Quebec separatist movement led by Premier René Lévesque, who failed to win a decisive referendum and mutilated his own party.

What had Canadians of both communities learned from the surmounted crises? Assuredly that the nation was one thing or nothing; that split into two or more fragments each would be sucked sooner or later into the hegemony of the United States, and that Canadians alone—barring nuclear war—could destroy their nation as they alone had made it.

Yet the twin ghosts of Quebec separatism and American Manifest Destiny have always haunted many Canadians. They even haunted a statesman as able as R. B. Bennett who told me, after his retirement, that I would live to see the nation split on the line of the Ottawa River. Shortly after our conversation he abandoned Canada in despair and fled to the ancestral womb of England, history triumphing over geography.

How the American people regard their neighbour's occasional self-torture and absurd masochism will be discussed later from a different angle of vision. Here it is timely to consider the plight of the oddest group among the anticontinentalists, the extreme "liberals" inside and outside the party of that name.

They preach mankind's brotherhood. They are all for peace (hardly an original sentiment) and the fairer distribution of the world's riches. They shed torrents of crocodile tears over the miseries of the Third World, but they would not allow it to pay its foreign debts or give it a chance of modest prosperity by exports to the Canadian market. They are frightened by Canada's excessive dependence on the market and capital of the United States but seldom admit that, lacking those benefits, the Canadian living standard must sink to a level unknown since the Great Depression.

Liberalism of that school, in all parties, usually turns into aggressive nationalism—this even though nationalism, wrongly construed, has been the recurring plague and cause of war throughout the ages and now is causing local wars throughout the world.

If the unsquared economic circle and anguish of such bastard liberalism is sad to look upon, the thin shadow line between patriotism and xenophobia is difficult to find and walk. But walk it we must or let sovereignty become xenophobia with resulting loss of influence in the world and limited prosperity at home.

The nationalism advocated by its more articulate voices is blind to the primary facts of the continent, of two nations forever locked within it by history, geography, language and common external danger. You may not like the facts but there they are, unalterable. To escape them, the outright nationalists often seek refuge in mean, visceral anti-Americanism which, they say, is nothing of the kind. On the contrary, it is enlightened patriotism directed not against the American society as a whole but only against its government.

That distinction is usually blurred in Canadian debate, replaced by gut prejudice. When anti-Reaganism is widespread on both sides of the border, the American people's long-run attitudes should not be confused with those of their short-run governors. Nor should the governed misunderstand, as they sometimes do, the attitudes of the sensible majority in Canada.

True enough, our nation at its beginning was largely a negative response to Manifest Destiny but could not have endured without a positive idea of its own. The old devil theory of politics cannot serve our needs today, though it still endures on the fringe of Canadian life.

How, then, should nationalism be rightly construed? Is it possible for Canadian citizens to believe in both nationhood and internationalism at the same time? Of course it is. All our most successful leaders were nationalists and internationalists. Men like Macdonald, Laurier, Borden, King, St. Laurent, Pearson and the aging Trudeau learned to walk the shadow line, often stumbling on one side or the other. So, we may expect, will Mulroney when he has mastered his job.

Many professed liberals ignore or fudge the facts. They refuse to see that a citizen may love Canada without hating foreigners, especially Americans, that an inwardly strong nation is a valuable building block in a changeable world as a weak nation cannot be. The wise nationalist is also an internationalist, seeing the world entire, not merely its parts. If this seems paradoxical, the paradox is Canada's Manifest Destiny, its only workable governing method—and the justification of its nationhood. To meet the needs of these skimblescamble times Canadians live perforce in a house under endless recon-struction, inconvenient to the householder and never finished.

In that process the issue of free trade versus protectionism will also remain unfinished despite all the partisan myths surrounding it. Prob-ably no living statesman has better described the endless sham battle between myth and reality than the Earl of Stockton, the former Harold Macmillan, prime minister of Britain. Elevated to the House of Lords, he warned it that "once you get a doctrine, that is the end of you. Pragmatic politics are the only good ones." Certainly they are the only good ones for Canada. The free-trade and protectionist doctrines, as absolute truths, have no place here.

To all problems of trade and foreign investment, the fringe of Cana-dian nationalism has a ready answer. Canada, it says, must reduce its dependence on the exporting industries and promote new, sophisti-cated, high-tech industries, the magic of computers, automation and superhuman robots. While no one, except the small minority who desire a less materialistic life, will quarrel with this advice, the facts get in the way of the argument.

Canada has suffered much luckless experience with megaprojects, some of a highly technical kind. The taxpayers' money invested in nuclear reactors, heavy water, airplane factories and more exotic ven-tures produced heavy losses. Since no industrial nation can resist the high-tech era, doubtless other projects will be successfully launched, but for a long time ahead the resource industries, Canada's naturally strong points, will be the underpinning of the economy. In them massive investment and more efficient machinery are needed to reduce costs and employment per unit of production. Lacking improved methods, these industries cannot meet the increasing challenge of foreign competitors. They, too, are mastering technology.

However its problems are solved, Canada will require large infusions of new capital to build new industries or expand old ones. A growing economy must seek investment money wherever it can be found on reasonable terms. The Canadian people's savings, high by world stan-dards, do not meet their needs or, at any rate, their demands for increasing wealth. When they commonly prefer safe guaranteed debt instruments like government bonds to stocks without any guaranteed returns, they depend on other nations for much risk capital. Without that enormous inflow, the present economy could not have been built and cannot enjoy adequate growth.

Most of the capital has come from the United States, which also buys most of Canada's exports. Unfortunately, too much of the imported funds has not been used to make the economy grow. It was used to cover the net deficits in total trade, visible and invisible, the Current Account, as economists call it. In recent years, with the advantage of a currency devalued in American terms, the exports of physical goods greatly exceeded the imports, but the surplus thus earned was too often spent, or overspent, on dividends and interest payments to foreign lenders, on Canadians' tourist travel, insurance, shipping and other service costs.

In some years Canada earned a small net surplus, in others not enough foreign money to finance necessary constructive investment and unnecessary extravagance. Instead, it borrowed to pay a large fraction of its housekeeping expenses, its grocery bill, by contracting and steadily increasing its foreign debt, governmental and private. A rich nation not always earning its livelihood in the world frequently lived beyond its current means. The Canadian people's appetite for a cake eaten and never reduced in volume still persists to deny the laws of arithmetic.

This vicious circle of debt financed by more and more debt unwisely used is a valid target of attack for nationalists and internationalists alike. Nationalists see in it not only financial and economic losses but political dangers. The United States, we are told, has failed to conquer Canada with arms and is now buying it with money until an excessive segment of our economy is owned by foreigners who couldn't care less about our nationhood. That is a legitimate fear, but Canada has the power to govern all capital when it arrives here by enforcing its own laws. For example, it preserves Canadian control of such vital services as the information media that cannot be safely alienated.

Who sought and still seeks foreign capital? Who invited it to move here in the first place? Only Canadians. They reaped the benefits and were able to invest substantial amounts of their own capital in the United States which welcomed it.

Recognizing no international boundary, capital is always hungry for profits wherever they can be earned and is poised for instant flight. If it is unfairly treated here, foreign investment will be curtailed or withdrawn. The consequences would be grave and, if the withdrawal were large and sudden enough, could be disastrous to Canada. Far short of this risk, we should not forget that foreign investors repatriate only their profits or interest earnings while they employ Canadian workers and develop Canadian resources.

Nevertheless, Canada has sold off too large a fraction of some important industries to make quick gains and will be stuck with the results until, over time, it finds enough money—and will—to buy part of them back. On a small but promising scale that process has begun already. Here a sense of proportion and timing, of long-term gains or losses, is required but has often been lacking in government and private life.

The Trudeau government took a long time to grasp, or admit, such obvious facts after it had established the Foreign Investment Review Agency to judge the benefits of imported capital or to even halt it. In its last years the government limited these restrictions and dulled the agency's teeth. The Mulroney government soon left the instrument virtually edentulous. Then it abolished a Liberal energy policy which, it said, had unfairly treated foreign investors and stifled economic growth in the western provinces.

The results have yet to appear. However they turn out, a sensible nationalism must always insist that the owners of foreign capital invested in Canada have no right to operate, even marginally, under foreign law. Extraterritoriality was asserted, or implied, by some former American governments, but it is intolerable to any self-respecting nation. It must be firmly suppressed. On the other hand, foreign capital must be treated without the discrimination sometimes enforced in the past.

What mainly concerns economic realists is not the presence of United States capital in Canada but its use, behaviour and motives. Do American investors, consciously or unconsciously, gobble up Canada's essential resources, having already depleted many of their own? Not content with profits, will they try to share and control too large a fraction of those resources, including clean water, the most precious among them? Is Canadian water to replace the rapidly diminishing underground storage basin that irrigates midwestern American farm land?

These are indeed momentous questions for the future. Canada possesses in its rivers, lakes and the vast sponge of the Pre-Cambrian Shield about a seventh of the world's fresh water but cannot safely export much more of it until the nation's own permanent needs have been fully guaranteed, and they are yet incalculable. No additional southward diversion should be allowed in volume sufficient to deplete one of Canada's unique assets and, as proposed by some American engineers, to change the native landscape and climate. The United States, they argue, must have increased supplies or its increasing population will go short and its food production will fall, ensuring starvation for millions of distant people.

These potential conflicts of interest could someday provoke the gravest friction the border has known in modern times (not to mention the "greenhouse effect" of carbon and other fumes in the atmosphere supposedly threatening the whole planet).

Meanwhile the more urgent threat is air, water and land pollution, emitted by industries and automobiles poisoning countless Canadian and American lakes and damaging Europe's forests. No doubt this clear and present danger will later invade our forests also.

Despite their friendship, Mulroney has not yet persuaded Reagan to co-operate, in more than gestures, against the menace of acid rain which emerges from Canadian as well as American industries. Oddly, the president, an out-of-doors man, does not seem to grasp these dangers and resists effective action because it involves too much money and too many votes. Although the cost of a remedy will be astronomical—far higher than governments in North America and elsewhere are yet ready to admit, or taxpayers to face—it must be paid eventually because the cost of neglect is still higher, the alternative truly calamitous.

Apart from all such relatively short-run problems, no theory, ideology or political promise will solve, or even comprehend, the long-run problems of the border. Neither Canadians nor Americans are theoretical by nature and training. To them, ideology is for college and professors, cranks and nuts.

Throughout North America a system evolves under varied names from the people's workaday habits while governments dance around the perimeter, articulate platitudes and have only the vaguest notion of what is really happening to mankind. But maybe governments deserve a little charity. After all, nobody knows what is happening below the surface at any given time.

In any event, Canadians will not begin to understand the United States until they have seen much more than its tourist haunts, known its diverse people far beyond the big cities and studied not just the daily utterance of governments but their real foreign policy now in rapid evolution. These things are very different from their popular image north of the border.

10

NEIGHBOURS GREAT AND SMALL

In Washington, when he was secretary of state, I first saw Dean Acheson at a press conference. He struck me as the coldest fish in the ocean—steely, unblinking eyes, mustachio of a Spanish grandee, clipped sentences of ice. But I was quite wrong about him as I had been about Graham Towers in Ottawa.

When I came to know Acheson well, thanks only to his daughter, Mary Bundy, and her husband, Bill, I found that he was a fellow of infinite jest, who kept any dinner table in a roar with his mischievous recollections. He was also a warm-hearted sentimentalist in other moods, a doting parent, a vulnerable human being, the least understood American public figure of his time. Later I realized, as apparently many did not, that in Acheson and Pearson the unending problems of the North American border were vividly symbolized.

Towards Canada Acheson seemed ambivalent. His ancestry was Canadian and in his youth he had worked on railway construction in Ontario. The mature statesman regarded Pearson with friendship but occasional doubt. Their minds and policies were bound to collide sooner or later and could not be easily reconciled in foreign affairs. Naturally enough, Acheson was irritated by moral sermons from Ottawa and took them to be unrealistic in a world of clashing super-powers.

About one thing Acheson was sure—if Canada, "stern daughter of the wrath of God," complained that it was taken for granted in the United States, it had better not take its neighbour for granted, either. He was also sure that the United States, as a superpower, need not expect foreign affection. It could command only respect and that was sufficient. But he believed that Harry Truman's successors were squandering his hard-won gains.

Still, through his years of trial, realism and sometimes misjudgement, Acheson kept his head while others lost theirs and blamed everything on him. He suffered fools in the Congress, the media and foreign governments if not gladly at least with steady nerves and dogged self-control.

His chief and idol, Truman, was given to outbursts of anger and had won the election of 1948 by his fiery attacks on a "do-nothing" Congress. Equally infuriated at times, Acheson did not permit himself this luxury except among trusted friends. He understood the awful responsibility of power, a responsibility that many Canadians do not understand when they have comparatively little of their own. But he knew that he had made mistakes and readily admitted them in conversation and print. I began to see that his reputation of arrogance cloaked an inner humility, the public posture often misrepresenting the private man.

When, for example, he had written a harsh commentary on Canadian policy in a book sponsored by Livingston Merchant, former ambassador to Canada and always its friend, Mary Bundy asked, or rather commanded, me to revise Acheson's chapter. In an act of supreme courage I bearded the lion, expecting to be eaten alive. Instead, he told me to rewrite the chapter. Still dubious, I did so, and he approved the new version without changing a word.

His years of office since Roosevelt's time had been strenuous and controversial, but afterward he could relax and enjoy life's ironies. While he, his wife, Alice, the Bundys and my wife, Dorothy, were guests in Pearson's apartment during Expo 67, an English lady among the crowds took Acheson for Anthony Eden. Could she have that great man's signature to commemorate the happy festival? Acheson signed Eden's name in her book. A gentleman, he told us, could not disappoint a lady. Hearing of the forgery, Eden was not amused. Acheson did not care. He had relished the little joke on his English friend.

One morning at breakfast, cooked by Acheson, I backed my chair against the small glass pane of a bookcase and cracked it. This, said the cook, was a grave affair. Guests from the United States would be blamed for damaging the Canadian government's property. An international crisis might well result. To forestall it I must confess my guilt and pay for it. So I wrote Pearson, explained the accident and sent him a cheque for five dollars which seemed more than adequate. The prime minister, then grappling with a political crisis in Ottawa, answered me in his own handwriting. Yes, he said, the affair was indeed grave. But he would try to hush it up, if possible, by returning my cheque and ordering his cabinet not to reveal a dangerous state secret.

Acheson and Truman, an odd but successful partnership between the aristocrat and the western dirt farmer, did not vary in their joint view of the world. Together they produced NATO, the Marshall Plan, the Truman Doctrine in the Mediterranean and the defence of Korea. When the Communist north invaded the south, Acheson and Truman saw at once that here was a challenge that must be resisted and only the United States could resist it. Acheson, though he had little faith in the United Nations, managed to involve it (thanks to the absence of the Russian delegate) and made the war a defence of collective security, of freedom everywhere. This decision was reached at a dramatic moment in American history—Acheson urging intervention, Gen. George Marshall skeptical of victory, Truman listening and finally deciding that the war would be fought, whatever the risks.

Canada entered it as a responsible member of the United Nations. Pearson, then minister of external affairs, warned the cabinet that it had no alternative. Prime Minister St. Laurent agreed.

Later, as the war long continued, Pearson sought to end it by diplomatic bargaining, and Acheson grew impatient with the Canadian's efforts, doubtless well intentioned but, at the time, impractical and unrealistic. Thus arises a question that still divides the admirers and critics of both men: Was Acheson the realist, actually more realistic than Pearson? Or had Pearson seen farther ahead than Acheson by recognizing the limits and risks of superpower, the inevitable diffusion of power among the newly armed states, some with nuclear weapons, in a world of rapid change?

As I understood Acheson, peace, stability and prosperity were just as important to him as to Pearson. But they could never be achieved if the peaceful nations lacked adequate power to curb the adventures of the unpeaceful.

Pearson, as I understood him, could not believe that military power of itself was enough to forestall the ultimate catastrophe, though power in responsible hands was an imperative need to meet the immediate threat. He did not waver in his loyalty to NATO; after all, he had been one of its first advocates. Nor did he waver in his support of the United States, but when its policy was mistaken in his judgement, he did not hesitate to question it publicly.

In his reckoning the time available to save the peace was shorter than Acheson seemed to believe. Certainly Pearson's faith in the United Nations and his hopes for a rudimentary world government of some kind in the distant future were much greater than Acheson ever professed.

Again, as I understood him, Pearson had begun to suspect that the organism called the nation state was becoming obsolete in its current form, the total sovereignty of old time no longer workable in the new closely knit world. Neither he nor any man could see far down that untravelled road, but he did not consider himself an idealist, only an internationalist and pragmatist as realistic as Acheson, perhaps more realistic, given the real human situation.

It is yet too early to judge between them, but on this record we must see that the public image of the Canadian idealist and the American realist is itself unreal. Their difference seemed to be a difference of timing and method, not of objectives. It is not too early to conclude that a synthesis of their views, however remote, is the only sure guarantee of world order. They did not live long enough to approach anything like a synthesis or to foresee the deepening crisis of the generation replacing them.

Along with Acheson I had luckily made a friend of another remarkable man. George Ball was then undersecretary, or second officer, of the State Department after Acheson's time, a tireless workhorse, optimist and globetrotter of liberal views and, as he thought, no illusions. But on his retirement to a home in Princeton, his judgement of the world underwent a profound change, undoubtedly influenced by his neighbour, George Kennan.

While quite unalike in character, these men combined their experience to the same end. Kennan looked shy, sensitive, inwardly tortured by mankind's prospects. Ball, the natural extrovert once known as a fervent anti-Communist, had concluded, like his friend, that American power, though essential, must not be used to threaten war on Russia but, over time, to negotiate peace. The alternative was mutual holocaust.

Both men had thought their way past an earlier and simpler view. Both concluded that the nuclear struggle was mad, the deterrent weapons unusable, only poker chips in a poker game played by reckless gamblers on either side. They agreed, too, that the game, as it was going, must end in human annihilation. All their prestige and influence, therefore, were exerted to cool the hot temper of official Washington, to warn Russia that it gambled with its own survival.

Kennan was evidently more alarmed and less hopeful than Ball. The former ambassador to Moscow and probably the greatest American expert on Russia delivered countless speeches and wrote countless articles and books of warning to the superpowers. For this work he paid a high price in leisure, health and peace of mind.

Luckiest among all breaks in my trade was a long friendship with the Bundys, whose house outside Princeton became my second home. As Dr. Johnson advised Boswell to "infiltrate" his ideas through other minds, so I tested mine with Bill. After his first career in government he now edited *Foreign Affairs*, knew most of the world's leaders, published their versions of events in his magazine and wrote his own. Although he gave me the benefit of his knowledge, he has no responsibility for anything in this book. With some of its conclusions, I guess, he will disagree.

Another distinguished resident of Princeton, and a man of ripe scholarship, was perhaps the best judge of current public opinion. The late George Gallup ("Ted" to his friends) had perfected the science of the opinion poll on the basis of mathematical law, which he vainly tried to explain to me. I doubted the wisdom of the polls, not because they were inaccurate but because they seemed to challenge the basis of representative government.

Edmund Burke, I reminded Gallup, had postulated representative government in a memorable address to his electors of Bristol, telling them that he would listen to their views but, in the end, as a member of Parliament and not a rubber stamp, he must sometimes vote against them. This, I suggested, was the whole meaning and responsibility of the democratic process whose agents were bound to act as they thought best on information unknown to their voters. Gallup did not agree. He well knew, from his polls, the vagaries of public opinion and accepted them as the price of democracy. For him the grand Jeffersonian premise, the ultimate wisdom of the voters, still held.

It did not hold for one of Princeton University's most eminent historians. He shocked me by declaring that all societies went through the same cycle—a tyrant like King John is disciplined by his nobles, the nobles are then disciplined by the people and the people, their affairs soon in chaos, elevate a new tyrant. The cycle, said the historian, would be repeated in the United States, a man on horseback arriving when needed. That counsel of despair was not widely shared but, far short of it, the United States obviously was in trouble unimaginable to Burke, Jefferson and the American Founders.

Their present successor faced worse trouble, and, playing by the political rules, Reagan had no time to learn about Canada. His meeting with Mulroney at the Quebec "Shamrock Summit" was embellished by gaudy theatricals somewhat overdone, not by serious work. Hosts and guests sang "When Irish Eyes Are Smiling" and also smiled for the television cameras, but the president's mind was elsewhere on his latest wrangle with the Congress. So nothing of real substance was accomplished, despite the usual optimistic communiqué.

If the Politburo and its new boss, Mikhail Gorbachev, watched this ceremony and thought it was a televised sham, they could not be expected to understand the paramount fact of the continental border. It is not economic or visible. It is a two-sided fact of mind and morality that can never be stated in words and is not yet fully grasped even by the world's most intimate neighbours.

Least of all do most Americans know Canada's past, the origin of its present and future. Why should they examine it when their own history is more exciting and violent, the durable stuff of drama? How should they know, in more than vague legend, that Canada's different mind was formed by a lonely struggle for a separate national existence, dubious until recent times, when Canadians themselves seldom look back, with well-earned pride, on their different adventure, though it conditions all today's events? These intangibles are not to be measured by statistics, business affairs or the ephemera of politics.

The early record shows that Canada repelled two American invasions, that the young Republic bought Louisiana, seized Texas and California from Mexico and thought briefly of seizing the Canadian

West. But its land hunger was already sated and a third northern invasion was never attempted.

Another fact of record is more reassuring: In modern times the United States, with all its foreign blunders, treated Canada as no great power of the past treated a defenceless nation living beside it with rich natural treasure easy to grasp. Canadians who distrust their neighbour's motives should remember that Russia engorged half of Europe after Hitler had conquered most of it, that Japan annexed a large part of China and that the British Empire, in its heyday, absorbed India, Canada and additional territories overseas.

Even now the days of imperialism have not ended. Russia is still expansive, Afghanistan its latest victim, the European satellites under its military and economic control. When North America's superpower does not threaten Canada, the people of both nations might usefully ask themselves what different neighbours they would prefer to have. Canadians might ask a second question: If they possessed superpower, how would they treat a powerless United States? And how would they regard sullen anti-Canadianism on the border?

Happily, no such question arises in practical affairs, and in them the power of the United States will be Canada's sole defence until the world regains its sanity. In the meantime, to what ends will that power be used?

It was overestimated in the Second World War, the days of Atlantic and Pacific victory. Sometimes it was misapplied, the world's needs misconstrued, appalling errors and even crimes committed. Against all this, foreigners should count the generosity of the Americans to other peoples. Acts of wisdom like the Marshall Plan and the revival of prostrate Germany and Japan must not be forgotten. The Canadian people benefited indirectly from the wise acts and suffered little directly from the errors overseas.

No matter how this record, wise and unwise, is judged, an imaginary parallel of North American latitude made not by nature but by man is a rare triumph of intelligence over geography and continental logic.

What forces drew that line? A school of Canadian historians has argued that Confederation was essentially a business deal with patriotic ornaments, negotiated by railway promoters and greedy entrepreneurs of the Laurentian heartland to exploit the hinterland, and by politicians who needed campaign funds.

Among the historians perhaps none was more articulate and persua-

sive than Frank Underhill. In an excellent book on the writing of
Canadian history, Carl Berger recalls Underhill's verdict that the
United States was only Canada "writ large." Must we then accept the
complementary side of the verdict—that Canada is only the United
States writ small? Was our nation made by economic ambition combined with negative resistance to American threats, the memory of
two failed invasions? Does it survive today on the mouse's fear of the
elephant? Is it truly a business proposition and nothing more?

Assuredly it is something more, something positive beyond the
negatives. All the power of business, all the motives of greed, cannot
explain the work of Macdonald, Brown and their fellow workmen. For
them Canada was not to be a second-class imitation and minor appendage of a Republic lately devastated by civil war. It was to be something better. Without that positive element there could have been no
nation in their time or ours.

Lacking an adequate word, we are forced to use a tattered cliché and
call the secret of our nationhood a Canadian Dream as powerful, if not
as pretentious, as our neighbour's unifying myth. On such an instinct,
hunch, character or spirit—call it what you please—Canada must and
will endure. Nothing less can serve. Anti-Americanism carried into
mere xenophobia is not enough for Canada's survival. And nothing
can change the facts of the border.

When frictions occur and Canadians grow impatient, they should
remember—and often do not—the cumbersome apparatus of the
American system, the ceaseless struggle between executive and legislature, the unpredictable Supreme Court decisions that sometimes frus-
trate both, the delayed and uncertain results.

Americans, on the other hand, should not have been surprised by
Canada's frustration when, for example, a fisheries treaty negotiated
with the United States president was rejected by the Senate; again,
when the Reagan government refused to do anything effective about
the acid rain that destroys the life of countless Canadian lakes; yet
again when the government's budgetary deficits raised interest rates
north of the border and impeded business recovery.

Contrasts between the systems, derived from different experience
and native attitudes, are not restricted to any written law, and they go
back more than two centuries. Having rejected a British king, the
Americans still clung to the theory of kingship. At first some of the
Founders thought of appointing a king, George Washington, of course.

He and the Philadelphia Congress were too wise to accept such an imitation, knowing that it would never work in a newly sovereign country. They created a Republic with a president as sovereign as any living king, much more powerful than the third George's successors.

In 1867 Canada took lessons from both Philadelphia and London to build a state as yet far short of independent sovereignty or the power to defend itself from attack. The Americans were more willing than the Canadians or the British to trust the wisdom of a single man. Political power in Canada, as in Britain, must be diffused through a company of men jointly and individually responsible to an elected Parliament. In the United States power was divided between a president, a Congress and a judiciary, each acting as a check on the others to ensure a continual balance. The balance varied as events and the strength of rival personalities directed. That same shift, regardless of constitutional theory, also changes the Canadian balance.

The Founding Fathers thought they had created a system of government by laws, not men; but great men, when they occasionally appeared, could never be suppressed. A Washington, a Lincoln or a Roosevelt, at least in times of crisis, had power that the Congress hardly dared to challenge so long as the people stood behind him. A Canadian prime minister, even the most powerful, can never defy Parliament. He is safe only when his party controls it. And three times, so far, Parliament has overthrown governments by its vote. Such a vote is sure to be repeated in the future.

All our Canadian experience—a small nation living in a world of giants—has made us more cautious and skeptical of concentrated power than our neighbours have been. Perhaps we may even claim that in our constitutional methods we are more democratic, more subject to the people's will despite the royal trappings of monarchy. Certainly our governments as a rule have been more stable. With one brief interruption, the Pearson-Trudeau regime outlasted five presidencies of alternating parties.

These abstract questions raise another of practical concern: How much trust should we give to the old axiom that any nation will get the kind of government it deserves? Over the long term the axiom may be reliable. Over the short it is highly dubious. Not many foreigners would think that Britain, for example, got the kind of government its people deserved between the world wars, that the United States deserved no truly great president in a span of about twenty years, or that

Canada was not entitled to better governmental management than it received in the last decade.

These, too, are abstract, unanswerable questions. What of the specific case of Ronald Reagan as his presidency affects Canada's immediate affairs? While the American people's business is for them alone to manage, they should know that in many Canadian eyes, including the official eyes of Ottawa—until Mulroney arrived— Reagan was a prize exhibit against the theory of government according to the people's deserts (although his splendid personal courage has been fully demonstrated).

On the diplomatic firing line stands the Canadian ambassador to Washington. Since the embassy was first opened there, all the ambassadors have served Canada well under any government because they were experts in their own subtle profession, not politicians, and their influence on foreign policy made in Ottawa was always great, though incalculable. All had unique entrée into the State Department, a "special relationship" denied to other nations. All were of smooth manner in public, in private exceedingly tough. Their often close personal friendships with American counterparts were never allowed to blunt their duty to Canada or their advice to Ottawa.

Mainly through such men the State Department formed its vision of Canada, sometimes overestimating, sometimes underestimating without fully understanding it. When Allan Gotlieb took charge of the embassy he changed its operating method though not its purpose. To the horror of the old hands in the External Affairs Department, he launched a campaign of "public diplomacy," defending Canadian policies in many speeches and hiring expert American lobbyists. They argued with members of the Congress against legislation, regulation and the fine print that, wittingly or unwittingly, damaged Canada.

As Gotlieb saw it, he was playing in a new ball game because most of the damage originates nowadays in the legislature, not the executive. Hence it was necessary to approach the legislature directly, and the approach required native experts well known to the legislators, not outsiders, always suspect. It is too early to judge the results of "public diplomacy," but it already has educated some ignorant congressmen and forestalled some dangerous moves against Canadian interests. In other areas it has failed, and lately new dangers have appeared.

However it works out, the basic facts of the border remain changeless, mandated by geography, history, massive travel, joint interests, external threat—a rich omelet beyond unscrambling. The "special relationship" of Canada and the United States, officially denied by Washington, remains, too. How can such unique ties ever be dissolved when they serve both neighbours and set an example for all nations to follow but have yet to follow? It is bootless to lament the imperfections of the continental friendship, imperfections common to private friendships.

The border was not made by nature but by man, an imaginary line, a triumph of human intelligence over geography, greed and all the known laws of logic. A deeper, unknown logic must have governed the process all the same or the outcome would have been quite different. The Canadians were satisfied with nothing more than survival— and it was always dubious until recent times. That they have survived as a people, despite their own mistakes and their neighbour's threats, is a wonderwork. It has no parallel elsewhere—the harvest of Canada's stubborn intent and its neighbour's belated wisdom.

Any Canadian who ventures to cite such facts, visible and invisible, is sure to be suspected of treason by the professional anti-Americans. He is probably in the pay of Wall Street or the CIA. Whatever his reputation may be, it will not change the facts.

Since no foreign policy can long succeed, even in authoritarian countries, without the broad consent of the people, we must look beyond Washington if we are to understand the policy of the United States in its continuing evolution or reversal. We must look to the American people. And since they are so diverse and volatile, the search is not easy.

A notion first mentioned to me, then a youngster, by Wickham Steed, the famous editor of the London *Times,* on a tour of Canada, put the general misunderstanding of its neighbour in a homely paradigm. The British people and their overseas kin, he said, do not criticize French people merely because they may eat peas with a knife, but the Americans are expected to use a fork because their culture had a British origin and they speak the English language. Instead, Americans should be understood for what they really are, a distinct breed with a distinct culture.

In this analogy Steed was not typical of his own nation. I know few English people who really like Americans, having never met them in their own land. As wryly observed by a typical American, E. B. White, the typical Englishman is never happy until he has explained the United States to its natives. The typical Canadian, on the other hand, is unhappy because he cannot explain himself to any foreigners. But through proximity and shared customs he knows the Americans better than any other foreigners can hope to do.

Even so, the American ethos is not sufficiently understood in Canada and, of course, distant peoples understand it still less. Although my understanding is also insufficient, I have seen something of the United States from coast to coast and found Americans more candid, outgoing and helpful than most peoples overseas. Fairly judged, these are good manners. Americans, you might say, wear their hearts on their sleeves for public inspection. And their society is as democratic as any massive society can be. Whether democracy has been pushed too far in common life and politics is a nice question that only Americans can answer.

Unfortunately, they are given a repulsive caricature abroad by some of their overrich tourists. Meeting such crude specimens, the native peoples, eager for their money, conclude that all Americans must be vulgar, boastful and greedy. That slander persists to distort the reality of a generous people. Seen at home, they are easy to meet on friendly terms, but the policies of their governments are hard for them, or visitors, to interpret when this changeable nation never ceases to experiment. It will try anything from the Darwinian economics of Herbert Hoover to Franklin Roosevelt's New Deal and, under Reagan, back again to the original faith, or at least its slogans—all in a single lifetime.

By nature and experience they have always been gamblers and now gamble with nothing less than the world's economy and peace. The American Revolution never stops. It only pauses to refuel itself, alters or reverses course and trades in an old vehicle of politics to buy a new one.

Perpetual motion has been the historical norm for upward of three centuries, and it produced the most unpredictable and affluent society in the democratic West. But is the norm a safe guide for the next century? Is it now threatened by a mind-change deeper than all the intermingled trials and errors of government?

Strangely enough, it was Russell Baker, a celebrated humourist and a very troubled citizen behind his printed persiflage, who raised the question in the midst of the Reagan boom. Have three decades of war preparation, Baker asked, become a habit, even an addiction, imprisoning the national mind? Do they offer nothing more than an eternity of improving machines of death? In their military habits, are the Americans becoming like the Russians or the Russians like the Americans? And is it true, as the old adage goes, that a man or nation finally adopts the thoughtways of the enemy?

Baker raises the question but cannot answer it. Nor can foreigners. But one oddity they will see immediately—Americans seem almost childlike in wanting to be loved as a great power never is. Contrary to their foreign image and political speeches, they harbour grave doubts about themselves. They constantly question the use of their power, the wisdom of their governments and the virtues of their society.

You will not find many doubts in Britain. The British people, justly esteemed for their good manners, their dignity, humour and quiet courage—the people who stood alone to resist the Nazi avalanche—seldom deny their special mission even in the darkest times. Neither do the French, the Chinese nor any other ancient civilization. The Canadian visitor to Britain is received with a touching kindness. He is also touched and awed by the British genius in the arts, the visible monuments to the days of lost power, the memory of greatness that his own nation has yet to equal and may never equal. But the typical Canadian does not feel entirely at home in Britain as he usually does in the United States, for he is at bottom a North American and cannot be anything else.

Burdened by an old inferiority complex, many Canadians find a poor kind of solace in claiming manners superior to those of their neighbours—a futile exercise, for manners alone are no true measure of quality. No people is accurately depicted by the image and protective carapace that it exhibits to the world.

One of our great prime ministers chose a diplomatic occasion to reveal his thoughts on the continental reality. Welcoming to Ottawa the president of France who had already visited Washington, Louis St. Laurent spoke to him about the United States with intentional candour: "You cannot fail to have been impressed by the strength of that great country and also the sincerity of the peaceful aspirations of its people. Here in Canada you will not fail to note the close friendly relations which bind us to our southern neighbours and also the untrammelled independence we enjoy in our own land. If our frontiers bordered on those of some grasping imperial neighbouring state, we might not have this opportunity of welcoming you to a free Parliament. . . . Canada is, I think, the best evidence of the peaceful purposes of the United States."

If St. Laurent were alive today, he would continue to defend Canada's interests against American blunders, but I doubt he would change a word of that speech. With a steady common sense inherited from his peasant ancestors, he would understand the practical necessities of the border to be faced by every Canadian government—that Canada must always maintain an independent foreign policy up to the limit of its actual means, always influence its neighbour as strongly as the means allow, speak out against American mistakes but never break the friendship essential to both nations as enforced by their joint manifest destiny.

There is still the paramount task of continental statesmanship in Washington and Ottawa today. So it will remain tomorrow long after Reagan, Mulroney and our generation are gone.

11

THE TEMPLE AND THE DREAM

Alone beside the Greek temple of Abraham Lincoln, the stranger may share a fragment of the American Dream. Here, if anywhere, it is incarnate, almost palpable. The carved marble presence of the man who saved the Union seems to brood over its future with eyes melancholy but serene. In the memory of his countryman he is eternal. So is the dream.

At midnight, below the temple's long steps, a basin of still water reflects and duplicates the soaring shaft that hallows the life and legend of George Washington. A mile distant the bulbous dome of the Capitol glistens under the winter moon. The White House and its temporary resident are hidden by a grove of trees, protected by human sentries and computerized missiles on instant alert.

What, the stranger will ask, would Lincoln think of his latest successor, of a world far outside the dreams of his time? There can be no answer, but history tells us that Lincoln fought a civil war limited to half a continent while Ronald Reagan has the power to destroy all planetary life at the touch of a button. Asleep now in his mansion, the president is never distant from the button. He has become more powerful than Washington, Lincoln or any living American, his task more dangerous.

Thence follows perhaps the most momentous question in the world of our time: How will Reagan use his power? Does he really know where he is going, taking his people and other peoples with him? Does he fully understand the burden of choice and responsibility inherited from all the days since a tiny ship anchored near the Plymouth beach?

Yes, he tells a reporter in a sudden moment of self-revelation, his task is understood and awesome. Supposing that enemy missiles are on their way and he has no means of stopping them? The only response, he says, is to "push the button before they get here even though you're all going to die. . . . There's something so immortal about it."

Like his great predecessor, Reagan is brooding. Although no two men could be more different in character and circumstance, each has tried to carry out his version of the American Dream. But if Canadians are to understand it, and the colossus sprawled along their southern flank, they could hardly pick a worse starting point than Washington, once a fetid swamp, today a metropolis of noble architecture, sculptured bronze heroes, leafy parks and grimy politics, the capital of world democracy.

On the main streets the crowds look well dressed, well fed and in a tearing hurry. The costly hotels and restaurants are jammed. The prevailing mood is smug and cocky. The leading citizen in the White House appears to be satisfied with his work. His leadership, he boasts, has cured a deep business slump, begun a second American Revolution, made his people stand tall and proud again. But their mood could change overnight. In this country public opinion swings like the regular pendulum of a grandfather clock.

The capital's surface is thin and deceptive. Stroll beyond the urban core and you find black squalour in the slums. Or, better, travel across the land among the small cities, towns, villages and ranches, talk to New Englanders, Midwesterners, Southerners and Californians. Then you encounter a people who bear faint resemblance to their worldwide image, or caricature, and Washington's sleek opulence. A Constitution, a rich economy and, still stronger, an abiding myth hold together several distinct nations, interests, attitudes and lifeways. Here is a prodigy without equivalent anywhere on earth. Unlike their governing centre, these varied elements of the Union are troubled by a process of change too fast for comprehension. Some regions suffer desperate poverty. All are divided in their political outlook and only about half a free electorate bothers to vote. Yet somehow the whole intricate fabric is united by a mysterious something called the dream.

Such imponderables will always involve Canada more directly than any other foreign nation. How, then, must Canadians judge their mighty neighbour? Should it be envied, imitated or resisted? And what does it think of the people north of the border?

The last question is not hard to answer. You might suppose, to hear the talk of the extreme Canadian nationalists, that Americans muse through sleepless nights on the possession of the continent entire. In fact, most of them regard Canada, if they think of it at all, as a good place for skiing or savouring the quaint old-world custom of the Quebec peasantry.

Naturally enough, their eyes are fixed, day by day, on trouble spots in Europe, Central America, the Middle East and Asia. Canada is rarely in the headlines, or even the back pages, because it makes no news of war, revolution, scandal or famine. Just as Canadians long turned a blind eye to countries south of the Rio Grande, Americans turned a blind eye to the north where the untroubled neighbours could be taken for granted, though actually they could not.

Among my many close friends in Washington only two have suggested that Canadians would be better off if they joined the Union.

An eminent professor of European history used to argue the case for continental unity as ordained by nature's scheme of things and wondered why Canadians had rejected a superior society—this at the very moment when the society was rent by Vietnam, Watergate, crime, drugs, environmental pollution and other familiar misfortunes. In answer to my questions, the professor showed that he knew no Canadian history, had seen no part of Canada west of Toronto. But he professed the highest respect for Canadians despite their wrongheadedness.

The second man, an influential White House adviser of two Democratic administrations, knew all about foreign politics, that of Canada alone excepted. He regretted the exception and, having often skied in Quebec, intended to tour the western provinces and see the Rockies. Preparing for the journey, he asked me if Calgary was east or west of Winnipeg. He understood already that Vancouver was on the Pacific Coast and quite a big town. But he could never understand why Canadians, a sensible folk, refused to accept the political logic of the continent. Oh well, doubtless they would accept it eventually and meanwhile should not be criticized, much less coerced.

In their continental ignorance these men are typical Americans. The State Department's experts, on the contrary, keep track of Canada's affairs, political, economic and military, with an information apparatus that would surprise most Canadians. Experienced foreign service officers like Willis Armstrong and his wife, Louise, authors of a penetrating book on the continent's affairs, know more about Canada than most of its natives will ever learn.

Unfortunately, such knowledge seldom percolates through the layers of the bureaucracy to the upper regions of government. Few men more accurately represented the uninformed public opinion of his time than the late U.S. Senator Robert Taft. In the election year of 1952 I asked him what he thought of the Reciprocity agreement with Canada negotiated by his father, William Howard. The question puzzled the son. What, he asked me in return, had the agreement proposed?

As he vaguely recollected, it had something to do with free trade which, he guessed, would still be a good idea. Was his memory correct? Yes, I said, it was correct, but I did not attempt to enlighten him further. If the abler son knew nothing about his father's misunderstanding of Canada, there was no use arguing a history that should be familiar to any Canadian high school student.

We have no right to sneer at this neighbourly ignorance. Typical citizens and governments of Canada needed almost a century to understand the apparently simple, though truly complex, North American relationship which, as Pearson warned, will never be easy or automatic. Today the learning process is by no means complete. But continental union has never been an issue of practical politics and today is less practical than ever on both sides of the border.

Only once in modern times has an American government, typically misjudging Canada, supposed that it might seek admission to the Republic. When the Quebec government threatened to break the Canadian union and establish a French-Canadian state astride the St. Lawrence River, Washington was forced to consider the possible results. Luckily, President Carter had the good sense to hope aloud that Canada would not break up and increase his already overwhelming problems.

He was right in believing that the broken pieces could not long resist the American magnet. In economic calculation each piece might possess enough wealth and territory to survive, but Canada is more than an economy and the sum of its often quarrelsome parts. It is a community, a kind of family, with typical household frictions and is based on a premise not to be explained or expressed to foreigners. If that spirit and its clustered memories ever die, then the nation will die, too, and deserve its death.

What ultimate truth have Canadians learned from their experience? Above all, that only they can destroy the nation as only they built it. Nevertheless, the ancient fear of Manifest Destiny still haunts some of our best citizens.

The latest doubts are focussed on Reagan, but there is no doubt that he has made himself one of the most popular presidents in American history. How should Canadians judge him? Is he nothing more than a second-class actor from Hollywood where, in the movie studios, the wind blows free across the open rangeland of the mythical Old West? An unequalled master of public relations? A televised salesman of soothing platitudes and witty one-liners fed to him by his speech writers? A simplistic man of good will but a danger to the world's peace?

Such judgements are common among foreigners and may be partially accurate, but they do not measure the man whole, for Reagan now possesses much more than the baggage he brought with him to Washington and keeps adding to it. With all his flamboyant language, dramatic postures and stumbles in action, he is an authentic phenomenon, inexplicable and infuriating to his enemies.

From his first days of office the true nature behind the grin perplexed and divided the government of Canada. Trudeau regarded him with skepticism verging on intellectual contempt, though it was carefully hidden at the start. Near the end, he barely troubled to hide his real opinion. Finally he expressed it, along with his low assessment of all the NATO leaders, in the peculiarly harsh Washington speech of late 1984.

The climate of the border changed, or seemed to change, as soon as Mulroney formed a government. Reagan became a personal friend, the two men drawn to each other by the same general view of human events. At this writing the friendship is under attack. The parliamentary opposition accuses the prime minister of subservience to the president; Mulroney denies the charge with hot indignation. In fact, he is boldly asserting Canada's sovereignty by rebuilding its economic and military strength long neglected by the Liberal predecessors.

So goes the many-sided debate, but its outcome will not be predicted here and cannot be predicted by anyone. Enough at the moment for Canadians to ponder the known Reagan record as fairly as possible when already in world affairs it is a strange medley of success and failure.

After he had made a clumsy beginning and frightened his nation's allies, Reagan realized that their voluntary support was essential to the United States since it could no longer dominate the world as it did in the early postwar years as the single owner of the Bomb. Hitherto ignorant of foreign affairs, Reagan learned slowly, but he learned. It must have been a hard cram course when the newborn establishment included few experienced advisers and they quarreled among themselves. Other presidential intimates, qualified only by personal loyalty, were as ignorant about foreign affairs as their boss.

The regime's original naivety was portrayed by an episode that nobody could believe if one of the two participants had not disclosed it in a public speech strangely overlooked by the media. George Ball, the chief foreign trouble-shooter of the Kennedy and Johnson administrations until he resigned in opposition to the Vietnam War, was sitting one day in his Princeton home, at work on his explosive memoirs. Answering a long-distance telephone call, he heard an unfamiliar voice from California. The caller introduced himself as Judge William Clark whose name Ball had never heard before.

"He was worried," Ball remembers, "because he said, 'I don't know anything about foreign policy. I've only been outside the United States once in my life.' " Nonetheless, Clark was to be nominated by the president as undersecretary of state, Ball's own post for nine years.

Astounded, Ball heard Clark ask, "What is the job all about and how should I respond to questions at my confirmation hearing [before a Senate committee]?"

Pitying his caller, Ball told Clark how to deal with the Senate. For half an hour Clark listened eagerly to the veteran of congressional in-fighting and begged a second favour. Would Ball give him a full day of counsel in New York? Ball agreed but, he says, "I never heard from him again."

Evidently Clark had discovered to his surprise that Ball was a Democrat, well known as such throughout the diplomatic world, a man for Republicans to avoid. How could this rather frightening little contretemps be explained? Ball concluded, in his subsequently unreported speech, that "our electoral procedures, complete with television and a multiplicity of [local] primaries, tend to provide us with leaders quite innocent of world politics and the diplomacy required of a leading nation. Prior to becoming president neither Jimmy Carter nor Ronald Reagan had ever been exposed to the complex problem of our relations with other nations. American naivety is bipartisan."

Against these long-standing obstacles, his built-in prejudices and the contrary advice of his experts, Reagan had to struggle as best he could, learning and unlearning on the job. From the struggle came a mixed bag.

His NATO allies had originally urged the United States to install its new and improved missiles in Europe—a request seldom remembered now. When many Europeans opposed this policy, their governments hesitated but finally accepted the missiles as the surest guarantee of American defence if it were ever needed. The Russians protested by walking out of the Geneva disarmament conference, but Reagan expected their new government to return once it recognized the allies' unity which it had hoped to split. He was right. The Russians returned with gestures of peace and long-term strategy unknown.

Before then a far more important event had changed the whole international climate. The president's decision to research antimissile weapons in space again frightened some of his allies and their restive peoples. Many scientists warned him that the project was both futile and dangerous, but he, and the American Congress, pressed ahead, at incalculable future costs and risks, fearing that Russia had its own similar research well underway, despite its fervid denial.

These mutual suspicions seemed to postpone any chance of an early breakthrough at Geneva. Under the best of circumstances, many years, perhaps a generation of tough bargaining, may be needed to negotiate a deal between the superpowers. Nothing better than a long stalemate, without war, is probably all we can hope for.

In the meantime Reagan had been moving on several fronts. After threatening to reject the SALT TWO arms limitation agreement negotiated by his predecessors, he continued to enforce it without the formal consent of the Senate but with certain specific reservations and obviously grave doubts.

He nurtured friendly relations with China where Communist dogma appeared, like Marx's ideal state, to be withering. He soothed Taiwan but not to the point of dangerously antagonizing Peking. He kept urging Japanese rearmament even though it was prohibited by a constitution made in the United States. At home he tried to fight off the congressional protectionists of both parties when Japan was running a huge trade surplus in the American market. He called for a further worldwide reduction of all commercial barriers against not only goods but services.

In the Falklands War he gave Britain strong support at the cost of antagonizing Argentina and other Latin American countries, but he had invaded Grenada with no advance notice to London. In Lebanon his search for peace ended in debacle and withdrawal. His strategy, overt and covert, in Central America reminded his critics of Leonid Brezhnev's doctrine that justified wars to "liberate" foreign peoples. The president brought no peace to a region of increasing anarchy, and his intervention there was attacked by many of his fellow citizens. Even the cordial Mulroney government bluntly disapproved it and already had been appalled by the notorious outrages of the CIA that included secret drug tests performed on unsuspecting Canadians.

All this time Reagan presided over the private and public feud between the "doves" of the State Department and the "hawks" of the Pentagon. Blandly ignoring their clash on foreign policy, he managed to keep George Shultz and Caspar Weinberger in his cabinet despite their clashing world views, while he appeared to stand above the White House factions and the power-hungry magnates of his party.

As foreigners in Ottawa and elsewhere watched a skillful operator, they detected a sea-change in the president's mind, or at any rate in his speeches. But they wondered how deep it went and how long it would last. Apparently the cold warrior of his first years, with his savage attacks on the Evil Communist Empire, the man who talked loosely about a winnable nuclear war, had become a passionate apostle of peace. A war of modern weapons, he now said, was unwinnable, unthinkable, and he continued to build up the armaments of the United States to prevent it.

His Star Wars experiment, or fantasy, compelled the Mulroney government to consider the gravest decision it had yet faced. Could space weapons make their possessors safe from their enemies? If only a minor fraction of the Russian missiles broke through the shield, would they not devastate any target? On the other hand, the Americans who had invented nuclear fission might perform another scientific miracle.

Pondering its options, the Canadian government proposed a compromise to buy time. Research, not the deployment, of space weapons was approved in principle as Britain and some European governments had approved it. Whether Canadian factories would be allowed to make parts for the weapons has yet to be decided. Deployment of the weapons, if any were perfected, would be subject to international negotiations at some uncertain future date.

That terrible decision was postponed, but the Mulroney compromise failed to satisfy the parliamentary opposition. Liberals and New Democrats, competing in speeches of alarm, insisted that, once created, space weapons were sure to be deployed. Even research must abort the Geneva negotiations and plunge the world into an unlimited armaments race. For the first time since a weaponry dispute wrecked the Diefenbaker government and ended in 1984 in the withdrawal of the last nuclear weapons from Canada, national politics was split on basic foreign policy.

So far we have heard only the opening round of a debate that, like research, will outlast Reagan's time and perhaps Mulroney's. Its immediate core is easy to ask, not easy to answer: Can it be safely assumed that space weapons, if perfected, would not be deployed after countless billions of dollars, great industries and multitudes of jobs had been invested in them and they had acquired a political momentum difficult if not impossible to stop? Again, is it realistic to suppose that Canada could avoid involvement in this escalating process if its own industries had received lucrative contracts to build parts for the weapons in a native military-industrial complex? Such an assumption is clearly unrealistic, not to say absurd.

Moreover, it is probable that some northern Canadian territory would be needed to make the space apparatus fully operational as it was needed for the test of cruise missiles. If Washington made a new and larger request, could any Canadian government refuse it? Then Canada would face an irrevocable decision touching its sovereignty (already questioned in the Arctic Ocean, the Northwest Passage). While that decision may lie some years ahead, there remains the undeniable key fact of Canada's defence—it is provided by the United States and no other nation has the means, or the will, to provide it by means decided in Washington. Has the Mulroney government thought its way through all the looming possibilities in approving research but not necessarily deployment? It seems unlikely when American policy, under Reagan's unknown successors, is also unknown. And soon he will enter his lame-duck years of declining power.

These and other confusing arguments pose a question that Reagan alone can answer: Is he sincere in his pursuit of peace? If so, will he offer Russia negotiable terms, using the threat of space weapons as a bargaining issue? Or do his terms make an arms bargain impossible? Does he believe, as some of his hawks believe, that Russian power will finally collapse under the costly burden of its armaments?

Such a hopeful notion is not shared by the president's more sophisticated advisers, including some who favour space weapons. On the contrary, they believe that foreign threats are likely to make the Russian people accept increasing sacrifices and thus strengthen their unity. But the Reagan government is determined to perfect its weaponry even if Russia can afford to duplicate it. In any case, the president says, the Anti-Ballistic Missile Treaty of 1972 does not apply to Star Wars research.

Many Canadians and the parliamentary opposition disagree with his legal reasoning, but his hawkish admirers discount all the risks of Star Wars research as dovish timidity and, worse, a retreat from future security. They say Reagan has always bargained reasonably with Russia and always will. Many of his critics think he has been unreasonable, reckless and truculent. But some of them, insiders of the Democratic Party, believe that his mental sea-change is genuine, that he hopes to go down in history as the great peacemaker, not merely the great communicator.

The evidence of his speeches is conflicting, sometimes chilling. For example, he scorned his opponent in the 1984 election by saying: "I know that Mr. [Walter] Mondale, in the past, has made statements as if they [the Russians] were just people like ourselves." At this, a foreign mind boggles. What else, the world public must inquire, are the Russians if not people like ourselves—and people who have suffered more from war than any Western people? Was the president's remark misunderstood? Was it only an off-the-cuff indiscretion like his joke about bombing Russia, when he thought that the microphones were closed, or was it a revealing Freudian slip? He alone can know.

In considering his real thoughts, as distinguished from his speeches, we must assume that he sincerely wants peace, for otherwise he would be a mad man as he certainly is not. We must assume, too, that the men in the Kremlin, however primitive, odious and stupid they may appear in Western eyes, are sane and prefer their own comfortable lives to sudden or lingering death by planetary incineration.

Even those who can push the last button, together with all peoples, high and low, free and downtrodden, will have to spend their little lives in a world that seems collectively mad. But now the inmates of a nuclear asylum, however sane they may be in private life, begin to take the political and military madness around them for normal behaviour among nations. If the world's temporary rulers do lose their sanity, as happened in Hitler's Reich, if they miscalculate each other's intentions, if some excited general fires the first missile, or some computer gives the wrong signal then, in Hobbes's phrase, human life would indeed be "solitary, poor, nasty, brutish and short."

Leaving aside these imaginable horrors, and trying to judge Reagan's immediate policies, we Canadians should not forget a record long preceding him. The magnificent success of the Marshall Plan that saved postwar Europe from chaos; the airlift that saved Berlin from a Russian blockade; the Korean War that thwarted the advance of Russian and Chinese communism; the Bay of Pigs fiasco that dimmed the legend of Kennedy's tinsel Camelot; his bold management of the Cuban missile crisis that foiled Nikita Khrushchev and finally ruined him; the Vietnam War that fractured American society and ended in humiliating disaster; the ugly American interventions in Guatemala and Chile that shocked the world; Jimmy Carter's Middle East peace initative at Camp David and his total misunderstanding of Iran's revolution—these mixed achievements and failures were no part of Reagan's responsibility. He has more than enough of his own to test any man, and not enough Canadians yet appreciate that burden when Canada bears none of comparable scope and danger.

But it is fair, I think, to conclude that Reagan, however well-meaning, has been too much obsessed with armaments, superfluous deterrence and overkill as the guarantors of peace; that he has diminished important social services, neglected the poor and deranged his nation's finances to build ever more weapons, unusable short of world suicide; that his Star Wars initiative could stifle any chance of disarmament, and that his personal friendship with Mulroney does not indicate any understanding of Canada (nor Mulroney's understanding of the United States).

All Canadian judgements are subject, of course, to galloping events now in the saddle everywhere and riding mankind. They recall, in Reagan's case, the Greek warning against hubris, endemic in presidents, as always followed by nemesis in varied forms. They also recall the warning of a greater president than Reagan. Americans, said George Washington, should beware of "inveterate antipathies against particular nations. The nation that indulges toward another an habitual hatred is in some degree a slave. It is a slave to its animosity which is sufficient to lead it astray from its duty and interests."

Let Canadians recall that warning when they judge Washington's present successor and the American nation. Let them, with their lesser responsibilities, beware of making themselves slaves to the hatred of their neighbours, that last tawdry comfort they can afford. Let them keep things in proportion without fastening all the blame for the world's trouble on the United States. Let them not forget, as many do, that Russia led the arms buildup from the start, flouted détente, engorged half of Europe, invaded Afghanistan and worked mischief from Africa to South America and Asia.

Before Canadians make any judgement, let them rethink the whole business of the border. It is growing more complex and perhaps less understood all the time.

12

COUNTERVAILING
FORCES

Long before he entered politics, Trudeau had found a reliable method for use in all his affairs, public and private. As his first major book explained, he instinctively distrusted popular opinions and invoked countervailing forces to increase his own strength. If he had defied the stock market and the advice of brokers, he might have made a fortune. Instead, he wrote, his method had given him power that he did not foresee or want (until it became the obsessive goal of his life).

In most of his political career he summed up enough votes to direct the nation's course where he thought it should go. But the master equilibrist sometimes stumbled on the tightrope, only to recover his balance by accepting the public will even when he thought it was wrong. On the whole the balancing act worked well for him if not always for the nation.

From the start, countervailing forces were applied to foreign policy. Though its overriding concern was, and is, the United States, Canada has interests, continually expanding interests, in many distant parts of the world. By making friends abroad, Trudeau hoped to offset, at least in some degree, the powerful presence beside him,

Other men wore the title, but Trudeau was his own foreign minister. Under his direction policy kept changing, not according to any fixed design, least of all to university textbooks and their writers in ivory towers, and it often contradicted official pronouncements. At moments of crisis policy was made on the spur of the moment by Trudeau alone, with a few anonymous counsellors, because events would not await leisurely decision. The great pragmatist reacted to them as they occurred. What else had any of his predecessors done since Macdonald built a nation by trial and error against all logic? And when events moved at increasing speed in Trudeau's time, so did his reactions, his diplomatic footwork and occasional gaucheries that irritated friends and comforted enemies.

His official policy had no sooner been printed in an unctuous document bearing flashes of his own unmistakable literary style before events superseded it. For instance, he vowed that Canada's role as an international broker and fixer was ended, and immediately afterward he became the decisive broker between the quarrelling white and nonwhite nations of the Commonwealth at the Singapore conference. The brokerage role, once transatlantic, had expanded and could not be easily resigned. From that beginning Trudeau went on to make himself, as he hoped, a broker between the superpowers.

This was pragmatic success of a sort, remarkable in a man who in youth had been an angry Quebec isolationist and, in his first days of office, was still ignorant of foreign affairs. He learned fast, but could his policy of reacting to events keep up with their momentum in the new world? And in his attempt to unloose countervailing forces, how much friction with the United States, strongest of all forces, dare he risk? That had always been Canada's riddle as a pawn in the old game of international chess now played under new rules. While distrusting the Reagan government, Trudeau found that he could not change the rules and summarized them in one of his last and best speeches as prime minister.

The world's interdependence had to be accepted, he said, for otherwise "tendencies of unilateralism and neutrality" would undermine the alliance of democratic nations. The resulting strains would have one inexorable result—the movement of Canada into the United States orbit. "The lesson for Canada, ironically, is that to preserve our political independence we have to recognize our economic interdependence and work to preserve the integrity and dynamism of the multilateral system." Canada, Trudeau added, must live with the international and continental realities. They could be shaped but not reversed. In other words, the countervailing forces, even when used skillfully, were limited.

While the power game and the forces and realities behind it have greatly changed, Macdonald understood them as they surrounded and buffeted him in his time. Playing the game without power, he watched helplessly when Britain sold out Canadian interests to the newly powerful American Republic.

Laurier had played for higher stakes and watched Britain surrender the Alaskan Panhandle to Teddy Roosevelt and his Big Stick. Borden had played the game with better results at Versailles and won Canada's independent status in the world. Bennett had played it, and lost, in the unworkable empire trade deal of 1932. King had played it with the best results in his unlikely friendship with Franklin Roosevelt and Winston Churchill after living between the wars without any policy. St. Laurent and Pearson had played it in the Suez crisis. Trudeau must play it by ear in the more dangerous clash of superpowers.

All of his predecessors had sometime clashed with the United States—Macdonald on the tariff and the fisheries; Laurier on Alaska; Diefenbaker on nuclear weapons in Canada; Pearson, most violently, on the American bombing of Vietnam. After this experience Trudeau moved gingerly but did not hesitate to back Margaret Thatcher in criticizing Reagan's invasion of Grenada and in making his own protest against the president's savage anti-Communist rhetoric. Always Canada was caught in the middle of the chess game. Never could Trudeau's countervailing forces outweigh the primary force on his nation's southern flank.

In all this varying experience there was at least one consistent element—Canada's foreign policy should be used to promote its world trade, the bedrock of its prosperity. Unlike a great power, it could not conquer foreign markets and command foreign materials by military action. It must win them by diplomacy, salesmanship and the price and quality of its goods. It must do business and seek friends wherever possible, even in Castro's Cuba, despite Washington's frown, and it could make friends easily because, lacking power, it threatened nobody. Canadians' own friendliness gave them a smug sense of virtue, and they generally forgot that they had no appetite for conquest, no envy of other peoples' resources, because they possessed at home more wealth and territory than they knew how to use.

Since economic gain had become, next to peace, the core of foreign policy, the External Affairs Department was forced to encumber itself with the management of international commerce against the protest of the trained diplomats who thought such business was beneath their dignity and distracted them from more important work. Salesmanship had been easy in the golden postwar years when the world was ravenous for Canada's goods. But the External Affairs Department was ill-prepared for its new role. The master diplomats like Pearson, Norman Robertson, Hume Wrong, Dana Wilgress and Escott Reid were gone, their times with them. Their successors might be just as able as they had been (though the remaining old hands doubted it) but the latest generation faced different problems when foreign policy became more and more a commercial proposition, the whole department an economic agency in its spare time, the ambassadors salesmen.

Usually the department was free of party politics. A few ambassadors in minor posts were rewarded for political service, but not many. A few civil servants—King, Pearson and Jack Pickersgill distinguished among them—had made themselves powerful politicians but, again, not many.

Politics of another sort never ceased in the department or, for that matter, in any public or private bureaucracy. The ferocious in-fighting of the ambitious diplomats and bureaucrats continued among themselves and, though always denied, could not always be hidden from Parliament and press. Trudeau watched it without visible worry. After all, countervailing forces were at work here as elsewhere. He sometimes promoted his favourite, even ignorant, politicians to unimportant foreign embassies, assured of their personal loyalty if not their talent.

Was the department thus improved or downgraded? On that question the old and the new hands naturally disagreed. Retired ambassadors thought the department was a mess, lacking their superior management. Their successors thought it was more competent and up-to-date than ever. In any case it was Trudeau's own instrument, serving as he, not the cabinet, directed. The foreign buck stopped on his desk. He was the master of personal diplomacy in the world and at home.

As such, he had to consider, next to the American giant, Canada's ties with Britain, one of its two original motherlands. The ties were loosened not by design or quarrel but by events that reduced Britain from the status of a great to a secondary power. It no longer possessed its empire, despite Churchill's pledge to preserve this clearly obsolete apparatus of power. If the liquidation of the empire had not been sufficiently demonstrated in the Second World War, the Suez crisis of 1956 nakedly and brutally revealed the altered British rank in the world. So did the independence of large old colonies like India and various little pseudonations in Africa and Asia.

Unlike most of his predecessors, Trudeau felt no strong emotional tug to Britain. That emotion was not in his origin and nature. His mother had been Scottish by descent, but he was all Canadian. He felt only the tug of France if he felt any foreign tug at all. His mind was moving, by fits and starts, towards a worldwide idea. Nevertheless, he understood (though he was never good with human beings) that Canadians of British descent still felt the transatlantic tug. History continued to struggle with geography—a fact of practical politics not to be ignored.

On the other hand, Trudeau found himself in ideological conflict with the latest government of Britain, he a quasi Liberal somewhat left of centre, Thatcher a right-wing Conservative like Reagan. The Iron Lady and the equally tough man could be personal friends and even political allies, however, when they jointly disagreed with the United States. These two might not cut great figures in the world's history, but in the age of leadership drought they looked greater than they were.

Trudeau, if he represented anything, represented, or tried to represent, a new world. Thatcher seemed, perhaps unfairly, to represent the old that could never be restored. For all her humble origins, Oxford accent, studied colloquial idiom and personal courage, she resembled, in hostile foreign eyes, a glamorous antique, a relic of the past.

When one of the tiny remaining fragments of the empire was invaded by Argentina, her response was as instinctive and automatic as Palmerston's would have been. The barren sheep pastures called the Falkland Islands, though few British citizens knew where they were, must be defended at any cost. The cost was high, wildly uneconomic, but it could not be avoided. British pride and also a primary principle of international law were at stake there. Having boldly vindicated the principle, Thatcher won her next election in a landslide. For the time being she looked invulnerable.

With all its courage and victory, the Falklands War stood at the outer margin of events, significant mainly because it brought the United States to Britain's side.

Before Thatcher's time events had moved far past such marginal concerns and carried Britain's foreign policy across the English Channel, committing it mainly to Europe for the first time since King John began the retreat from the Continent, and Britain, thus isolated, as Macaulay wrote, evolved its distinct civilization.

That was the long-term meaning of British membership in the European Common Market, secured after long hesitation at home and the rebuff of Charles de Gaulle. The membership was of such practical and emotional concern to the government of Canada that Diefenbaker had fought it as if he alone understood Britain's true interests. He did not see that for Britain, without its empire or sufficient markets in the Commonwealth, the tug of economics and geography was far too strong for the tug of history and ancient glory. A highly practical species, despite their tight upper lips, the British folk knew where they could best earn their livelihood, not in a distant Commonwealth but nearby in Europe or, additionally, in the United States and the Third World.

The United States, of course, must never be neglected when it provided Britain's ultimate defence. Accordingly, Thatcher cultivated Reagan's support and found in him a natural friend who articulated her own ideology. Their friendship, however wise or unwise their outlook on the world around them, was valuable to both their nations as Thatcher well knew and Reagan came to realize. In her trips to Washington, the British prime minister became almost a spokeswoman for all of Western Europe because she spoke the president's language and shared his conservative views.

Already Britain had ceased to be Canada's second largest trade partner, replaced by Japan. The originally Canadian invention of empire or Commonwealth tariff preferences (Laurier's response to American protectionism later expanded and then diminished by Bennett) had dwindled to relatively minor significance, replaced by the multilateral instrument of the General Agreement on Tariffs and Trade.

What, then, was really happening in Britain behind the political façade and the brief glory of the Falklands? At least in a visiting Canadian's eyes the answer seemed very simple: Britain was trying, on the one hand, to maintain its kindly, tolerant, decent society, its old ways of the pub, the weekend cricket and soccer games, politics also a game for sportsmen. But on the other hand it had to play the new game of brutal competition with the upstart rivals of Europe and Asia. It wanted to enjoy the living standards of such nations as Germany and France, even of Switzerland, Sweden and Denmark, without working as hard as they did. Britain was trying to have its cake and eat it and was steadily falling behind in the competitive race.

Walter Bagehot had written that the Englishman was an enjoying man, a good thing to be. But in the times of post—industrial revolution, unforeseen by Bagehot, enjoyment and the Pursuit of Happiness demand the high price of unhappy self-discipline, efficiency, improved industrial methods, the sacrifice of some fine old customs. Was the price too high for Britain to pay? Thatcher thought not. While fighting her Common Market partners on various issues with all the fury of a woman scorned, she disciplined the British labour unions and their employers alike. She was determined to make Britain as efficient, productive and rich as its European neighbours, no matter what the price in enjoyment.

Her reaction to Argentina, Britain's former friend and current enemy, was like that of a great power. Her reaction to business competitors was strictly in accordance with the facts of lost power. Like all contemporary politicians, she had become ambivalent, pragmatic and puzzled by those facts. Canadians watched her with a mixture of admiration and alarm.

The facts had been explained to me in a different fashion by Richard Crossman, then leading a Labour government in the House of Commons and quarrelling with Prime Minister Harold Wilson over membership in the Common Market. Crossman, a Socialist who resembled a rumpled, tweedy country gentleman, was candid with a fellow journalist in his opposition to membership.

"The trouble," he said, "is that we had the bad luck to win the war. And look at the losers! Germany and Japan had nowhere else to go but up and so they did. But we went down. What should we do now? We should stay out of Europe and make some money, that's what." In other words, Britain should make itself another cozy Switzerland or Sweden, demiparadise safe behind the moat of the Channel as if it were still as wide and impassable as in John of Gaunt's time. The ambivalent Crossman, a classic Little Englander rejoicing in his modern practicality, seemed even more nostalgic than Thatcher, then an opposition backbencher.

After talking to him in his Whitehall office, I found myself at lunch in a London bank at the heart of the City. The bankers were gentlemen of England, all except one director who spoke with a cockney accent and evidently was admitted to this upper-class company because he had the credentials of money and brains.

The gentlemen of England would gladly summon up the blood and fight a foreign enemy. Some of them had fought in the world wars as bravely as Henry V and his bowmen at Agincourt, leaving many comrades dead in victory. Now they must fight the grimy battle of economics, no business for a gentleman but, alas, inescapable in a grimy age.

Unlike Crossman, they recognized the changing facts of economic power and the competition of the Common Market while still trying to enjoy the old days, the long country weekends, the life of London's clubs. In Roy Thomson, a brash outsider from Canada, there was no ambivalence. He knew how to eat his cake and not only have but expand it, with a title of nobility, because he was not a gentleman of England. The gentlemen, he told me, were too lazy and inefficient to offer him serious competition.

That night I dined with Victor Feather who was supposed to be Britain's most influential labour leader. He looked rumpled like Crossman but spoke in a workingman's idiom and was equally ambivalent as he fought Labour's enemies in Big Business. Of course, he said, they usually "fiddled" with the tax laws. What of it? This cheating, the chauffeured Rolls-Royces, the conspicuous consumption, the country estates, the pathetic gentry, did not amount to much. Feather laughed at them and drank as heartily as any banker.

In both the upper and lower classes the geniality, the give-and-take, the enjoyment of a naturally happy breed remained. Without them Britain could not have carried through a social revolution and avoided bloodshed, even a bloody nose. An enjoying, great and indestructible breed.

Something else struck us as my wife and I travelled by car three times around Britain from the Channel to the Highlands. Outside the politics of London hardly anyone seemed to be interested in the Commonwealth. All were interested in Britain and, by necessity, in Europe. Imperialism was as dead as Queen Victoria. But the loss of a nonviable empire and the discovery of no comparable role in the new world was a grievous wound of the spirit. Although never admitted, the wound could not be hidden from the stranger.

Unlike the empire, the real glory of Britain was not dead. At Coventry, amid the ruins of the bombed cathedral and its splendid replacement, I beheld an exhibit that must reduce any decent stranger to tears. Probably nowhere else would some nameless man, after the night of the bombing, have erected a crudely scribbled placard with the words, "Father, Forgive." That placard spoke more eloquently of Britain's spirit than even Shakespeare or Churchill could speak.

Mixed with the indestructible British spirit, its forgiveness of enemies, was the ugly spectacle of Piccadilly Circus and Soho at midnight. There, it had been said in the postwar boom years, was the authentic image of "Swinging Britain," the second Elizabethan Age invented by the headline writers of the gutter press. The crowds of revellers, drunks, whores, pimps and drug addicts certainly swung, but they looked even more frightening, more degenerate, than the denizens of Times Square, New York—this a few blocks from Buckingham Palace, home of a second and worthy Elizabeth. If a minor part of London was swinging, it swung, I thought, from an invisible gibbet. In the small towns, villages and lovely, manicured countryside, heartland of Britain and perhaps its supreme achievement, we found no swingers, only the common folk, and only their kind could have scribbled that poignant message at Coventry.

Doubtless a believing Christian had scribbled it. But the stranger found less Christianity, less religious feeling, in Britain than in the United States or even in Canada. Once Britain had worshipped God, as revealed in the King James Version of the Bible, greatest of all books. In God's name it had fought a civil war and beheaded a king. Now, to many sophisticated people, God seemed obsolete like the empire, outlawed by science and economic imperatives. His worship seemed to be replaced, lacking higher authority, by secular worship of a more reliable institution, the Crown, and a deserving Queen who still worshipped Him.

How would this change in Britain, material and spiritual, affect its friendship with Canada? Would it have any effect at all? For the time being it had little or none in constitution and practical politics. Elizabeth, a constitutionally split personality, is Queen of Canada and, within it, is advised solely by her Canadian prime minister.

When she visits her North American Dominion she is treated with at least as much outward respect as in Britain, where cartoonists lampoon her and photographers of the gutter press invade her privacy, just as the British Parliament is more disorderly than the Canadian, soccer games more riotous. British phlegm is less evident at home than it looks to foreigners.

This curious society, broadening down from precedent to precedent, has worked well for Britain and is attractive to most Canadians. A Canadian prime minister in his senses, who rules, is far less respected than a Queen who only reigns, and he would never propose to abolish the monarchial system. Or if he did, his government would be instantly rejected by the present generation.

If the monarchy, with all its oddities, is the best system of government so far invented, will it always satisfy the next Canadian generations? Will our children, and theirs, be content with a monarch who lives in another country, visiting Canada infrequently, a Canadian only in law? It seems improbable. Certainly the next generation will feel the ancient tug less than its parents do. Even I felt it a little when I reported two coronations and saw two monarchs, father and daughter, on a display that no other nation could imitate.

My own immigrant father, son of rich English parents who gave him nothing but steamship fare, felt the tug so strongly that in the dusty Canadian cowtown where we then were living, he marked the King's birthday by borrowing a rifle and discharging a royal salute at the sagebrush hills. No one paid the least attention. He came home with a dislocated shoulder, happy to have asserted his loyalty in exile. Although a great-hearted man, he, like his kind, never ceased to be an Englishman. His son is totally Canadian. The son's children, and especially his grandchildren, seem to feel no tug at all.

Even if the next, or a succeeding, generation decides to change the system in favour of a native head of state, what better system can replace it? A hereditary dynasty enthroning some big contributor to the campaign funds of the ruling party? A powerful elected president as in the United States and France or a ceremonial president as in some European countries?

There is no agreement on that possible issue and none is yet needed. Such problems are for the future beyond the business of most living Canadians. No sane politicians would now question the existing system, whatever their long thoughts might be. Canada has a sufficiency of immediate problems to solve without raising another sure to split and convulse it. But some day the constitutional and emotional ambiguity surrounding a monarch who resides across the ocean may become a political issue of uncertain result.

Nowadays Canada admires, welcomes and needs Britain as a still important countervailing force (and a major market) even when it is a secondary power. The United States, too, must always reckon with Britain, as Reagan found in the Falklands and again in Grenada.

The old Atlantic Triangle, by which Canada ran a trade surplus in Britain to cover deficits in the United States, has perished with many other supposedly permanent economic structures, but the Atlantic community of thought and instinct, with no written laws, survives, driven closer together by a blundering Russia. At its heart is Bismarck's dictum, the common language of the British, American and Canadian people.

France has always been a prickly partner in the European Economic Community, always unpredictable, sometimes an insider, sometimes almost an outsider, but always essential to the whole partnership. Its geography in the European heartland, if nothing else, made it so. And its ancestral roots are deep in Canada.

The American Revolution could not have succeeded, at least not then, if it had lacked the alliance with prerevoluntionary France. Yorktown was as much a French as an American victory. But Jefferson, a leading revolutionist, foresaw that in another time of peril the infant United States might be compelled to "marry" the British fleet. He understood the primary Atlantic fact before Bismarck's birth.

Although Washington, in his last years, had warned against all entangling alliances, the emotional ties with France, personified by Lafayette, long remained a folk memory, and they were revived when, in two world wars, the United States rescued its original ally. "Lafayette, we are here!" cried an officer as Gen. "Black Jack" Pershing landed his troops on French soil. No such nostalgic slogan was uttered by Eisenhower when the Allied armada crossed the English Channel in the second war, but the imperatives had not changed. They had only been recognized as unchangeable.

The character of the French had not changed much, either, and it bears a special relevance to Canada in our time. Throughout the centuries the French were a difficult people to deal with and understand, if they understood themselves. They had never managed to complete their own revolution or, as Carlyle wrote, to make their many democratic constitutions march. Hilaire Belloc, himself half-French, put that history in a better phrase. Again and again, he said, Frenchmen marched across Europe and returned, having accomplished only an epic. So did their kinsmen in New France, marching and paddling across America to the Gulf of Mexico and the Rockies, only to be conquered at home on the St. Lawrence.

Charles de Gaulle was the last epic maker, but he totally misconstrued French Canada. His shout of *"Vive le Québec libre!"* in Montreal was no help to the Quebec people, even the separatists. Rejecting de Gaulle's effrontery and sending him back to France, Pearson could have won a national election next day, hands down.

With all his glamour and genius, de Gaulle failed to understand that the French Canadians were Canadians first, French second. France had deserted them in the Seven Years War and, in its revolution, deserted their church, too. That ancient gulf was hard, if not impossible, to bridge, and de Gaulle was the last man capable of bridging it.

After returning to Paris, he promptly froze France's relations with Canada. The Canadian ambassador, Jules Léger, was left outside in the cold. That freeze, as the crusty American ambassador Chip Bohlen told me, could not be thawed "until after the funeral." The United States, Britain and Canada must await de Gaulle's departure.

Before then he had also frozen Britain out of the Common Market and forced the NATO command out of Paris. He could never forgive his American, British, Canadian and other allies for twice rescuing France from Germany.

The thaw did come after the funeral as Bohlen had predicted. De Gaulle's successors, a little weary of *grandeur* and its folly, were less grand but more practical. They ceased, at least in public, to support *le Québec libre* despite all pleas by Premier René Lévesque

Lévesque was given the red carpet treatment in Paris and not much else. While France no longer recommended a separatist Quebec, it was sullen and cold in its treatment of Canada. Trudeau undertook to rewarm the old friendship. He defended Canada's unity and defeated Lévesque in the sovereignty-association referendum, but he embraced the vague concept of a worldwide francophone community so long as Quebec did not pursue a sovereign foreign policy. That could never be permitted if Canada were truly a nation, but a nation in need of any useful countervailing force. France supplied one among many.

So did West Germany, arisen from the ashes of war to make itself the most powerful nation in Europe. It, too, must be cultivated. The ablest of Ottawa's diplomats were sent to Bonn where the former enemy was encouraged to trade with Canada, and its NATO troops trained on the Canadian prairies. Peace, like war, makes strange bed-fellows. Moreover, Canadian voters of German origin could not be ignored.

The same was also true of Italy. Italian voters controlled several constituencies in the Toronto metropolis and the Pope, a mighty countervailing force in politics as in religion, lived in Rome. He must be cultivated for reasons religious, political and economic. But the Canadian government, in its latest spell of nationalism, protected the footwear industries of Quebec and Ontario from inexpensive, excellent Italian imports at the cost of the consumer.

As a countervailing force the rest of Europe did not matter so much to Canada. Switzerland was a good place for Trudeau's skis, Spain and the Scandinavian countries good places for a holiday, and they imported some Canadian goods. Even they could not be neglected. Nor could the Russian satellites behind the Iron Curtain where Trudeau carried his peace mission hoping they would carry it, or part of it, to Moscow.

Meanwhile the focus of Canadian foreign policy had been moving steadily from the Atlantic to the Pacific since Canada discovered its large and growing stake in Asia. There stood Japan above its miracle, the world's third or perhaps even its second economic giant. To the Japanese market moved vast quantities of Canadian coal, grain, paper and forest products that nourished the prosperity of the western provinces. To the Canadian market moved a smaller traffic of Japanese exports, usually giving Canada a favourable trade balance. Despite this surplus, it put quotas on Japanese automobiles and harassed their exporters with nit-picking customs regulations, complaining that Japan imported raw Canadian products without restriction but few finished goods, which was true.

Japan, complaining in turn against Canadian protectionism while continuing its own, exported capital as well as goods to Canada. It bought substantial shares in Canadian mineral and forest industries to ensure future supplies while hedging its bets by similar investments elsewhere. It sought Canadian trade and friendship, but the former enemy would not put all its eggs in any single basket, not even in the

United States where it enjoyed a huge trade surplus and antagonized the American employers and labour unions.

Japan was willing to negotiate the reduction of trade barriers, or so it said, but it knew that in Pacific strategy its islands and industries were absolutely vital to the United States. On the Pacific Japan had become as strong a countervailing force as Britain on the Atlantic.

Then there was China, Napoleon's sleeping giant who, awakening, must shake the world. Pearson, in his latter years, had grasped the future power of China and held that world power would soon be centred in the Pacific. Since his youthful vagabond journeys in the Chinese hinterland, Trudeau had recognized the Chinese Fact before Pearson. With almost romantic enthusiasm, he felt its ancient heritage and suffered a guilty conscience because the West had treated China shamefully and Canada had virtually enslaved Chinese labourers to build the CPR.

Japan and China were the great countervailing forces of the Pacific but, as in Europe, lesser forces could not be overlooked. Trudeau travelled restlessly through Korea and Southeast Asia always on the lookout for friends and trade. He also dealt with India, perhaps another awakening giant that already had betrayed Canada by purchasing its technology and making a nuclear explosive, if not quite a bomb, in violation of solemn contract.

What of Canada's other Commonwealth associates? Australia and New Zealand were among the older Dominions, white-skinned, usually prosperous, eager to trade but restricted by protectionist devices in the Canadian market. The colony of Hong Kong, however, was welcome to invest its capital and export some of its richer people to Canada.

Canadian governments were not much interested in these areas individually. Ottawa's interest was in the Commonwealth as a whole, most of the inhabitants nonwhite and poor. Acting together, they could be a countervailing force worth vigorous cultivation. Trudeau vigorously cultivated them as an honest broker, and seemed to replace the British prime minister as the Commonwealth's tacitly accepted leader. In his judgement it was not only the bridge between the northern rich and the southern poor but a countervailing force of vital importance to his pragmatic foreign policy.

Apparently J. W. Dafoe had been wrong in warning that a Commonwealth of disparate, quarrelling peoples could not survive without some kind of world government and law after the failure of the League of Nations. Without them the Commonwealth did survive after his death. It survived under the protection of the American nuclear umbrella, the uneasy *pax Americana*. Even the umbrella may not be strong enough, or well managed enough, to reconcile such a miscellany of races, histories, cultures and tribal quarrels. But Trudeau still hoped that they would maintain a collectivity of sorts if they understood their own interests.

Anyhow, he had done what he could to help them with advice, financial subsidies and vain preachments to the rich North on the necessity of aid to the poor South. (Mulroney has maintained Trudeau's general attitude—and the same barriers in the Canadian market against the exports of the poor.)

Outside the Commonwealth there remained Canada's blind eye long turned on Latin America. There Trudeau's own eyes were clearing. He negotiated oil imports from Mexico and Venezuela in case Middle Eastern supplies were interrupted; he flattered and wooed Mexican leaders; he sold wheat to Mexico and welcomed Mexican imports so long as they did not seriously compete with Canadian products. Ranged against the southern boundary of the United States, Mexico and its neighbours could be especially useful countervailing forces that, in Canada's view, Reagan had misunderstood and embittered.

What weight, then, did Canada have in the scales of changing world power not just in its own imagination? Not as much as it had once hoped but possibly more than it yet realizes. Today, Canada is indeed a Middle Power as King had blandly assumed at San Francisco. It has become a significant countervailing force of its own which the great powers cannot ignore.

Could it ever be more than that? Was it already more than that? Two Canadian professors, David DeWitt of the University of Alberta and John Kirton of the University of Toronto, argue that their nation already is a "principal power" because the power of the United States has declined and world power is newly diffused. This pushes our real status beyond the present facts. But assuredly Canada is far more successful in the world than most of its citizens yet realize. The national inferiority complex dies hard.

13

THE
FUNNY
GAME

In trying to judge where their nation stands in the world and how it is managing, or mismanaging, its business at home, Canadians are driven back to the agency which supposedly solves, or worsens, its problems.

The agency is called government, an apparatus so vast and intricate that literally no one, not even the mechanics in charge, know all its parts and functions. But when time can be spared from more interesting entertainment like sports, television, love affairs and the neighbours' domestic squabbles, we argue the success and failure of government as if we were examining some branch of a reliable science.

This method of examination serves well enough for physics, mathematics and chemistry, each with its known laws. For politics it is largely irrelevant and misses the mark, because the political process differs from any other. Its laws—or rather its vagaries—are never reliable. They produce results good and bad, prosperity or depression, peace and war, constructive works and ruinous destruction, apparently without rhyme or reason.

Politics, to be sure, does not control the ultimate concerns of individual life, thought and habit, but it penetrates and delineates the communal life of society which only a savage or a hermit can escape.

How odd, then, after countless centuries of experiment, that the process is so widely misunderstood, so often bungled and despised like an unworthy, even shameful pursuit, almost a vice. And odd, too, that politics since the days of ancient Greece has hardly given us a new and original idea.

While every problem solved in ancient or modern times produces at least two new ones, the task of government must be done, one way or another. Few of us would prefer anarchy. So we are lucky to find men and women prepared to do it while the majority disparage them, snickering or jeering at a safe distance. Nonetheless, the ignorant citizen rarely lacks an opinion on all passing issues though knowing little or nothing about them. Such a cranky, spasmodic attention to public business raises a fundamental question of our time: Can governments, policies and society as a whole adjust themselves to the evolving anatomy of the new world?

In Canada the beginning, only the beginning, of an answer has lately appeared. The citizenry suddenly suspects the importance, without fully understanding the machinery, of modern politics. This awakening interest comes very late. Has it come *too* late? If not, will the Canadian political method be sufficient for our need in the hard days ahead? Or, like the economic method, is it out of sync with events?

Only Canadians will finally answer that question. Their answer will depend, at times, on themselves, at other times on events outside their control. The dilemma of all times was best described by Abraham Lincoln, the greatest political genius produced so far in North America, when he said: "I claim not to have controlled events but confess plainly that events have controlled me." Few contemporary politicians are so frank, none so able. Few dare to admit the dictum of the scholarly British Liberal statesman, John Morley. He found that in politics there is no perfect answer to any problem. Always the answer is a second-best, a choice of the lesser evil.

What, then, is politics stripped of its myths and pretences? Many nonpoliticians have tried to define it, but not one fully succeeded. Even Shakespeare, who seemed to understand life entire, failed in that attempt. Doubtless with a highly political and tyrannical queen in mind, he could only make one of his fictitious characters grumble: "Get thee glass eyes and like a scurvy politician seem to see the things thou dost not." He scorned "the pate of a politician, one who could circumvent God."

As Shakespeare must have known, the ablest politician of his or any time cannot circumvent the pressures surrounding him at all times. Perhaps no one understood that fact better than Benjamin Disraeli, subtlest English politician of the nineteenth century and favourite adviser to another queen. "Finality," he said, "is not the language of politics." And in a wry aside he recalled that King Louis Philippe of France "attributed the great success of the British nation in political life to their talking politics after dinner."

Much virtue in this remark, for politics, beneath its outer skin, consists largely in private bargaining between its rival practitioners while they appear to be irreconcilable in public. Even a dinner with wine in Ottawa's parliamentary restaurant (subsidized by the taxpayers) often produces a deal later consummated, with suitable flourishes and sham battles, in the House of Commons.

Robert Louis Stevenson, a romantic of literature but a canny Scot in life, offered his own shrewd definition of the political process: "These are my politics—to change what we can, to better what we can but still to bear in mind that man is but a devil weakly fettered by some generous beliefs and impositions, and for no word, however sounding, and no cause, however just and pious, to relax the structure of these bonds . . . Man is a creature who lives not upon bread alone but principally by catchwords."

Many are the catchwords, all the way from Trudeau's sounding metaphors down to the humble aphorism reputedly uttered by the late Joseph Clarihue who, in the British Columbia Legislature, warned his fellow Liberals that "we must march breast forward, heads erect and ears to the ground." His advice was not so foolish as it then sounded, for the politician must always sniff the spoor of public desire and, if possible, fulfil it.

Sidney Hillman, the American labour leader, defined politics still better as "the science of who gets what, when, and why." There is the whole process in a nutshell.

But how to define the politician, least understood of all craftsmen? Is he ever the master of events? No, he is not. He is essentially a broker between competing interests, and if he can keep them in reasonable balance, short of violent collision, he will have done well. Even the second-best choice often eludes him. He is driven to a third-best, or worse, a solution that, clearly, will not work but perhaps will buy a little time until events change again.

This was usually John A. Macdonald's method, the only workable method in a country of such diverse regions and interests as Canada. Not without a shrewd folk wisdom did his people call him "Old Tomorrow," for today will pass in politics at every sundown; tomorrow will present new dilemmas and, with luck, new second-bests.

The average Canadian seems to think that the politician is a creature apart from common life. On the contrary, every human being is necessarily a politician. All of us must learn the ageless art of the possible, or impossible, if we are to live in domestic peace. As Aristotle put it long ago, "man is by nature a political animal." He must be to survive common life. Even in the bosom of his family he plays a clumsy sort of politics with flattery, mutual forgiveness, evasions and innocent white lies. So must his wife. No household, rich or poor, could endure without life's essential lubricant. Nor could society.

Among political animals the amateur is always distinguished from the professional. Most men and women are not born as natural politicians. But they are compelled to practise politics subconsciously day by day, hour by hour, never conscious of their habits. The natural, instinctive politician—a Lincoln, a Disraeli, a Reagan, a Thatcher or, in Canada, a Macdonald, Laurier, King, Trudeau or Mulroney—is a different animal. He goes about the business with conscious intent. And why?

There is the abiding mystery of the profession. What sane man or woman would voluntarily bear the whips and scorns of politics, the small rewards, the common heartbreak, and usually the pursebreak at the end, but for some subtle satisfaction unknown to others?

Once, in a brash moment, I asked the late Senator Henry Jackson why he wanted to be president of the United States. He blushed, looked sheepish and said he did not know. An honest answer from an honest man. Of course he did not know. No politician can ever know. His motives are always mixed, ideals struggling against ambition. The ego, often the megalomania, is torn this way and that, beyond understanding.

In such persons, you might say, politics is a disease incurable, frequently terminal. The microbe yields to no antibiotic, nor even to surgery. But always fame, as Milton, a born politician, confessed, is "the spur that the clear spirit doth raise (that last infirmity of noble mind) to scorn delights, and live laborious days." For the less noble mind of James Grainger, poet of the eighteenth century, fame was an "empty bubble."

The born politician never ceases to blow bubbles, to seek the spur and strive for the summit reached by only eighteen Canadians since the nation began.

If fame is the spur, power is the goal, its perks agreeable but incidental. If the public watches the strife with mystification or contempt, the politician's morals are generally as disparaged as they are misunderstood. It is all very well for the businessman to treat the political breed with contempt as if he were morally superior when he is not. All very well for him to denounce government as stupid and corrupt, probably both. In fact, as I have seen him, the businessman, practising politics in his own corporation, is generally no more honest than the man who practises it in the goldfish bowl and illuminated aquarium of Parliament.

With a few exceptions, businessmen generally fail in politics because business and politics are different arts. Nothing can be more absurd than to imagine that government is merely a Big Business. Its bottom line cannot be reckoned in money as the board room reckons it but only in the welfare of society. The two things are not the same at all.

In a rather long experience the honesty of politics has greatly advanced since my youthful reporting days in British Columbia, a province wrongly supposed to be less honest than the others. In those days the politicians commonly stretched the law out of joint, and the public expected nothing else. Once, for example, Premier "Honest John" Oliver came home from Ottawa to find that, in his absence, his cabinet had arranged a peculiarly malodorous campaign fund deal by purchasing, at exorbitant price, a warehouse of little value to store the government's liquor supply. Oliver called the attorney-general, the late J. W. de B. Farris, to his office and told him that a royal commission would investigate the scandal.

"Mr. Premier," said Farris, "it won't stand it," and he left the office.

"After that," Senator Farris told me with glee years later in Ottawa, "I never heard anything more about a royal commission."

The warehouse deal had been scandalous all right, but it was not investigated or changed. John was honest but he understood politics, and Farris, too, was honest by the standards of those times, his personal word always trustworthy

Since then the standards have improved. Such crude little bargains as the warehouse deal, and others like it, are rare nowadays in any province or in Ottawa where corruption on a larger scale takes the form of bribing voters, quite legally, with their own money.

Alas, the rollicking, adolescent days of politics and journalism are gone. Never again will an inspirited reporter like the late beloved Billy de Graves stand up in the Victoria press gallery and begin to address the legislature in rhymed insults before I could throw him down the dark, narrow stairs, fearing that his neck was broken. Happily it was not, but that night, after a lavish Conservative banquet, when all my fellow reporters were apparently inebriated, since they lay prostrate and snoring on the floor, I, then a teetotaller, wrote reports for five newspapers with fake signatures and the partisan slant required by each editor. None suspected the deception of my all-night labour.

Oh, those were rough days and rougher nights. So rough and so jolly that a banquet with plenteous liquid refreshments, given in Victoria to the legislature of dry, thirsty Washington State, ended in something like a riot of broken glasses and cutlery, one eminent British Columbia politician crawling under the long table to pinch the screaming ladies' legs, another carried out and desposited, sleeping peacefully, in the wet gutter, Oliver, cold sober, shaking his beard in despair. The planned gesture of international friendship could hardly be called a success. But it was as jolly as it was rough.

Today, I believe, few countries, if any, sustain more honest politics than does Canada. Some may have more polished manners, some less polished as in the United States where many elected persons ended in jail. So far as I recall a British Columbia cabinet minister was the only politician imprisoned for malfeasance in Canada. There has been no great Canadian money scandal since Beauharnois in the 1930s when the honest Bennett watched King and the Liberal Party walk "the valley of humiliation" only to emerge triumphantly as they had emerged from the Customs Scandal.

Let the citizen who considers politics inherently dishonest ask himself if his own honesty is beyond question. Has he never cheated, chiselled, bluffed and deceived in the little affairs of private life where he is safe, as the politician is not, from public scrutiny? We all need some charity, all being human. Few of us have the right to hurl the first stone.

In sum, as John Nance Garner, the American politician of many scars, remarked when he lost the Democratic presidential nomination to Roosevelt, "Politics, son, is a funny game." Lacking better, that definition will serve everywhere.

A funny game, often sad, not easily mastered. Macdonald, its supreme Canadian master, said that a new member needed several sessions of Parliament before he learned to hang his hat in the cloakroom, much longer to hang his career on a policy, still longer to realize that all policies must change with the changing problems.

In politics nothing is permanent, no theory sacred. The ablest government must operate on the relatively short term, from crisis to crisis, lurching blindly through unmapped territory while it pretends to have a map and answers to all questions. One step in the dark enough for it, and the steps are circular like those of a man lost. The process resembles a merry-go-round though represented in debate as a straight line.

A funny game. Its player, the genus *Politicus,* is *sui generis* a craftsman of a unique trade. But original ideas rarely, if ever, originate in the game. They originate in the minds of thinkers with names generally forgotten—a saint in the plains of India, a ragged philosopher like Socrates in the slums of ancient Athens, a carpenter in Asia Minor, a shepherd in the Arabian desert, a rebel in the countryside of England, a German heretic brooding on communism in the British Museum.

From all available ideas the Founding Fathers of the American Republic took what they thought they might require, remodelled it for a yet unborn state and evolved a constitution supposed to be original but which, in essentials, was not. So did the Fathers of Confederation who took the British parliamentary system and added to it the American federal device, the single truly new idea—and the last one—to emerge from later political experiment. Nowadays Canadian governments practise the same larceny at home, stealing ideas from opposition parties or any other source, claiming them as their own inventions that can always be changed or abandoned to fit the fell grip of circumstance.

It is never easy for the layman to read the confusing signals of politics when banners herald an advance and the troops already are in full retreat. Even the humble elected foot soldier of the party is often baffled by contradictory orders, but he seldom disobeys them. He follows his leader, like the heroes of the Light Brigade, without asking the reason why.

Besides, he is so busy in the daily grind of Ottawa that he has little time to think much for himself, to read anything more than the newspapers, the dull pages of Hansard, the countless, incomprehensible reports of the official experts, the whining letters from his constituents. For the most part he depends on the learning of others. As the acerbic John Maynard Keynes put it, practical men, especially politicians, are mostly the slaves of some defunct economist. Many of them were long Keynes's slaves without understanding or living up to his theory.

But it is a common mistake to think that the member of Parliament does little work because the House of Commons suddenly empties, leaving hardly a quorum behind, as soon as the daily fireworks of Question Period have faded. In fact, he is upstairs in his office dictating soft answers to his constituents and trying to get a pension for an ungrateful voter. Or he is attending a committee, or wrestling with a pompous bureaucrat who inhabits a luxurious skyscraper. The average member of Parliament is not lazy. He is overworked. He lives most of the day and half the night in a suffocating hothouse while the bitter wind comes roaring out of the Gatineau Hills and the city shivers.

This is an unhealthy life. It often makes a sedentary politician soft in body, even in mind. Ottawa, supposed to be the heart and mirror of Canada, becomes, like most capitals, strangely isolated from the people. To know and serve them, the politician must go home frequently, his travel expenses paid by the public, mix with the local voters and regain the common touch lost in Parliament. Taking one consideration with another, such a life, at best, is miserable, not to be envied or imitated by a smug citizenry. But it has its rewards in fame and at least the sense of power.

Some members, a small minority, neglect their duty, as some citizens do also. They drink too much, eat too much, wench too much, break up their distant families, end in divorce court or passing scandal, a day's wonder on the front page, soon forgotten. But the great majority live like monks in their marble-lined fortress. A funny game but grim.

Its tasks and trials are little known outside the capital. Among them is the necessity for leading politicians to speak four languages— English, French, the formal jargon of Parliament and the colloquial argot of the street. Quadrilingualism is uniquely required in Canada by the English and French facts, by the age of politics as theatre, by the harsh television cameras that replace the long parliamentary debate with one-minute flashes, ghostwritten wisecracks, punchy one-liners like a cartoon in *The New Yorker,* plastic grins or sagacious frowns to titillate the groundlings of the networks coast to coast.

In all times and nations the great politician must be an actor, as was Roosevelt, greatest of our time. So was Churchill with his own bulldog act and carefully written speeches that sounded spontaneous. So was King with the different act of the dull man, comfortable as an old shoe. And so was Trudeau with many acts ranging from sublimity to vulgarity according to his vagrant moods. But Stanfield, who should have been prime minister, would never try to act, was always himself, and his fine character, his learning and his private wit were lost to the public eye.

The best actors suffer their off-days. Roosevelt could slip in moments of anger but not often. Reagan, trained in Hollywood, still needed a well-rehearsed speech text and hidden teleprompters in the House of Representatives.

Much depends on the mood of the speaker and the listeners, the ambience of the moment, favourable or unfavourable. At Gettysburg, for instance, the greatest speech in American history, lasting perhaps two minutes, went over with a hush, was forgotten in a deluge of inferior oratory. But soon the people came to realize that Lincoln's few words were immortal.

In modern Canada debate too often moves from the House of Commons to the corridors where the kleig lights flare, the cameras grind and the mischievous interviewers try to catch their victims with some unanswerable question like, "Have you stopped betraying your leader?" Thus is Parliament diminished, and newspapers deplore its sorry state without adequately reporting its often excellent speeches. The fruit of long research is buried forever in the tomb of Hansard. And thus also appearance becomes more important than substance, the public easily distracted from its urgent business by televised drama.

The politician's worst task is to make himself heard above the synthetic clamour, to explain his views, to correct lies when they are far down the road before the truth can put its boots on. How he yearns to be understood! How he strives to use his knowledge, experience and talent to serve his constituents! What a hope!

The public attention span on any dull but important statement is reckoned in minutes. No issue short of a national emergency or a juicy scandal can compete with a Grey or Stanley Cup final. Only a vivid personality like Trudeau could keep himself constantly in the front of the people's collective mind because he knew how to stir up the support of friends, the anger of enemies and the interest of neutrals. He used controversy, sophistry and irony when required as the cutting tools of his trade to make headlines and blur the legitimate questions of the hour.

For the average politician wielding a rubber sword, competition with such a duellist was as hopeless as with the stars of football or hockey. But sometimes Trudeau's brilliance cost him dearly. When he called the opposition a gaggle of "nobodies," that outburst was not soon forgiven by his friends or by the public. Neither was his indecent gesture from a railway car in British Columbia.

In the political theatre of our times stage business, elaborate scenery, contrived suspense and thunder and lightning in the wings often substitute for thought. The citizens expect the plumber to clear a drain, the carpenter to build a house, the surgeon to penetrate heart or brain. From the politician they have begun to expect cant, sweet-talk and occasional comedy. They could get much more if they would only listen to the quadrilingual voices crying in the wilderness.

Once politics was a task for unpaid gentlemen of scant learning, as Wellington insisted. Now a successful member of the Canadian Parliament, with few exceptions, is a university graduate paid well but usually less than he could earn in private business. He cannot afford to be a gentleman of the old school, and a woman finds it difficult to remain a lady in the parliamentary rough-and-tumble. Both sexes must mingle with the common citizenry as if they were typical of it, though they are not and otherwise would spend short lives at Ottawa.

Yet gentility still prevails there, little known to the voters. King well understood its necessity when, for example, he told his intimates that his powerful colleague, Jim Gardiner, was unfit to lead the Liberal Party because he was not a "gentleman." In his own mind, of course, King was a true gentleman who smoothly cut other gentlemen's throats as occasion demanded. No other treatment, he once said in Parliament, could deal with "certain classes" of people. Gentility survives in a nameless but staunch parliamentary club that enforces its own unwritten rules and cuts across party lines. Friendships are often bipartisan and close despite the public clashes in the House.

To be sure, blood feuds do exist and have always existed. Famous among them were those between Macdonald and Brown, King and

Meighen, Pearson and Diefenbaker, but they are rare nowadays and usually waged within the same party. Without an off-duty truce between on-duty enemies, the system would become unworkable as it is in most countries.

Political Ottawa, unlike the nonpolitical city around it, hardly talks anything else but politics from the cabinet minister's office down to the cleaning women's rest room. All these people are employed by government and their jobs depend upon it. In this vast chamber of echoes, ceaseless speculation, rumour and wild surmise provide conversation day and night. Gossip is Ottawa's amusement, vice and major product, unfortunately noneconomic but inexhaustible. Such incestuous argument, the talkers wrongly imagine, creates public opinion which unfolds far from the capital in its own mysterious fashion.

However opinion is made, party leaders and the rank and file alike have to learn the tricks of their curious trade. It may not take a new member several sessions to hang his hat properly in the cloakroom, but it may take him years to learn the four political languages. Nowadays any man or woman aspiring to party leadership and supreme office must have at least a working knowledge of both official languages. The English-speaking politician usually has trouble learning French, though Stanfield and Clark mastered it after much secret labour, as King and Diefenbaker did not, while Mulroney was bilingual from his youth and Turner acquired a second language in his Montreal law practice. The French Canadian's more sensitive ear, however, seems to accommodate itself to the English rhythm with comparative ease.

Ernest Lapointe came to Ottawa from the Quebec countryside without a word of English. In a few years he made himself one of Parliament's finest orators in both languages. Jean Chrétien was also unilingual when he reached Ottawa, and he learned a second language more heavily accented than Lapointe's (sometimes deliberately accented for comic relief) to make himself popular even in the West where the naturally bilingual Trudeau was anathema.

Beside language there are other essential tricks of the trade, among them the use of words to disguise intention or the lack of intention. Probably no man since King mastered this trick as well as Paul Martin who, in Pearson's government, was the able and popular Minister of Obfuscation. In Question Period, when questions were aimed across the aisle like bullets, they seldom penetrated Martin's bullet-proof vest. His statements from the treasury benches, in both languages, were long, ponderous and eloquent, and the weary questioner gave up in despair, having received no answer. Only Allan MacEachen, one of Martin's successors, could equal that sleek double talk and then only in English, his second language being unusable Cape Breton Gaelic.

Even more powerful than wordy obfuscation is silence, if you know how to use it. Trudeau always knew but sometimes, his temper roused, he burst into outrageous speech, a moment later regretted but long remembered by the public. King's slips were few, as in the notorious five-cent speech which he vainly tried to correct next day. He used to tell his intimates, "The most useful things I've done are the things I refused to do." He waited, silent, until his mind, or rather his gut, told him that the moment was ripe for decision and public opinion ready for it. With him timing was as important as action.

When the time had come to strike he struck instantly, without warning. In 1940 he summoned Parliament, gave no advance word to any minister except Lapointe and, having solemnly introduced a newly elected member, dissolved the House to win a wartime election. The new member, struck dumb and bewildered, did not know what had happened to him. The opposition, caught unaware, could only squirm, squeak and gibber into defeat. King, the supposedly timid little man, could be the most reckless of gamblers.

His successor, St. Laurent, also knew the power of silence, the importance of timing. He slipped only once, in the "supermen" speech when he was old, grief-stricken, weary and sick.

Along with silence the official leak is an effective trick or instrument. Every minister swears on the Bible never to discuss the monarch's business outside the cabinet chamber. The oath is sometimes violated by intent, a balloon of rumour launched through a chosen reporter to test the atmosphere of public opinion. If opinion seems hostile to a certain policy, the rumour is indignantly denied by the leaker. The reporter is deflated with the balloon.

More often the leak is not deliberate but unintentional after a minister has been indiscreet among friends. Pearson used to complain that his cabinet was a sieve full of holes impossible to plug. Trudeau had watched those leaks and warned his own ministers, at their first meeting, that if he identified a leaker the man would be fired. But like Pearson, he could never plug the sieve. He soon found the silent civil service leaking on its own account to bring pressure against the government's intended policies. Brown envelopes, without address or signature, appeared on some reporter's desk. They contained a high official secret, perhaps a cabinet paper, the monarch's inviolable business. When it was printed the responsible minister might be furious, but what could he tell the jeering opposition? Usually that the leak was spurious, that it did not represent government policy as yet undecided.

Sometimes, when it did represent policy, the policy was slightly revised to discredit the leaker as in the classic case of Marc Lalonde who indiscreetly flourished a text of his approaching budget speech before the eyes of the reporters, assuming that they could not read it but forgetting the television cameras. They photographed, in midair, some of his figures and policies. In clumsy repair of a leak traditionally ruinous to finance ministers, he increased his planned expenditures by $200 million—this in a budget of restraint—to prove that the camera was mistaken. An expensive repair.

Next to silence and timing in politics the most valuable trick, or talent, is a sense of humour. Lacking it, the politician could hardly endure his life. Not many politicians have enough of that saving quality. Trudeau had corrosive wit aplenty, the natural bent of the Gallic mind, but wit is not humour. King, with little wit, had humour of a sort, though strictly in private, and he never laughed at himself. Pearson was the single prime minister of my acquaintance who laughed at himself, and the world, to hide his deepening despair. If Trudeau did the same, humour overcoming wit, the public never heard of it, but disappointment, hurt and lost hopes were clearly engraved on his aging features and on those of all his predecessors.

In all the tricks of the trade and the rules of the funny game, the original question continues to nag us: Does our governing system fit the new age? Clearly, it does not. If it should be made to fit, when and where shall we begin to improve it? And what parts most need revision?

14

THE
STRANGE
ORGANISM

The parliamentary process in its varied forms, even democracy itself, could not survive, much less flourish in the modern world, if they lacked political parties. They were one of Britain's many gifts to free peoples as they spread across the ocean to the American Republic and the monarchial Canadian Confederation. While unmentioned in their constitutions, parties supplied the bone structure, flesh and governing brain of the living organism called the state.

Each party is also an organism and in Canada, as we shall see, all parties now approach their latest realignment with consequences not yet foreseeable by the politican or the voter and likely to surprise both.

Enforcing its own laws, rewards and punishments, the successful party is a state within the state and, like all organisms from the worm to the human, it has a compulsion to live, preferably in office or, if necessary, in opposition until it is re-elected.

The cells of the organism are invisible to the public most of the time. They become visible, and vocal, only in election times and then briefly. At other times they are little noted as they argue, divide and struggle within themselves. But unlike animal bodies so afflicted, the party remains healthy in its division. It defies the laws of anatomy and scientific analysis.

In operating method it resembles a private club. Its candidates are usually nominated by a handful of card-carrying party members and their nominating conventions attract small public interest. But the men and women then elected to control Parliament will frame the country's laws governing everybody. If the citizens feel neglected in the process, the fault is largely their own. If they want better candidates and law makers, they should join the existing parties or form new ones instead of leaving the basic humdrum work of democracy to the clubs that will persist and go about their business whether victorious or defeated.

In one respect a law of longevity prevails over the laws of the party. Canadian governments lead comparatively short lives, perhaps about ten years on average. Their allotted span resembles that of cats and dogs. They age fast, losing their quality and usefulness before they lose office. The party is quite different. Its life is measured not in years or decades but, if it is lucky, in centuries.

According to theory, J. W. Dafoe wryly observed, parties exchange places by the will of the voters without complaint. They accept the natural cycle of democracy. In fact, no party leaves office without a sense of outrage as if nature's laws had been violated. It must be a brave, unusual politician who, on the night of electoral defeat, retains his democratic faith in the wisdom of the people. A still braver and more unlikely politician will agree with Dafoe that there are only two kinds of government—the barely tolerable and all the others.

The prairie Homer sometimes nodded. His work on Laurier (flawed hero of his youth) was written as a mere review of O. D. Skelton's official biography published just after the First World War. The review expanded into the most perceptive study of Canadian politics up to that time. In it Dafoe seemed to commit an error uncharacteristic of such a profound student.

The conscription crisis of 1917, he wrote, had ended the era of the Great Parties. Of course it had not. Under King, Laurier's then hardly known successor, the Liberal Party held office longer than under Laurier. King's record beat even that of Robert Walpole who, in England, planted the seeds of the first Great Party. Was Dafoe wrong in this judgement or only premature? For some years he seemed to be right. King formed two minority governments and Meighen, though gaining ground, never won a majority. But after 1926 King had a majority in Parliament with credible support across the nation and could claim to lead a Great Party again.

Minority government returned in Diefenbaker's last year of office and continued throughout Pearson's term. At first the young Trudeau commanded a majority, but Liberalism was later almost extinguished in the West and Conservatism in Quebec. No truly national party existed.

The 1984 election transformed both organisms. Now the Conservative Party was dominant everywhere. It had shattered the historical Liberal hold on Quebec, reduced its enemy to a parliamentary rump and may have ensured the final decline of organized Liberalism in Canada as in Britain. The cards of politics were thus reshuffled in a new deal expected by no one. The grand Liberal coalition of English-speaking and French-speaking voters that embraced other ethnic and interest groups was bankrupt, replaced by Mulroney's triumphant coalition that hoped to be grand, and long-lived, in its turn.

In its euphoria did it stop to consider the long-term prospects? If it destroyed the Liberal Party, the New Democratic Party would become the official opposition and, some day, probably the government. This has always been the left-wing strategy and the last result any true Conservative wishes to see. The wiser Conservative heads understand the strategy and do not intend to foster it, but the Liberal Party could destroy itself without help from either of its enemies.

All these possibilities belong to the future. In 1985 something else occurred. The three parties and the public, too, were turning their attention away from the debate of constitution and threatened national breakup to the bread and butter problems of the economy.

Where, then, does the party system now stand? An Englishman tried to foresee and answer the current question in the first years of this century. Viscount Bryce, the British ambassador to the United States, who had studied Canadian politics as a hobby, concluded that in Canada "party seems to exist for its own sake . . . Ideas are not needed to make parties, for these can live by heredity and, like the Guelphs and Ghibellines of mediaeval Italy, by memories of past combats; attachment to leaders of such striking gifts as were Sir John Macdonald and Sir Wilfrid Laurier created a personal loyalty which exposed a man to reproach as a deserter when he voted against his party."

Bryce could not foresee that after his time most Canadians would adhere to no party. It is an uncommon voter nowadays who feels the least pangs of disloyalty in switching his or her vote from one election to the next. The old English rhyme—that every child born alive is either a little Liberal or a little Conservative—no longer holds true in Canada. Bryce was mistaken if he supposed that Canada's parties would continue to depend only on memories and exceptional leaders.

The Conservative Party survived Macdonald and the Liberal Party survived Laurier. Some inner force besides myth and men kept them so much alive that no third party has been able to dislodge either. Even the farmers' Progressive Party, with its sweep of 1921, a rebellion within the Liberal Party, soon returned like a prodigal to the old home.

A backward glance tells us that the everlasting irony of politics always was, and still is, at work.

The Liberal Party had been the unlikely child of a British parent whose teacher was Adam Smith. That Scots genius invented, or perfected, the Economic Man before Marx discovered such an imaginary species. In the new state of Canada, Liberalism joined Smith's almost mystical worship of a market as free as a weak human nature allowed. King and his three successors, St. Laurent, Pearson and Trudeau, questioned the original faith, and their governments gave the nation a social welfare system, regardless of the market, with few equals anywhere (and with costs overwhelming today's budget).

The Conservative Party, traditionally the defender of Big Business, had not hesitated to invade the market, had used its cash and credit to subsidize the Canadian Pacific Railway, despite the Liberal Party's somewhat comical horror, and provided the enduring subsidy of tariff protection. In recent times, however, Conservatism preached the Liberal market creed, the minimum presence of the state, while rescuing many bankrupt corporations and assuring the poor that they would not be neglected whatever the cost.

Such is Canada's latest political transformation. It may intrigue scholars of history, but the public is more concerned with jobs, wages, profits, taxes and living standards. Abstract ideas are for residents of ivory towers. Canadians as a whole think primarily of life's common round. They have little time for the irony or the day-to-day tactics of the politicians. And party leaders struggle to keep up with the public's demand for increasing expenditure.

Macdonald had little schooling, but his reading was voracious and he must have known that the civilizations of the past were never without parties in primitive guise, though as yet they had no names or doctrines, only lust for rewards. The men surrounding a Pharaoh of Egypt, a Caesar of Rome, a king or Lord Protector of England, a Hitler of Germany, a Stalin of Russia and rulers of all varieties needed a party whether named or nameless, to rally their friends and suppress their enemies. But the party became a recognized institution of democratic parliaments only in modern times.

Not until Walpole organized the Whig dynasty in Britain and began to Anglicize the imported monarchs from Hanover, was a true party born. Even then it was no more than a rudimentary apparatus held together by the king's placemen and royal bribes. Walpole did not know or ask whether he had hatched a paragon or a cockatrice. But the lasting division between the Whigs and their opposition, the Tories, was emerging.

The Whigs vaguely represented the new business class of the industrial revolution. The Tories represented the rural land-owning class, the squirearchy. Neither represented what we now call democracy. Government was still for gentlemen only under both parties, and the franchise was restricted to voters with substantial property.

Inchoate and as yet unrecognized, a shift of economic power not confined to gentry produced a middle class, the bourgeoisie as Marx called it, that balance wheel of any free society. To the rising democratic wave of the future the parties adjusted themselves in the genial, compromising absent-minded fashion of the nation's character until, towards the end of the nineteenth century, the Tories under Disraeli (a Jew and hardly a gentleman) had built the modern Conservative Party and the Whigs, under Gladstone, the Liberal Party. Thus, in contemporary idiom, British politics was divided between Right and Left. The division became clearer with the rise of the Labour Party, the new organ of the Left, which replaced the Liberal Party as the alternative government.

Superficially different, though basically the same, was the party system imported from Britain into the newborn American Republic. The Founders and constitution builders, with all their political genius, had not planned that import. To them party warfare seemed almost as dangerous as King George, and they took precautions to curb it. Government would be managed by gentlemen only in the United States as in Britain. Washington himself, the first president, was instinctively an overseas English gentleman before stupid English governments made him the complete American. So, for that matter, was the ambivalent Thomas Jefferson, aristocrat of democracy and orginator of the American party system.

While the Founding Fathers had not even trusted the presidency (or elected monarchy) to a popular vote and left it to the decision of an Electoral College of propertied men, a durable party system emerged with Jefferson's election as the third president in 1800. Already, when he was a member of Washington's cabinet, the rudiments of a Republican Party, the future Democratic Party, had gathered around him and his liberal views. Around his rival, Alexander Hamilton, had gathered the conservative Federalists, or future Republican Party of Lincoln's time. Alternating in office and changing their names, these parties established themselves so firmly that every attempt in modern times to start a third party, even by such a mighty Republican rebel as Theodore Roosevelt and his Bull Moose Party, has failed.

Since their earliest days the groping leaders of the British colonies in a Canada restricted to the Laurentian Valley and the Maritimes had watched events on both sides of the Atlantic. They admired British politics and imported from it what seemed valuable to them on the outer rim of empire. They beheld American politics with so much alarm that they used the danger of a newly armed United States to unite four of the colonies and found a dubious structure known as Confederation. But it contained American as well as British imports modified to suit Canada's peculiar needs.

Before this time the embryo of a Conservative Party had appeared in the Family Compact of Upper Canada and the Chateau Clique of Lower Canada. A Liberal embryo can be traced to the struggle for responsible government in the first four decades of the nineteenth century. Liberal ideas, or vague yearnings, could be dimly detected in the 1837 Rebellion when William Lyon Mackenzie was a Liberal of sorts though he called himself only a reformer.

Liberalism lacked a coherent party until the organized reformers of Ontario appeared, calling themselves Clear Grits because their mix contained no adulterating mud. In George Brown they discovered a natural leader of high intelligence, unquestioned honesty but flawed by his stubborn prejudice against Catholics and French Canadians. His reward was murder by a disgruntled employee of his fearless newspaper, the *Globe* of Toronto.

In Macdonald, the young, roistering, mourning widower from Kingston, the Conservatives discovered a superior politician. He became the chief architect of Confederation with Brown's patriotic, essential and temporary help. As the first Canadian prime minister he was briefly exiled by the Pacific Scandal, but Macdonald understood the art of the possible. His immediate rival, Edward Blake, the sea-green incorruptible and erratic prophet of Liberalism, did not. Disgusted with an ungrateful Canada, he fled to England where he favoured the British Parliament with his boring hairsplitting argument.

When Macdonald returned from exile and defeated the luckless government of Alexander Mackenzie, the new establishment calling itself Liberal Conservative included friends and enemies alike in a coalition that lasted to the end of its maker's life. But as Macdonald complained, the purchasable partners were never sufficiently loyal to the party. The coalition remained at the mercy of "loose fish" who dishonestly refused to stay bought.

In the meantime the Liberal Party had found its greatest leader, an obscure French Canadian unknown outside Quebec until Macdonald committed his worst error by hanging the half-mad Louis Riel—a political not a judicial execution. Hearing the news from Regina, Wilfrid Laurier addressed a clamorous multitude of protest in Montreal and declared that, had he lived as a French Canadian Metis beside the Saskatchewan River, he would have joined Riel and shouldered his own musket against the bloodthirsty government. A single speech made Laurier the first real alternative to Macdonald. The young Quebec politician, so tall, so handsome and ethereal in looks, so eloquent in speech, so subtle in mind, was certain to succeed, though at the beginning he despaired after losing a series of elections.

Macdonald's Conservative Party was invulnerable but only until its leader's death in 1891. Without him the aging establishment disintegrated. Laurier and the Liberal Party reached office in 1896 and stayed there for fifteen years to be defeated in turn by the Reciprocity gambit of 1911.

The Regina gallows had released political currents more enduring than Laurier's regime. Thenceforth the Conservative Party, elsewhere victorious, was largely excluded from Quebec, its natural fortress, that never forgave the hanging of Riel. The familiar world of politics was stood upside-down as happened again in 1984.

With his unprecedented sweep of 1958, Diefenbaker deeply penetrated Quebec, but this was an aberration quickly regretted by the
voters who, in Trudeau's last triumph, elected a solitary Conservative.
Macdonald's party turned, not without grave doubt and some ugly
convention deals, to Mulroney, a Quebec native of Irish descent.
Perhaps he might be the catalyst needed to revive the coalition established by the original master. The new leader fulfilled all these hopes
and seemed to have destroyed Laurier's lifework.

When the greatest Liberal died in 1919, what had he bequeathed to
his successors, including Turner? A party controlling Quebec but almost annihilated elsewhere by the conscription crisis of 1917. Only a
genius of politics as remarkable as Laurier could put the broken
Humpty Dumpty together again. That genius appeared in King, part of
whose unlikely tale has been told here already. To understand our
present situation, we should remember that King's whole career was
built on his party. Without it he could not have risen to power, much
less held it into his old age.

An event more important to Canada than King's success in politics
occurred some three decades after his departure. Quebec's rejection of
separatism in the 1980 referendum was one of the most important
political events in Canadian history since it preserved the union of
1867 from piecemeal destruction.

For the nation's success in crossing that perilous watershed much
credit must go to both parties; to Trudeau, his unanswerable logic and
stirring oratory; to Jean Chrétien, who organized the antiseparatist
campaign; to Claude Ryan, the Quebec Liberal leader, who stifled his
dislike of Trudeau and co-operated in the work of salvation; to Clark,
the federal Conservative leader, who knew and admired Quebec. But
the final credit must go, of course, to the Quebec people. They, as its
first pioneers, understood that they belonged to Canada. They also
understood party politics.

While all this Canadian experience and the imports from abroad
seemed to have built two durable Great Parties, both of them ceased,
by the 1980s, to be truly national when Liberalism dominated Quebec
and Conservatism the West. A national party must have a credible
presence across the nation, above all in the political fulcrum of Ontario where support kept shifting from one party to the other. The last
election changed that unstable balance only to create a worse imbal-
ance. To understand it, another backward glance is required, for

Canada's democratic learning process was not quick or easy. Despite the changing times, the old partisan memories and loyalties dwindled slowly.

Even today a minority clings to them, like my Ontario friend, otherwise intelligent, who explains that he is a Conservative because his father was a Conservative and trained his son in the true faith. Now he needs nothing more than a label to guide his vote.

My western friend and philosopher of the Pacific rain forest, known only as Archie, appeared to be equally reasonable in explaining why he was a bachelor. His father, grandfather and ancestors back to the mists of antiquity, he said, were all bachelors. Their loyal descendant could not break a fine old family tradition.

At any rate, a similiar tradition is unquestioned within the party bosom, that secure hierarchy of laws, rewards and punishments. With a strong leader the hierarchy becomes an oligarchy whether it wins or loses elections. Trudeau was the latest real oligarch in succession to Macdonald, Laurier and King. All four of them relished and throve on the queen-making royal jelly of J. W. Dafoe's famous metaphor and acquired a craving for it (as Mulroney may find in his time). Only leaders of short-term office or naturally modest men like Borden, St. Laurent and Pearson were immune to the addiction. Others needed ever-increasing gobbets of jelly, their appetites insatiable.

They also needed flexibility and elbowroom. While describing every swerve of direction as a logical installment of their unalterable lifelong goal, they kept changing their minds, which should not surprise us. Who doesn't? Only fools or mystics.

The political process in a free society is for the most part a change of mind. If it were not, the society must soon lose its freedom and end in the prison of unchangeable minds. Any politician who is right half the time is like a baseball star who bats .500 in the big leagues. Even Babe Ruth could not reach that figure. Nor can the amateur batters in the minor leagues of private life.

We should not be surprised, either, if politicians seldom admit their mistakes when few of us do. What business manager has recently emerged from his board room to announce that he is responsible for his corporation's collapse? What householder has informed the neighbourhood that he has squandered his savings and reduced his wife and children to dire poverty? What honest man will say he never bends the truth a little, as politicians bend it?

The politician cannot expect much sympathy when he blunders or fibs. The voters demand more of the politician than of themselves. In the current national mood (not least in the media) cynicism and disparagement of politics become a habit, a collective jeer, almost a way of life. The modern crop of politicians may disappoint a citizen who knew the departed titans, but they did not have to grapple with the problems now baffling every government in the world.

The worst of all mistakes is to suppose that any of us can escape the mistakes of our public servants. Yet some citizens seem to rejoice when things go wrong at the top, as a mountaineer clinging to a rope from above might rejoice if it broke. We all cling to the rope of government. This mood, with the troubles now besetting us, will pass. Our children will forget them, having to face others of their own. But a party leader deals with things as they are today, not as he hopes they may be tomorrow. And the strongest leader is vulnerable to his party's laws or even its punishments.

First a prime minister must command the obedience of his cabinet where he will have few, if any, real friends. He has only colleagues who commonly dislike him, fight an endless civil war and maintain in public the fiction of solidarity vital to the system.

Second, the prime minister must command the loyalty of his elected supporters. The caucus is a suborganism inside the party organism. Sworn to secrecy, the inner conclave, like every vessel in Ottawa, always leaks. A prime minister who understands the system expects nothing else. He knows that the caucus, however leaky, is a tool required in his management of power. Through it the conflicts of separate ideas and interests can usually be reconciled, a makeshift compromise arranged and promulgated as the party's sacred canon.

The cabinet is generally easier to manage. Once well established, the queen bee seldom loses control of his ministers who seldom resign on issues of principle, though they often resign for reasons of personal ambition or because they cannot abide the regnant leader.

The resignation of C. G. Power, for reasons of principle alone, was an unusual event, especially because he had been a loyal party politician, a rough campaigner but a man of shining honour. When King finally enforced overseas conscription in 1944, Power, a terribly wounded veteran of the first war, resigned his Air Force portfolio of the second and his admirable career. With no French blood in his Irish heredity, he had promised Quebec that he would never vote for overseas conscription to retain office. The oath was kept.

King vainly implored him to stay. "Chubby," he said in tears, "I need you." He did, too, but he had underestimated Chubby's honour as he had underestimated the honour of J. L. Ralston whose throat he had cut in the middle of a cabinet meeting. King and Ralston (a larger human being) were never reconciled. After the war King, this time not in tears but in the Chateau Frontenac and his flannel underwear, embraced Power and then saved him from honourable poverty by appointment to the Senate.

Besides cabinet and caucus, the leader of a national party must deal with its provincial branches across the country. These grassroots are not easily nourished since the local voters often support one party in their legislature and another in Parliament, thus keeping a foot in each.

So long as the national party finds governments of its own stripe controlling many of the provinces, it need not worry much about inevitable disagreements on specific issues. But when all provinces are controlled by the enemy, the grassroots wither. So they did at the end of the Trudeau regime. John Turner is now trying to restore Liberal strength wherever possible. The Conservative Party long dominated the legislatures of at least half the provinces, sedulously cultivating their friendship. In 1985, however, Conservatism lost control of Ontario after more than four decades of power.

Certainly there are grave faults in the party system. It usually compels the backbenchers of Parliament to vote for their party even if they privately oppose some aspect of its policy. Or, if they vote against it—a very rare step—they must accept the resentment of their friends and their leader whose displeasure may fatally punish the deserter. Not many politicians take that risk.

Another fault is Parliament's loss of its historical control over public spending—unless it is prepared to defeat a government's budget as it defeated the Clark government and John Crosbie's sensible budget in 1979. Modern budgets, totalling more than $100 billion, are so vast and intricate that Parliament cannot examine or comprehend the details. Most cabinet ministers do not understand them beyond the features relevant to their own departments. Yet these budgets, framed by a group of anonymous advisers, have eviscerated the treasury, damaging public and private business alike.

So far, all the talk of diluting the power of the front benches to increase that of the back has produced little change. Power keeps flowing to the executive as the nation's problems become more and more intractable and less understood by the public. But a current depth study of parliamentary reform may bring marginal changes before long. For example, governments could safely allow amendments to some of their legislation without making them a test of confidence. Other procedural reforms could be effected without undermining the party system.

Despite its faults, the system provides a balancing mechanism lacked by other systems. In the official opposition it sustains an alternative government ready to take office without delay or violence. Tradition stronger than written law ensures a smooth change of government in obedience to Parliament or the voters, except at a time of extraordinary crisis like the King-Byng affair of 1926.

To make certain that the mechanism is strong and constantly available, the public treasury pays the opposition leader a high salary. His party's work of research is also financed by the state. Awaiting power, the opposition can often force the government to rethink its policy, correct its mistakes and alter its course while pretending to follow a straight line. In 1985 the Mulroney government retreated, under fire, from some important aspects of its first budget.

With all the system's flaws it works because it does not live on a formulation of abstract principles in some never-never land. The party is an empirical amalgam of widely varying persons and interests concerned only with what we call the real world. So it has always been in Canada from Macdonald's Liberal-Conservative coalition to the present day when his successors describe themselves as Progressive Conservatives. So it must be if any government is to last long. This necessity should be remembered now when new political combinations are forming and new personalities replace old.

Canada has no lack of precedents for such a natural evolution. Looking back again, we can discern some reliable guide posts to the future—the coalition of Robert Baldwin and Louis Hippolyte Lafontaine that began the fight for responsible government; the coalition of Macdonald and George Etienne Cartier that stretched a young nation from the Atlantic to the Pacific; the coalition of Laurier and William Stevens Fielding that governed successfully for fifteen years and broke on the issue of Reciprocity; the coalition of King and Ernest Lapointe that took Canada into a world war and laid the foundation of a welfare state; the coalition of St. Laurent and C. D. Howe that gave us sound postwar government and many important reforms until it succumbed to old age, the pipeline debacle and the Suez crisis.

Diefenbaker saw no need of a strong Quebec lieutenant to build a new coalition and share his power. That flaw in his government was bound to wreck it after a short life. Pearson repeatedly sought a French Canadian partner, chose several but none succeeded. While Trudeau lost Turner and did not seriously try to find an English-speaking replacement, he held office for the next nine years with one brief interruption. The price of his success was high: he broke the national party which he had long neglected.

In its original habitat, Latin logic seems to fit ill with parliamentary government but it fits pretty well in Canada. No Canadians better than those of Quebec have thrived on the system, despite former logicians like René Lévesque who became an outright pragmatist. Parties that rejected pragmatism in favour of rigid principle never won a federal election. The Co-operative Commonwealth Federation and its successor, the New Democratic Party, are classic exhibits of history's unchanged law. After their promising start they would not compromise policies already out of date. Instead, they allowed themselves to become, or appear to become, the agents of a single theory, socialism. They failed to recognize, as a great leader like M. J. Coldwell did not, that politics is only human nature roughly organized and by instinct hostile to theory.

Edward Broadbent gradually learned where office can be won. He moved to the centre and is no longer a recognizable Socialist but a pragmatic reformer, a practical politician who advocates social democracy without clearly defining it. His party has been valuable in politics. Its disappearance would be a grave loss to the nation which needs a leftist critic rebuking the laches and sins of the major parties.

All parties also have their family troubles, especially those accruing from too long a spell in office or opposition. Trudeau's government was the victim of geriatric decay. The Conservative Party needed more than two decades to recover from Diefenbaker's *Götterdämmerung* of 1963, unload him, lose the election of 1972 by a hair's breadth under Robert Stanfield, win transient office under Clark and find Mulroney at last.

Few nations, mostly English-speaking or Scandinavian, have grasped the workable method of coalition and its instrument, the Great Party. France and Italy, for instance, built countless coalitions

and were passionately free by nature but they could not build Great
Parties where conflict is privately defused, stable government established. They usually bred small quarrelsome parties that bred governments of short life, ceaseless turmoil and, in Italy, the tragicomedy of
Mussolini.

As Leon Blum, the French statesman who once headed a common-
front government, put his nation's dilemma: "If parliamentarianism
has succeeded in England and failed in France, it is essentially because
there existed an old and strong organization of parties the like of
which we in France—with rare exceptions which prove the rule—
have never been able to create for a century and a half."

Canada's political experience was more fortunate, but a habit of
regicide and suicide combined with the worst of luck to bar the Conservative Party from office for most of the present century. This dismal
record goes all the way back to the hopeless Prime Minister Mackenzie
Bowell and his cabinet rebellion or "nest of traitors" in 1896. Then
followed the awesome catalogue of leaders unhorsed by their followers
or worn out by electoral defeat—Charles Tupper, Arthur Meighen,
R. B. Bennett, Robert Manion, John Bracken, George Drew, Diefenbaker, Stanfield and Clark, nine men in less than a century. They
were the victims of their own mistakes, bad luck, hard times and the
broken rhythm of politics.

A spell too long out of office induced desperation, irresponsible
promises to the voters and a dearth of new talent when bright
youngsters saw the Conservative Party as a hearse and preferred a
Liberal bandwagon until the fortunes of both were suddenly reversed.

During the same period the Liberal Party, enjoying the undeserved
luck of its enemy's disarray, produced five successful leaders and slew
none of them. In its own mind it became the natural governing party
until age, hubris and internal rot sapped its earlier strength and made
it a mockery of Liberalism. An old government, like an old man, is
rheumatic, short-sighted, lazy and arrogant. It reels and finally col-
lapses *sans* discipline, *sans* policy, *sans* everything.

After its excessive term of power, the Liberal Party needed a spell in
the cleansing air of opposition to repair its health, repent its sins,
rethink its future, recruit young talent and devise policy for changed
times, for only in opposition are ideas likely to sprout, nourished,
unlike vegetable growth, by the cold of winter. Lord Acton's law of
power's corruption holds eternal in all seasons and places and often in

Canadian prime ministers. Although money could not corrupt any of them, power corrupted the ethics and the methods of several. Acton, oddly enough, was Trudeau's favourite philosopher.

Only a man or woman of peculiar wisdom realizes that more serenity can be found in opposition than in office where responsibility is a heavy burden. Without the responsibility of government, an opposition member of Parliament is a comparatively free spirit. But no politician relishes the so-called wilderness. Power is always the prize and sacred grail.

Once in office the party magnates begin to quarrel among themselves, and nothing causes more quarrels than the patronage which governments alone dispense. And probably nothing is so widely misunderstood and resented. If patronage did not exist it would have to be invented, but it has existed in all civilized and barbarous communities. To suppose that men of power will not help their friends and punish their enemies is to suppose that the old Adam of human nature has died. It is to suppose that a party, indispensable mechanism of democratic government, can live without nourishment and win power without campaign funds. This notion is absurd in an age when the campaigns of television are costly beyond the credence of Macdonald who was temporarily dislodged by the mean little Pacific Scandal and a sum of money not worth talking about nowadays.

Besides television, newspaper advertising, pamphlets, the candidate's travel, the telephone bills, the polling services, the rent of offices and meeting halls must be financed. The poorest workers at the grassroots who keep the party alive between elections must be paid something for their campaign work, and certainly earn it. They lick stamps, ring doorbells, distribute handbills, run errands, man telephones, applaud the candidate's speeches or heckle his opponent.

The candidate is seldom chosen by some broadly based, democratic assembly, but has merely to win a majority in a small, obscure meeting of the faithful, most voters hardly aware that it is taking place. Then the typical candidate is front-page news for a day or two, a local celebrity hitherto little known or unknown to the nation.

Most of the party's workers are not told much about its high policy and a government's legal method of bribing the electorate with public works, extra services, reduced taxes or other goodies at the cost of the taxpayers who accept them gladly before the bills come in. Then their protest is too late. Nor can most workers expect the glittering prizes of

Senate or royal commission appointments, secure civil service jobs and
the perquisites enjoyed by the magnates who usually forget most of
their foul-weather friends after the election, the nameless folk who are
the garrison troops and cannon fodder of political war.

Clifford Sifton, hardest-boiled politician of his era, said that no
problem of government gave him so much trouble as the award of
patronage. He awarded it without scruple to enrich his friends but
towards the end actually suggested that the national treasury contribute to party funds. The time for this now commonplace idea did not
come until long after his departure. Before Sifton's time Macdonald
was continually distracted from important affairs by the appointment
of a minor clerk, a customs inspector, a ferryman, a collector of canal
tolls, a janitor or cleaning woman—the grimy, unavoidable chores of a
prime minister's life then and now when the rewards are far more
lavish.

Of course patronage can be an evil if it is misused—as it often is,
especially by dying governments—an evil to be fought like others but
not to be eliminated so long as the old Adam lives. In earlier times
cheap patronage was a worse canker in the body politic than it is
today. Steadily over the years it has been reduced in a civil service
among the best in the Western world. The civil servant is appointed
after competitive examination and promoted as a rule on merit
(though the backroom friendship of a party boss is always helpful). In
the dropsical anatomy of modern government there remain only about
thirty-five hundred patronage jobs for distribution to the faithful. And
in the competition for them you might think that a kingdom was the
reward.

The unseemly struggle for jobs is not confined to the humble aspir-
ants on the party fringe. It is still more competitive and ferocious in
the higher regions of politics. The competitors, who often could earn
larger salaries in private business, seek appointment to royal commissions, agencies of the Crown, foreign embassies and even to the Senate, that nirvana and last resort of noble minds. There is no account-
ing for such curious ambitions ceaselessly nagging all governments.
Trudeau's appointments, some good, many of them bad, earned him
more public anger than all his policies combined.

Having promised more jobs than he can deliver, any new prime
minister finds that their distribution is a bane instead of a benediction,

since not only individuals but whole regions and voting groups must be placated and the pork barrel is limited. So Mulroney found, and to deodorize a mass of unsavoury appointments he gave a few others to his political enemies. Like all prime ministers he also found that the barrel was too small for his followers' appetite.

Patronage can be a useful tool but a tool only. For enduring success a party needs a spine of philosophical doctrine or at least its outward appearance. This is asking a lot from politicians who, in their trade, are men and women of action rather than cerebration. The thinking minority knows that personalities, however charismatic, soon disappear. The party lives on and history proves that after the hysteria of elections the decisive vote had usually turned not on men or women but on the winning party's record and reputation, its philosophy dimmed by the rough-and-tumble of the game.

The young Trudeau was called a philosopher-king. Such an image in the newspapers must have amused him and did not last long when he was leading a one-man government and swinging so often from one image or theory to another.

No party lacks a few expositors of its philosophy. Among the best in the Conservative ranks is John Fraser who represents Vancouver South in the Mulroney government. As he explained in a notable but little noted speech, historical conservatism took full account of human beings and neither excused their evil side nor exaggerated their virtue. The party stood for political realism, not reaction, and in some ways was liberalism brought up to date. After all, he said, Conservative governments established the government-owned Canadian National Railways, founded the central Bank of Canada and, in Diefenbaker's time, enacted the first Bill of Rights. Conservatism, Fraser argued, was politics seen in the round without illusion but not without hope.

By coincidence, soon after the Fraser speech, liberalism found an equally articulate defender in Senator Jack Austin who also comes from Vancouver (the two men thus denying British Columbia's false image as a thoughtless, anti-intellectual region). Senator Austin, a highly practical politician most of the time, held that liberalism was human nature's agent and true hope for the future. Since it did not regard government as a remedy for all society's diseases, it rejected socialism. On the other hand, it recognized more clearly than did conservatism that private enterprise was not a total remedy, either.

It pursued the middle way, the only workable way, placing more confidence than did conservatism in human possibilities, the Eternal Verities.

The exchange between Fraser and Austin was too lofty for an occasional observer of politics on its margin. I watched the activists at work and reached my own murky conclusions. Among its philosophers, liberalism, I found, was often imprisoned by rigid theories inherited from a time long past. Theorists with closed minds were thereby able to avoid creative thought, a fate worse than death, or even life. They sought refuge in a cavern of prejudice and platitude. Some indeed were suckled on creeds outworn as if a new age could still live on such liberal achievements as the repeal of the Corn Laws, free trade, manhood suffrage, civil rights and mankind's inevitable progress—all fine old ideals well worth preserving but not the stuff of contemporary politics.

On the other side I found many honest and elected Conservatives with equally closed minds who had no remote idea of what conservatism meant. Enough for them that it meant the chance of power and power's satisfactions. They also had their cavern of refuge in a folk memory of the good old days, of lost gentility and family compacts. Enough for them a flickering torch of nostalgia and the nostalgia ached. Only electoral success relieved that pain.

The public does not experience the pain or the relief and is skeptical of partisanship in all forms. It does not share and may not remember the black-and-white political dogma of Dr. Sam Johnson who indicted some harmless acquaintance as "a bottomless Whig." In today's Canada there are not many bottomless Grits, Tories or Socialists, only bewildered politicians and voters. The ranks of true believers in politics or anything else have been sadly depleted.

Governments come and go with trumpet peals of victory or groans of defeat but the change is mostly cosmetic, the fundamentals unchanged, except in rare times of crisis. Even then the change is usually far less important than its makers suppose. Every historian will make his own list of fundamental events according to his individual philosophy or prejudice. But no layman can be immune to the consequences of party politics.

George Orwell, a disillusioned philosopher, once warned: "All issues are political issues and politics itself is a mass of lies, evasions, folly, hatred and schizophrenia." Hence all political language was used "to make lies sound truthful and murder respectable and to give an apparent solidity to pure wind." A case-hardened political reporter, less hagridden by conscience than Orwell, would put the thing much less bitterly if less accurately. In party politics, he would argue, the myth, not the lie, is dominant and almost always more compelling than the fact.

A newborn Canadian state had to survive largely on myths if it were to survive at all. But then, every human is a bundle and churning vortex of myths never clearly expressed or admitted. How powerful is the myth of our happy days beyond recall, our childhood memories how easily aroused by a sight, a sound, a springtime perfume when politics has been forgotten! And how tough an integument we need to shelter us from the reality of the mad world!

Have mercy, therefore, on the politician who lives and must live most of the time on party myths, not facts, creeds or issues.

Canadians are not very good myth makers. In that craft the British and the Americans have been much more successful. They built countless myths and heroes. We chose few. Champlain, Frontenac, Radisson, La Salle and Montcalm are the only mythical survivors of New France still in the Anglo-Saxon memory, while the French Canadians nourish many other local myths. Among most English-speaking citizens there remain from early times only Wolfe, Brock, Tecumseh and the transcontinental explorer, Mackenzie; from later times Macdonald, Laurier and Riel; from recent times King, an improbable candidate now a rich ore vein for historians, the brilliant but failed Meighen whom Conservative mythology tries in vain to represent as a greater man than his rival, and Diefenbaker, also a failure after he had governed for six years on catchwords with meagre substance.

Already Trudeau has joined the round table of mythdom, despite his current unpopularity. A finer man, St. Laurent, has not yet joined and perhaps never will because he never sought the bubble of reputation, nor felt the spur of fame.

If the Americans, best of mythologists, had produced some of our forgotten heroes, they would have written books and erected monuments to celebrate such figures and make them immortal. Slight and evil characters like Jesse James, Judge Lynch and Billy the Kid provided the durable stuff of myth along with the evil. They sprang from the supermyth of the Wild West, of cowboys and Indians, that lives today in the nation's politics, even in its president.

All parties have their myths, but the party system itself is not a myth. It is a living fact, the workplace and operating machinery of free government where the latest master mechanic will be tested. And before Mulroney is fairly judged we must study the men who preceded him with their individual methods, their achievements and their failures.

15

THE
LONESOME
PINNACLE

In theory the leader of a Canadian government is *primus inter pares*, first among equals. In practical politics he is something else entirely. No constitution defines his real powers. They are what he makes them, provided that he does not break the law, and they vary as the occupants of the supreme office follow one another with personal strength or weakness. In their time all these men have illuminated or darkened, advanced or obstructed, the political process and the society revolving around it.

The prime minister's public life is spent on a pinnacle which, by its nature, must be stark, cold and lonesome, however carefree he may look on the television screen. Unique power dwells beside him and so does heartbreak.

None yet glimpsed the possible sweep, the majesty and the squalid underside of the office when most of the British North America Act was written, in pen and ink, by Macdonald, the indispensable man alone fit to implement it. All the people saw on the first day of July 1867 were the rockets, bonfires and parades. All they heard were the music of bands and the throb of cannons, muffling the solemn proclamation of Queen Victoria who would never see or remotely understand her new Dominion.

Few of the four million Canadians spread from the Great Lakes to the Atlantic read Section 11 of the Act, under the title "Executive Power," sixty-seven words containing unlikely explosives: "There shall be a Council to aid and advise in the Government of Canada, to be styled the Queen's Privy Council for Canada; and the Persons who are to be Members of that Council shall be from Time to Time chosen and summoned by the Governor General and sworn in as Privy Councillors, and members thereof may be from Time to Time removed by the Governor General."

What did those words mean? Even their author did not know. Macdonald, knighted that very day, had no time now for constitutional thought. He was smoothing over a nasty little quarrel that almost broke his cabinet before it could start work. He was also mollifying a pompous Governor General, Lord Monck, who had turned up for the birthday celebration in a business suit as if Canada were not worth a Windsor uniform of gold braid and feathers, as expected.

But such as it was, the supreme office, in fact, not theory and written words, could be filled by no man except the immigrant boy from Scotland, the hard drinker and tortured genius from Kingston. Macdonald, with his homely face, mane of black curls, empurpled whiskey nose, bittersweet grin, tall, gangling figure and flashy clothes ("a rum 'un to look at, a rare 'un to go") had begun already to make his office unique.

The beginning was so smooth and subtle that all his successors down to our time imitated the original model, improving or degrading it. They could do no other. Each in his own fashion was a kind of tribal chieftain. Whatever the written words may intend, that most ancient title of command still lives in Canada.

It took many years and many men to explore and expand the office unspecified in the Constitution. What, after all, was the Queen's Privy Council? Who would be its members? Among its members who, if anyone, would be *primus inter pares?*

The last question was settled with Macdonald's arrival on the first day of a Confederation so frail and impoverished, so widely scattered and quarrelsome, that few practical politicians in Britain, or their Queen, could be sure of its survival which, at best, seemed dubious. All the other questions were not to be answered for a long time and were still not permanently answered as Mulroney devised his own experimental answers.

But one thing at least was clear from the beginning—the chief adviser of the Queen had a power possessed by no one else. He could advise her, at any moment, to dissolve Parliament and call an election. Experience was to prove in her successors' time that the monarch could not reject such advice. Accordingly, the prime minister held that whip of dissolution over his cabinet, his party, his caucus and the entire course of political events. In the pinch he could always flourish the whip and the mere rumour of it seldom failed to bring his followers into line.

Behind him, in loyalty or betrayal, stood his cabinet, but what was the cabinet? Who, among the Privy Councillors, would be members of it? How would the chosen men execute their undefined duties? And how many of them, more equal than the others, would form the unacknowledged inner cabinet where the big decisions would be made?

Of these questions Macdonald was suddenly and bitterly aware on the birthday of Confederation. He had almost failed to choose a cabinet, that committee of Parliament responsible to it, and he thought in despair of resigning. But resignation was impossible, though geography and religion, not Constitution, threatened to disrupt all his plans. Obeying the unwritten law of politics, he must fill round holes with square pegs. He must choose three ministers from Protestant Ontario, two faithful Conservatives, one Reformer (to give some faint reality to his new Liberal Conservative Party). Catholic Quebec demanded and received the same number, led by George Etienne Cartier. New Brunswick got one and so did Nova Scotia.

The arithmetic would not add up. A delegate from the vital Irish Catholic vote was missing. At the last moment Charles Tupper generously withdrew his undoubted claim. An unknown man of the required origin and faith represented Nova Scotia.

Certainly this was not the cabinet Macdonald wanted. As he said, half in earnest, he would have preferred "highly respectable parties whom I could send to the penitentiary if I liked." But luckily George Brown was absent, in the arms of a young Scottish bride, the world of politics well lost. And Macdonald could truthfully boast on a public platform that, anyhow, the electorate would rather have *him* drunk than his only serious rival sober.

The unwritten law of geography, the appointment of men who might not be fit for office but controlled their own regions, is as imperative today as it was in 1867, a law beyond repeal. So is the law of the cabinet's age: old prime ministers want old friends around them, colleagues as comfortable as old clothes, not talented youngsters who make trouble. That decline was to mark especially Laurier's cabinets in his latter years and those of most successors.

There were many other enduring laws yet to be interpreted when the first national government was formed. Among them is the Law of Method, as it may be called. Only two prime ministerial methods are available, the method of the logical mind and the method of the illogical gut, and both have been used by different men with different results.

Our three supposedly greatest prime ministers, Macdonald, Laurier and King, always used the gut method. They trusted their hunches more than the advice of experts and usually they were right. Lesser men like Mackenzie, Meighen and Bennett, even a more successful man like Trudeau, depended too much on their minds and the apparent logic of the immediate situation. Very often they were wrong.

An artist of true genius, as Carlyle wrote, resembles a normal, healthy man unaware of his bodily organs. So, too, is the artist unaware of his genius. He paints a picture, carves a sculpture, designs a cathedral, writes a book or symphony but cannot explain how he did it. Only the inferior craftsman can explain his inferior work. The true artist of politics can never explain his superior work. King, a true artist of politics whatever else he may have been, understood that mystery. "Either I see a thing at once or I don't see it at all," he said. Macdonald and Laurier did the same. The arguments marshalled to justify a secret daemon were dragged in by the heels for documentation of a *fait accompli.*

A second law, stemming from the first, may be called the Law of Invisible Currents. The great prime minister must be able to see through the superficial scum and recognize, deep down, the flow of events that escape the eyes of lesser men.

Where are events actually flowing? Not, as a rule, where the people or the minor politicians suppose. Not where the public opinion polls generally indicate. The ability to disregard the deceptive scum and recognize the real currents has marked great leaders in all times, places and governing systems. Without it an inferior leader may survive by honest work or trickery for a little while but not for long because he does not really lead.

In a governing system like Canada's, the great leader must also sense the changing daily mood of Parliament. On some good days he can easily get what he wants. On some bad days he can get nothing and, if he is wise, will postpone decision until the next good day appears.

Macdonald and Laurier were masters of mood. In this curious art King was their equal. He would slide into the House with a bland, disarming, false smile for the opposition like a man treading gingerly on eggs. Then, testing the mood, he would direct business to suit it, pushing forward or retreating as occasion demanded. Emanation, not speech, was his guide. He played on the House as on a violin.

Thence comes a third law that may be called the Law of Strategic Retreat. No one better than Wellington, greatest British soldier of his time, though an inferior politician, understood that law. He said the paramount virtue of a military commander was his ability to retreat without losing his army. King, no soldier, applied the same law to politics. Over and over again he retreated (as did Macdonald and Laurier) under a smoke screen of obfuscation, but he saved his army for future advance when events permitted. Above all, a commander must have infinite patience or he is likely to lose everything.

A fourth law, which may be called the Law of Inevitable Contradiction, holds that any leader achieving office will usually do the opposite of his election promises and his own sincere intentions because changed events leave him no alternative. History in all free nations is replete with such reversals.

Woodrow Wilson won the 1916 election on the promise to keep his nation out of a foreign war and promptly took it in. Roosevelt promised to balance the budget and unbalanced it. Lyndon Johnson promised a great society of peace and launched the disastrous Vietnam War. Richard Nixon promised law and order and doomed his illustrious career at Watergate. Ronald Reagan repeated the familiar promise of a balanced budget and accumulated a record deficit.

In Canada Macdonald promised justice for everyone and hanged Riel. He said of the French Canadians, "Treat them as a nation and they will act as a free people generally do. Call them a faction and they become factious." Then, in a momentary, fatal lapse, he treated them almost as fellow rebels of the Saskatchewan traitor. Laurier predicted that the twentieth century would belong to Canada and lived just long enough to see the folly of his hope. He visited London, was overwhelmed by duchesses, and said that in his proudest day he might see a

Canadian elected to a parliament of the empire. Then he came home to fight for his nation's independence.

King promised to be governed by the ruthless, all-wise competitive market and produced the welfare state of government subsidy. Trudeau promised to work for a Just Society and it remains unjust like individual life; he promised to wrestle inflation to the ground and wrestled it to an unprecedented peak. The Law of Inevitable Contradiction still prevails and is unlikely ever to be reversed.

So, too, a fifth law which may be called the Law of Durable Democracy. It holds that the people can seldom understand a complex process like central banking, budgetary finance or economic projections, for example, but they will always understand the man in supreme office if he stays there long enough to shed his electoral disguise. Of him, indeed, the people's judgement, it may almost be said, is the judgement of God, *vox populi vox Dei*, infallible.

Among the ten prime ministers known to me personally—more than half the entire list at this writing—Diefenbaker is perhaps the classic illustration of this fifth law. When he was a backbencher of Parliament I spent a day with him on a westbound train and brashly asserted that the public might be fooled all the time about the details of government business but rarely about the man at the head of it. He seemed to be surprised and kept coming back to our conversation for years afterward. Yet no prime minister more than he was damaged by the people's instinct, though it had been postponed for six years.

Pearson often kidded me about my faith in that instinct, though he, too, was judged by it, and quite accurately (barring public knowledge of his inner toughness) before his voluntary retirement in 1968. And so was Trudeau in his time, when he understood everything except the people.

Even if a prime minister obeys the known laws, he cannot succeed without luck—the essential quality of Napoleon's marshals—in the breaks of the game. Apparently Macdonald did not have it in the Pacific Scandal when his Liberal enemies stole those damning telegrams from Kingston and wrecked his second government. But in his last election he was blessed with the luck of the Conservative theft of a more damning Liberal document. Meanwhile he had enjoyed the luck of the depression years that wrecked Mackenzie who had no luck at all, public or personal.

Laurier, at first unlucky, rode to office on a world boom and took full credit for it until his serendipity ended in the losing gamble of Reciprocity. Borden's fortunes also started badly but the tariff deal of 1911 reversed them. Meighen's career was as ill starred as Mackenzie's, while King had far more luck than any politician in our history. St. Laurent thus inherited the nation's ablest government, a smoothly working party machine and prosperous times. But his luck ran out in the bungled pipeline argument, the Suez crisis and finally in sickness and private sorrows, trouble coming in battalions.

Diefenbaker's luck was spotty. At the beginning it seemed limitless, but the house of cards built in 1958 collapsed within five years. He never emerged from the ruins. There followed the nationwide spasm known as Trudeaumania, but it had passed within four years. From then on its beneficiary lived on a roller coaster of rising or falling hopes.

Fickle fortune can best be tolerated if a man has that saving grace, a sense of humour. Few men have it. You can accuse a man of almost any fault and he will forgive you. Tell him that he has no sense of humour and he will never forget that worst of all insults.

No prime minister had so much puckish, winking, grinning humour as Macdonald, though it was a disguise for lifelong, personal anguish. King's disguise as a dull, humourless, competent workhorse concealed no heartbreak but served him so well that only once did he discard it momentarily in Parliament when Bennett, also a bachelor, though a celebrated beau, rose to ask what the prime minister would do if he confronted a parade of naked Doukhobor women. Quick as a flash King replied: "I'd send for the leader of the opposition." That flash was never repeated in public. In private, the disguise removed, King would laugh at his enemies and colleagues alike but not at King, God's servant. His humour was one-sided.

So was Diefenbaker's. As a political beginner and gifted mimic he could people his office with all the leading figures of Parliament until you saw them in the flesh and heard their voices. But on the platform his jokes were sodden with bitter ironies. His backbench modesty had disappeared by this time. His ego had exploded. Pearson giggled at the world and himself lest he weep for mankind. Trudeau's sparkling wit usually was barbed and flawed by a lack of true humour, sometimes by vulgarity.

Macdonald, the humourist, had taught another lesson that no successor could afford to neglect. A party leader, he said, must never seek revenge on today's enemies because they might be tomorrow's friends. Now and then he forgot his own lesson and roundly cursed men like Donald Smith, "the biggest liar I ever met," who deserted him in the Pacific Scandal, and Oliver Mowat, the "damned pup" from Ontario whose Liberal "chops" he threatened to "slap." Moreover, he boasted that he could destroy other enemies faster than hell singed a feather. Then he would sit back and grin at the eternal cussedness of things.

To many of his successors revenge was sweet, especially to King, Meighen and Diefenbaker, but not to Laurier, Borden, St. Laurent or Pearson. They were poor haters. Trudeau seemed to have little capacity for either hatred or affection; no prime minister was as secretive and self-contained as he.

Even more than humour and forgiveness, a leader needs physical health. Macdonald rarely enjoyed it. Often he took to his bed with sciatica and stomach disorders. Once, prostrate in his office for weeks with inoperable gallstones, he nearly died. Drink, the final escape from heartbreak, had undermined the lean strong body of his youth. Mackenzie, seldom drinking, was physically destroyed by worry, a nagging conscience, poverty and friends' betrayal. Even Macdonald pitied his enemy's dismal end. Laurier appeared so sickly in his middle age that friends and enemies did not expect him to live long. But he lived for seventy-eight years until he dropped dead, murmuring to his wife, "*C'est fini.*"

Borden was healthy until overwork forced his retirement and he enjoyed a vigorous old age. The same was true of Meighen until his final years of sickness. No one could be healthier than Laurier's heir. King made sure of that by guarding the prime ministerial health as a sacred duty to government and nation, while ruthlessly overstraining his cabinet and his secretaries. "I never work," he told me, "when I'm tired." He actually hung on the wall of the bathroom in his Kingsmere country house a placard advising guests to keep their bowels open. Always he ate food more like a glutton than a gourmet, though he drank little alcohol.

St. Laurent, Bennett, Diefenbaker and Pearson also drank little or no alcohol but age and sickness overwhelmed all of them at last. Trudeau was an athlete, swimmer, diver, skier and canoeist on dangerous waters, but his physical health could not protect him from frequent bouts of nervous exhaustion and resulting fits of bad temper in Parliament.

Certain similarities can be detected in most of these men. Except for Trudeau, they were sedentary by habit, preferring the indoors to the outdoors. As youngsters they did the physical work of summer holidays but only Mackenzie, the stonemason, was a true workingman, his own nature carved in brittle stone. All of them, except Trudeau, were raised in comparative, some in dire, poverty; the lack of this experience remained a gaping lacuna in Trudeau's knowledge of human nature.

Another similarity ran through all their careers. They rose, slow or fast, from apprenticeship in Parliament. Until Mulroney arrived every prime minister had been previously elected and served his time in Parliament (though Trudeau's time was remarkably brief). In his literary profession Caxton had found "the lyf so short, the craft so long to lerne." Few men ever learn it completely in the profession or craft of politics.

Nowadays, however, a prime minister can call on help denied to his early predecessors. He has around him swarms of expert advisers who sometimes are as dangerous as they are expert since political, like military, war is too important to be left to generals. The prime minister also has computers, secret opinion polls, the whole equipment of so-called communication to keep him informed or misinformed. He trusts them at his peril.

No leader in wars of all sorts can escape the blunders of his lieutenants. A cabinet colleague commits some stupid indiscretion in Parliament or press conference and must be defended even if his case is indefensible. A civil servant writes a foolish report and it leaks. He, too, must be rescued, demoted to an inferior job or fired. A well-meaning secretary gives his boss some inaccurate figures and they must be corrected, to the opposition's jeers, or somehow made to seem accurate. But men and women must be guilty of grave faults before they are dismissed.

Laurier dismissed the potent Israel Tarte who had double-crossed him. Borden dismissed Sam Hughes, his wartime defence minister, who was crazed with megalomania (though George Foster wrote in his diary that the prime minister "seems helpless on the surf . . . irresolute and fearful"). Pearson dismissed an erring Quebec colleague. Even Diefenbaker, a man of perpetual rancour, seldom dismissed, only demoted, his ministers who hated him in return. Trudeau publicly dismissed no colleague and did not have to. Some of the best among them retired because, like Turner, they found him intolerable. Others were not reappointed when the cabinet was reorganized after elections.

While dismissal is rare in modern government, its leader must not count too much on colleagues, experts, assistants and computerized figures. Only his own instinct, his sense of ordinary people's feelings, the sponge that absorbs them, the mirror that reflects them, the seismograph that registers the faintest tremor will serve a prime minister in the crunch. Always the pinnacle of power is lonesome, windswept and chill.

At least its modern occupant commands a reassuring new craft, the ghostwriters. King was perhaps the first prime minister to rely on them but with his close supervision. In Jack Pickersgill (who, unique among assistants, refused to be bullied) King found the perfect ghost. He had reached an abstract, subliminal decision in solitary prayer. Now it must be buttressed with concrete arguments to convince a nonsubliminal Parliament and nation.

Pickersgill supplied them in four-hour speeches that dragged in every conceivable fact, including, as the weary cabinet and opposition thought, the kitchen sink. But when King hired Leonard Brockington, most eloquent of Canadian orators, to write stirring wartime speeches, the experiment was an immediate failure. Wisely, King saw that the public would recognize the fraud, and he decided not to use the ghostly product.

Once, he made his own kind of speech and, afterward, asked Brockington's opinion of it.

"Mr. Prime Minister," said Brockington, "you went in like the power and the glory. You came out like a trickle of weasel piss."

The ghost soon faded from government but his reputation for wit was secure. He had first won it in Calgary by a vicious pun against Bennett, the inheritor of a famous match-making industry. "There is a tide in the affairs of men," said Brockington, "which, taken at the Eddy, leads on to fortune." Bennett never forgave that penetrating arrow. Brockington, bent and crippled by arthritis, continued to deliver his own sparkling orations, brave to the end, forever in love more with words than with substance.

After King's time the last Edwardian, or even Victorian, political rhetoric suddenly changed. He had spoken in the antique, pretentious, richly upholstered manner of the nineteenth century. St. Laurent, the lawyer and man of business, rarely spoke for more than half an hour and then in short, crisp sentences, full of substance. He never bored the House. Diefenbaker's manner was different and more effusive. He faced the House, or an audience outside it, with a pack of cue cards in hand and alternated them as the occasion seemed to indicate, often veering off dangerous ground in midsentence when he perceived the mood of the audience. Pearson was no orator, disliked ghostwritten material and achieved his best results in really extemporaneous speeches or offhand press conferences.

Style changed again with Trudeau. He seldom raised his voice, spoke in a dozen varied idioms and several languages all the way from classic quotations down to the argot of the gutter. Only when nervously exhausted, his temper lost, did he insult the opposition and the public with inexcusable outbursts of fury. The pinnacle had both chilled and heated him.

Something more than Trudeau's style and personality had begun long before his arrival to change the link between leader and led. First came radio which even King learned to use effectively. Then television transformed politics everywhere, and Trudeau proved to be its matchless virtuoso. In his time only Reagan, a trained actor, could compete with an actor untrained but born for the age of theatrical politics.

When he took office Trudeau already knew all the tricks of the new trade—the quiet, conversational voice, the modest relaxed manner, the folksy appearance as if he were sitting beside the viewer's fireplace. Then the offhand, deadly asides hardly noticed at the moment but remembered next morning like a Hollywood double take, the mix of light banter and sudden *gravitas,* the smile followed by the frown and merciless thrust. As complete master, Trudeau could switch effortlessly from great to petty concerns, from his homemade Constitution to a hockey score. The world of knowledge was his province and he roamed all over the visible world.

Most deadly of all were his replies to the interviewers who attempted to trap him with the overloaded question. Always they were hoist on their own petards. Even Jack Webster, the publicly ferocious and privately tender-hearted gadfly of Vancouver, learned to fear his frequent guest from Ottawa. In Jack's experience Trudeau was a meat chopper that chopped the questioner exceeding fine, making every reply look like a self-evident truth. Trudeau enjoyed these little triumphs, for he was a bad loser in any game. Jack sought this guest and dreaded him. So did all the interviewers. But Trudeau was good theatre however fine he chopped. The television age had found a natural.

Actors of less talent also had acquired or imitated most of the tricks. They knew how to answer an unanswerable question by talking around it, fudging it, worrying it as a dog worries a bone until the interviewer lost the trigger of his well-baited trap. If the intended victim escaped, he would avoid the next trap by talking endlessly and using up the available time before the interviewer could resume the duel of words.

For all this entertainment a high admission charge is levied, not just in taxpayers' money but in the erosion of serious debate, of Parliament itself. In earlier, simpler times parliamentary debating points cut the thickest ice of politics from coast to coast when amusement was scarce. In our time the public pays little or no attention to them. Instead, it watches the mini-dramas and capsule simplicities televised outside the House. Except for the one-hour spectacle of Question Period, Parliament is hardly reported in the newspapers.

As soon as the hour ends the press gallery empties, perhaps only one or two reporters left on duty by the Canadian Press. The House empties, too, a mere quorum, or less than a quorum, of members left on duty with a bored cabinet watchdog in case of emergencies. And most of the quorum is reading newspapers, writing letters or pondering private affairs. Among ordinary citizens, who reads Hansard nowadays, the record of some excellent speeches? Almost nobody.

To be sure, television cameras impartially record Question Period, or its hotter exchanges, attract a considerable public audience and force members to improve their clothes, language and deportment. On the other hand, the chance of a national audience encourages mere acting and posturing instead of attention to the facts. This is not debate. Nor, of course, is the half-minute television spot that confuses more than it clarifies any serious issue. It is a struggle to make headlines and evening camera images. Debate has become the first casualty in the age of instantaneous communication and free entertainment. The backbencher must live with the marvellous new technology.

After Question Period a member faces an almost vacant House to make speeches reported only in Hansard, not the press. But the speaker can send free copies of Hansard to the home folk in case anyone cares to read them—a faint hope at best.

The prime minister has an opposite problem. He should never look too grand. A sophisticated public suspects grandeur, preferring its leaders to be one of the common people, though by nature he is quite different. Again, the leader should admit a few, not many, errors to prove his candour which the public admires. But on the whole, the party, dependent upon it, has always been right.

Besides his own talent and his ghosts, the prime minister possesses in the bureaucracy a tool as old as civilization. In our time it has become a kind of new art form. The bureaucracy of Ottawa is the second layer of government just below, or sometimes above, the cabinet. By the verdict of foreign governments Canada has one of the best bureaucracies in the world despite its empire-building proliferation and recurring derangement by efficiency experts. Without its experience and skill, government as we know it could hardly function.

Some inexperienced mediocrity is appointed to the cabinet for political reasons and knows little or nothing about the departmental job. Almost invariably the deputy minister, the so-called mandarin, must teach the neophyte minister how to perform in the department and in the House. If the minister is too stupid to learn, the deputy soon becomes dominant, willy-nilly. Even the strongest character, arriving with vows of personal independence, can seldom override the deputy who has also fed on bureaucratic royal jelly to become an autocratic bee.

Thence a grave danger for the politician—the danger of plausibility. How much trust can the minister give the expert advisers when he knows far less than they about the minutiae of government? While they are nearly always skilled and loyal, the advisers can unwittingly let the minister down, miscalculate figures, err in economic prediction and compile unworkable budgets.

To help the ministers, or correct their mistakes, hundreds of independent "consultants" are employed at enormous cost that the taxpayer cannot reckon. Royal commissions, task forces and studies of all kinds have become a growth industry beyond the control or knowledge of Parliament and public. The industry keeps growing to supply ministers with ideas or warn them against illusory policies however attractive they may be. Whether the results are worth their price will never be known, but it is willingly paid for by governments lacking time to do their own research. They can only judge what policies the nation will tolerate—a difficult and often erring choice.

The consultants need not worry. They are sure of full employment while many private industries decline. Consultation, useful or worthless, is a permanent fixture in a society too complex for ordinary citizens and politicians to understand. But in the end it is they who will make the great decisions to the approval or horror of the anonymous experts.

Here the public should note, but usually does not, the difference between the nonpartisan civil servants and the partisan staff of the Prime Minister's Office, the throbbing engine room of politics. Its mechanics are hired to inform their boss and explain his policies to the voters. He can accept, reject or modify the counsel of the back-room politicians whom the taxpayers support but never identify until some egregious blunder is committed and there is political hell to pay.

Among blunders, few were more egregious in our time than those of Jim Coutts, then fixer-in-chief of the Liberal back room. After sudden inspiration Coutts gradually lured Jack Horner, a Conservative M.P. from Alberta, into the Trudeau government, hoping that the unlikely recruit would bring western votes with him. He did not, was rejected by his own voters but found ample reward in other official jobs. Undaur.ted, Coutts, himself a native Albertan, arranged for a Liberal M.P. of Ontario to be named a senator, thus opening the Spadina constituency in Toronto. There Coutts ran for Parliament in a by-election and was defeated. Nothing could have better pleased the government's enemies, nationwide.

This fiasco—repeated in the last general election—seemed in passing strange when Coutts was one of the most competent craftsmen of his trade and also a bold, original left-wing thinker of acute intelligence. If even he could go so far wrong, a party leader will always be a chary of back-room expertise.

The line between political and nonpolitical advisers should be clearly drawn but sometimes is not, and the well-meaning bureaucrat may cross it unawares. Above all, in theory, the Prime Minister's Office, the secret PMO, is divided from that of the Privy Council housed in the same Langevin Block on Wellington Street. The secretary of the Privy Council, towering over his fellow mandarins, should take no part in politics. Some of these men do not. Others do, most notable among them in recent times the brooding Michael Pitfield, like the calm centre of a hurricane.

Under Trudeau's patronage, Pitfield was the accepted originator of ideas, the reputed genius and *éminence grise* of government, the prime minister's alter ego much closer to him than any cabinet colleague. As Pitfield saw it, his duty was to protect his boss and in so doing he protected a Liberal Party indistinguishable from the welfare of the state. He plunged up to the neck in to politics. As a result of his unequalled power, he attracted the jealousy of equally able or abler mandarins who thought his ideas had brought disorder, sometimes even havoc, to the civil service. However that may or may not have been, his partisan reward, on the eve of Trudeau's departure, was an "independent" senatorship.

In fairness it must be said that politics can hardly be avoided when an official works with the prime minister from day to day and hour to hour on the nation's vital business. It takes a remarkable man or woman to separate the nonpartisan and the partisan duties that often merge. But mandarins of every sort are seldom fired. With their own unacknowledged trade union, they are generally moved, as in a game of musical chairs, between one important job and another because their trained talent is needed by all governments. The prime minister can listen or not listen to them, hire or fire, advance or retreat. In the end he finds, like Harry Truman, that the buck stops on his desk.

But the chief magistrate, with all his power and all the mystery of leadership throughout the ages, can never do exactly what he wants to do, often what needs doing. Always he is subject to higher unwritten laws, the notions and whims of his time, the insoluble problems, the second-best choice quaintly known as the decision-making process.

In fact, he is likely to have more publicity and less effect on the nation's society than do some little-remembered men like the Canadian doctors who discovered insulin, or the inventors of television, the polluters of earth, water and air, the growers of food, the teachers of the young, the entrepreneurs of business, the leaders of trade unions and other hardly recognized persons who are quietly revolutionizing our collective life.

A prime minister may recognize such long-run movements, but his mind is necessarily focussed on the immediate concerns of government. And it must often be confused and obfuscated by a pullulating, overflowing bureaucracy that he can never fully control.

When reality becomes too oppressive, the unceasing talk of structures, utopias and other might-have-beens is perhaps briefly diverting. In reality, what structure have Canadian governments built over the years? All that the average voter, taxpayer and supposed master of government can see is its stately pleasure-domes, its turrets, battlements, donjon keeps, shady courtyards, gushing fountains and terraced gardens measureless to man.

However viewed, this structure, if it can be called a structure, was measureless even to Auditor General Kenneth Dye. He described the Crown corporations and the casual outposts of the establishment as "enormous icebergs floating in the foggy Atlantic, silent, majestic, awesome."

Awesome indeed when about 315 known icebergs float, their precise number uncounted as they spend, and frequently lose, the taxpayers' dollars in hundreds of millions every year. Dye calls the bureaucratic structure a "sub-government" larger in its payroll than the visible government, with more employees than the government's total of about 240,000. The structure has grown from only twenty-eight Crown corporations two decades ago and had assets of $74 billion at last count. No prime minister will take time to count them. He has more urgent questions to test his qualities, apart from the daily grind of politics—three questions above all.

The first, of course, is whether mankind can avoid nuclear destruction; the second whether democracy can long survive even in the nations dedicated to freedom; the third whether the free peoples have the wisdom to maintain, or create, a society where freedom, with reasonable prosperity, will live and thrive in safety.

Every prime minister must give his own answers, or none, but he will not be as regnant, wise or unwise as he may look in the latest news. From the funny political game, the lonely pinnacle and mere accident he can never be free. Nor can his work be explained, justified or contemned by the abstract rules of power, only by concrete and mostly *ad hoc* action as chance permits.

To understand, even in the broadest terms, the men who have governed Canada, we must recall from yet another angle of vision their individual strengths, weaknesses, triumphs and failures, their day-to-day performance. Then perhaps we may see how the supreme office, its methods, personalities and nature evolved, ourselves the beneficiaries or victims.

16

THE
BITTER
LESSONS

The election of 1984, spectacular and momentous as it seemed at the time, was a passing episode in the nation's history. Although its results will be long with us, it decided no important issue and changed nothing fundamental in our affairs.

Few elections ever do. During this century the electorate answered specific questions only twice, rejecting continental free trade in 1911 and approving wartime conscription in 1917. Having won the other elections, the victorious party did, as government, what it had to do, frequently the opposite of its promises because they were impossible or outdated by unforeseen events.

Doubtless our latest government will do the same and in some areas has begun to do so already. But where should Brian Mulroney look for guidance? He can find it, of course, in the immediate events surrounding him and, if he is wise, in the lessons of the past. Those lessons are focussed and vividly portrayed by the achievements and mistakes of Mulroney's predecessors. To succeed, he must examine the record of all the men who held the prime minister's office—the written record, mostly forgotten, and also the unwritten record known to few living Canadians.

Such an examination will show that the public images of the great

Canadian leaders usually masked quite different men. In most cases their mistakes and eccentricities are vaguely remembered, their successful work either exaggerated or misconstrued by friends and enemies together. "The evil that men do lives after them, the good is oft interred with their bones."

Wherever Mulroney looks he will find no safer guide than Macdonald whose lessons in another time remain valid and unmistakable in ours. So long as the nation lives it will judge or misjudge him in his reality and in his legend. They are contradictory. It is generally supposed, for example, that he invented Confederation. He did not. On the contrary, he opposed the idea when lesser men advocated it. Until his fiftieth birthday, at the earliest, he was unconvinced that a transcontinental state could be built or, if built, could work.

"The opening of the prairie lands," he said, "would drain away our youth and strength. I am perfectly willing personally to leave the whole country a wilderness for the next half century." But once persuaded that the wilderness must be grasped, governed and peopled before the United States absorbed it in peace or war, he was better equipped than any of his peers to write a national constitution, build the CPR and extend Canada from Atlantic to Pacific—*A Mari usque ad Mare.* At the time for decision the indispensable man had arrived.

Even more improbable were his origin and upbringing. Birth in Glasgow in 1815; a strong, kindly mother whom he adored; a father given to drink and business failures; immigration to Canada at the age of five and settlement in Kingston; five years in primitive schools; "no boyhood," as he later recalled, and "from the age of fifteen I began to earn my own living"; apprenticeship to a lawyer of the village and a law degree after vast reading and trumpery examination; early addiction to barrooms, liquor and low company—these were the beginnings of a life apparently sure to be insignificant if not worse.

The beginnings, like everything else about him, were deceptive.

A youngster carrying his musket against the Rebellion of 1837; the only lawyer willing to defend Nils Szoltecky Von Schoultz, sincere but mad invader of Canada at the Battle of the Prescott Windmill; the defence hopeless, the prisoner condemned, his counsel escorting him to the gallows and refusing any fee—these were the more impressive beginnings. Perhaps, the town guessed, the roistering, overdressed youth had some stuff in him? Possibly he might even find a humble place in politics?

The stuff soon appeared. Better material lacking, Macdonald was elected as a Tory to the Canadian Assembly, then equally divided between Upper and Lower Canada, rotten with graft, frequently deadlocked and paralyzed. Here he learned how to purchase votes on the cheap, win local elections and make himself the ablest administrator of his time. But he was himself unpurchasable as his poverty attested. Already his lifelong private agonies had begun.

In Scotland he met his cousin, Isabella Clark, married her in Kingston and watched her slowly die over the next dozen years. The son born of this first marriage died, too, in infancy. A second son, Hugh John, was to outlive the father. But the father must live nine years without a real home, in solitary widowerhood, partially relieved by politics and alcohol. In politics, rough as it was, he had stumbled upon his natural habitat.

Alliance with Cartier, the brisk, staccato terrier of Quebec; invention of the Liberal Conservative Party; brief coalition with George Brown; their joint trip to England where they attended the Derby and spattered the crowds with flour; ultimately Confederation; Macdonald's first government; suddenly unbelievable news from a Fort Garry seized by Riel who, in tail coat, starched white shirt and beaded moccasins, raised the flag of an independent state and executed an obstreperous Ontario youth—what was the new prime minister to make of all this?

What was he to make of his colleague, "Wandering Willie" McDougall, who, appointed lieutenant governor of Rupert's Land, had reached the West through the United States, had been turned back by Riel's horsemen at the Canadian border and, in a final act of lunacy, crossed it in a midnight blizzard to read a forged royal authority from Queen Victoria, only to retreat again?

It was easy to fire McDougall but not to understand Riel. He, surprisingly enough, had refused to let the American agents of Manifest Destiny coerce his provisional government which protested its loyalty to the Crown. At least Macdonald, as a lawyer, knew that the Metis leader was not a rebel. In a vacuum of local authority he had committed no treason. And when Canada's military expedition toiled westward to Fort Garry, through the swamps and jungles of Ontario, Riel fled to exile in the United States. Evidently he was out of the way for good.

Manitoba, "the God that speaks," entered Confederation on Riel's terms with separate Catholic schools, later to be abolished in breach of a contract that the Supreme Court has lately restored. No, Riel was not out of the way for good. He was teaching school in Montana before he heard a summons to treason.

Macdonald had learned some permanent lessons from these adventures. He had convinced himself that the United States would always be tempted to penetrate the Candian West, preferably short of war, that the West was essential to Canada and that it could be held only with steel rails.

After Canada's Atlantic fisheries had been opened to the United States by the imperial government and "overwashed Englishmen utterly ignorant of the country and full of crotchets as all Englishmen are," he had learned that a Canadian prime minister could never reproduce his British counterpart, as London assumed. Burke, at Bristol, had been wise to repudiate direct democracy, misgoverned by the whims of ignorant voters. It was impossible, especially in a sprawling, divided country like Canada. Only strong, centralized representative government could work and then seldom well.

Macdonald had also learned that only a coalition of rival interests could manage a transcontinental state. So he made himself the best party manager and caucus boss in our history—except for King—supplying his candidates with "good buncombe arguments," even luring the Nova Scotia titan, Joseph Howe, enemy of Confederation, into the government.

Then the original CPR deal with Hugh Allan; treachery and double-cross; breaks in the coalition; a second election in 1872; Macdonald's own Kingston seat endangered; the telegraphed requests of a desperate, drunken man for railway campaign funds; victory of the government by a narrow majority; the death of Cartier; the Kingston telegrams stolen from the Montreal office of the CPR lawyer, John Abbott, and sold to the Liberals for $5,000; Macdonald's five-hour speech of defence when, half-drunk, almost too sick to stand, supported by glasses of water innumerable, laced invisibly with gin; the full-blown Pacific Scandal; the desertion of friends like Donald Smith; Macdonald's resignation and disgrace; a broken man "tottering down the hill to the East Gate alone" in "a Red River sash and coat and the old historic mink-skin cap" while everyone passed him "with a wide sweep."

This was the end of his career. Or so it seemed. But there was one great compensation. In England to ease the British North America Act through Parliament, Macdonald had met, on a London street, a youthful friend, Susan Agnes Bernard, married her a few days later and, in Ottawa, possessed a home at last.

Even Agnes's lifelong devotion could not end his sorrows. Their daughter remained mentally a child, the parents wheeling her in baby carriage, the father still keeping the hidden toys of his lost infant son. And by now, with debts of some $80,000, he would be a bankrupt if creditors pressed their claims.

Having summoned Alexander Mackenzie to form a Liberal government, Governor General Lord Dufferin reported to London that his new prime minister was "a poor creature and under the thumb of George Brown . . . a puppet." This judgement was soon reversed. But Mackenzie may well have been the most unfortunate creature ever to occupy the great office, his sorrows even worse than Macdonald's.

In some ways the lives of the two men ran parallel. Mackenzie was born in 1822 among the Perthshire hills, son of a poor crofter. He attended the local schools for six years, learned his stonemason's trade and, at the age of twenty, arrived in Kingston, Macdonald's home town, with his tools and sixteen shillings as his material possessions.

He had wealth of another sort. Mackenzie's stony look hid a passionate nature; it had compelled him to follow his sweetheart, Helen Neil, to Canada. He possessed also a shrewd, practical, if narrow, mind, the most honest in Canadian politics, more honest than Macdonald's. And honesty, in the corruption of the time, doomed him from the start.

A winter of homesteading with Helen's family in the Ontario bush; mason's work on the St. Lawrence canals; small building contracts; intensive reading of history; mother and six brothers brought to Canada with his savings; marriage to Helen; death of their first child, Helen's soon following; his own repeated illness relieved by opium and a Baptist's prayer, morning and night—such was the unpromising apprenticeship of a man now prematurely aged with deeply graven face, tangled, reddish beard, clean-shaven upper lip, clear blue eyes, Scottish burr and no personal ambition. For already he had become in the Liberal Party the devoted intellectual slave of Brown.

That the slave was more steadfast and durable than the master no one then suspected, least of all Mackenzie who, overestimating Brown, fatally underestimated Macdonald as a mere scallawag and "debauchee." Still worse, for the trade of politics, was Mackenzie's naive faith in human nature, logic, free trade and the Economic Man of Liberal myth.

Nonetheless he grew, made himself the party's second man, sometimes led the parliamentary opposition, though overawed by the greater mind of Edward Blake, greatest mind in Canada. Unfortunately, it could seldom be made up while the owner's moon face was often wet with tears under the tiny, steel-rimmed spectacles.

When the summons came from Dufferin, Mackenzie recommended Blake who had replaced Brown as his idol. The great mind still not made up, Blake refused. Mackenzie settled down as prime minister and minister of public works behind the stone façade of the West Block. There he craftily installed a secret staircase that enabled him to escape the swarms of patronage-seekers. Lunching at the Rideau Club, he could go home at night to a comfortable house and his second wife. She had kept all his wildly romantic love letters but the first comfort he had ever known was short-lived.

Electoral victory for the new government in 1874; onslaught of a world depression; terrifying budgetary deficit above $24 million; spreading unemployment; the transcontinental railway, "a monstrous scheme," in disjointed fragments and no money to complete it; British Columbia demanding completion, appealing to the Queen; riotous mobs in Victoria threatening secession from Canada; an unworkable compromise; Blake dismissing the whole project as worse than the possible loss of the Pacific Coast, the railway "two streaks of rust across the wilderness," resigning from the cabinet, withdrawing his resignation, offering to replace the prime minister who quietly rejected the generous offer—this unbroken chain of misfortune was enough to wreck any government.

But Mackenzie still persisted in his impossible dream of free trade. The opposition awaited the next budget; Charles Tupper, its bulldog and battering ram, had two speeches ready, one demanding reduced tariffs, the other demanding the opposite. When the budget was brought down it proposed "a tariff for revenue only" and no protection. Macdonald had his issue for use at leisure. That "old cat," as the Liberals called him, was on the prowl again, remaining sober, inventing the political picnic, talking little politics, telling jokes to the farmers, discussing in the vaguest terms his National Policy of disguised protectionism.

Now the life of a Parliament in all-night turmoil ran out. The election of 1878 and the nation's first secret ballot finished Mackenzie's career in office. Depression, Macdonald's temporary friend, had done its work.

What had the ruined stonemason really achieved? More than his enemies and later historians recognized. He had given the nation's politics a first spell of honesty and the secret ballot; he had given its judiciary a Supreme Court; he had discovered a handsome young Quebec lieutenant in Wilfrid Laurier. By this respectable work Mackenzie had impoverished himself and destroyed his health. Towards the end he could speak only in a whisper from the opposition bench, finally in unintelligible croaks. Before his resignation as Liberal Party leader he had become "a washed-out rag and limp enough to hang upon a clothes line," Dufferin reported to London.

Back in office, Macdonald was not surprised by his victory, for he understood human nature as Mackenzie never did. But the new government had inherited a national estate close to bankruptcy when, suddenly and magically, the depression lifted as a result, Macdonald pretended, of the National Policy. His luck had returned after long absence.

British money secured by George Stephen, the melancholy Montreal financier, to complete the CPR within ten years; Mackenzie replaced by Blake whose logical speeches bored the voters who re-elected the government in 1882 by a two-to-one majority; William Van Horne pushing rails across the prairies, sometimes several miles a day, before a pass through the Rockies had been found—altogether things were going well for Macdonald.

And yet, unbelievably, the CPR was insolvent by 1885, the government unable to get more money from Parliament or in Britain where a desperate Stephen cabled "Stand fast, Craigellachie!"—the war cry of clan Grant—without anything to stand on. Then, again miraculously, luck returned with Riel's first true rebellion.

Van Horne's unfinished railroad and, where necessary, sleighs on tracks laid on river ice carried an army to capture the rebel at Batoche. Parliament, finally convinced, voted the required CPR funds. Donald Smith drove the last spike at Craigellachie in the high mountains. The first train arrived in Port Moody. All these hairbreadth escapes meant that Canada was a transcontinental state, even if a prairie vacuum still gaped between East and West. Macdonald had been installed in office for the rest of his life.

He and his wife rode westward in 1886, sometimes travelling on a locomotive's cowcatcher through the Rockies, and reached Victoria, his new parliamentary seat. He drove the last spike of the Esquimalt and Nanaimo Railway and descended the coal mine of its owner, Robert Dunsmuir, to enjoy strong drink safe from their teetotalling wives.

Soon, however, Macdonald's luck turned fickle. The world depression returned and the National Policy seemed powerless to resist it. Then luck of a sort also returned.

Parading through the blizzards of February, Macdonald won the 1887 election with a bare majority, thanks for the most part to Blake's logical speeches. But now the Liberals had the sense to make Laurier their leader. Already Macdonald was old, sick, half the time a prisoner in Earnscliffe, his house, desperately anxious to retire, knowing that death alone could relieve him. Perhaps he knew, too, that Riel's execution had left a subterranean fire smouldering in Quebec, though he had temporarily postponed the explosion.

In any case, he must face another election in 1891, his seventy-seventh year. Again he led the parades through freezing weather, a frozen smile on his face. And again he was given luck in two lavish helpings.

When Laurier proposed unlimited Reciprocity with the United States, Macdonald saw at once that it was a grave, probably fatal, mistake (to be repeated two decades later). If it might not be quite enough to save the government, Edward Farrer, one of the Toronto *Globe*'s editors, wrote a confidential pamphlet explaining how the United States could easily dominate Canada. In poetic revenge for the Liberal theft of the Kingston telegrams, a printer stole the Farrer pamphlet and gave it to the Conservative bosses.

Instantly Macdonald pounced on this "veiled treason" and declared (stealing a phrase from Robert Baldwin), "A British subject I was born—a British subject I hope to die." That did the business. Macdonald won his last election but, as a British subject, he was dying.

Paralyzed and speechless in Earnscliffe, he could answer simple questions only by the pressure of his left hand. At a quarter past ten on the night of 6 June relief came at last. He was buried beside his parents, his first wife and infant son in the Cataraqui graveyard at Kingston while the nation mourned its indispensable man. A few months later Mackenzie also died, crying, "Oh, take me home!" Two great Canadians, each with his separate kind of greatness, were home together.

Macdonald had gone, but the Conservative government felt assured of a prosperous future if it could find a man fit to replace him. On his deathbed Macdonald had first recommended Senator John Abbott, then decided that the CPR solicitor was "too selfish," that the party leader should be John Sparrow David Thompson, the Nova Scotia judge whom he regarded as the best recruit he had ever brought to the cabinet.

The party sachems, and Thompson himself, feared that the nation was not ready for a Catholic prime minister. So Abbott, a grim, grizzled old man, took office as a stop-gap custodian, though he declared, "I hate politics." No wonder, when the Liberal politicians had rifled his office for the Kingston telegrams.

Two things were wrong with this arrangement. Abbott, as a senator, could not sit in the Commons and lead it. The government, seemingly in good health, was dying with the nineteenth century and no politician was prepared for the twentieth. Abbott resigned in disgust at the end of 1892. Thompson replaced him and, with his fine mind, his wit, his chubby, cheerful look, seemed likely to make a successful prime minister at the age of forty-eight. But just as he began to face the eruption of the Manitoba Schools Question, he dropped dead at luncheon with Queen Victoria at Windsor Castle.

Charles Tupper, his natural heir, was reluctant to abandon the easy life of high commissioner in London. Perforce, the Conservative caucus, with grave doubt, appointed the nation's worst leader. Mackenzie Bowell, then sixty-one years old, had been brought to Canada from Britain by his parents in childhood, had gradually worked his way upward in local politics as an anti-Catholic zealot in Belleville, and behind a flowing white beard, his nature offered nothing more than ignorant bigotry.

While the Manitoba Schools Question reeled into legal limbo and the government ceased to govern, it was not long before a "nest of traitors" among his colleagues forced Bowell to resign. The traitors summoned Tupper and he came home, too late.

Macdonald's lifelong partner was now old, his time ebbing with the century. But the bulldog face with bushy white sideburns still looked formidable, much more formidable than the pale, languid Laurier who had sunk into despair for himself and the nation. That mood was premature. In 1896, using the methods of Machiavelli instead of Galahad, Laurier fudged the schools question, defeated Tupper and opened fifteen years of Liberal glory.

Even the world's economic weather had changed. As Laurier took office the rising barometer of Canada was set fair, the nation's first real Happy Time about to dawn with the new century. The first French Canadian prime minister had a long way to go before the barometer fell, ending his life in exile and anguish, but not in the nation's memory.

Laurier's peasant ancestry stretched back nine generations in Canada to the early 1600s. By the time he was born in the dusty village of St. Lin in 1841, his father had graduated, as a land surveyor, into the petty bourgeoisie. The family was still poor, the son's bedroom a narrow, dark closet. Yet even in boyhood he showed promise.

Life with a family of Scottish Presbyterians at the village of New Glasgow where he mastered the English language; seven years at the modest college, L'Assomption; failing health with lung hemorrhages that might soon kill him; partial recovery and apprenticeship in a Montreal law office; on doctors' orders a move to the fresh air of the Eastern Townships; improved health; election to the Quebec legislature, then to Parliament and Mackenzie's cabinet; enduring, childless marriage to Zoe Lafontaine; a love affair, supposedly platonic, with Emilie Lavergne; a Catholic's ever-memorable speech attacking the ultramontane bishops—this rapid rise had made Laurier the successor to Blake and the Canadian of the future.

But Laurier was never the man of his legend, not a true religious believer, not as scrupulous as his worshippers imagined, nor as wicked as his enemies believed, or hoped. By the chaotic year of 1896, the real man of mixed qualities had only begun to appear in the Manitoba school issue.

Bowell, a Protestant prime minister on his last legs, finds the snarling courage to risk the loss of Conservative Ontario and issues a "remedial order" forcing the Manitoba government to re-establish the separate Catholic schools that it had abolished in defiance of the provincial constitution. Manitoba ignores the order. Laurier remains silent except for a few platitudes and fatuous reliance on his own "sunny ways" because he has no strategy, no means of winning Ontario if he stands by the Manitoba Catholics, no means of holding Quebec if he supports Bowell.

Fortunately, the arch-manipulator, Israel Tarte, has a strategy as rough as anything known, so far, in Canadian politics. The Liberal candidates outside Quebec will stand for or against separate schools to win their own local elections. Quebec will vote for Laurier no matter where he stands, or even if he takes no stand at all. Tarte's strategy, with Laurier's blessing, proves to be a masterpiece.

The remedial order failing, Tupper introduces compulsory legislation to reopen the separate schools. Parliament's life ends before the legislation can be passed. Tupper, the Protestant Conservative, fights the seminal 1896 election as the champion of the Manitoba Catholics; Laurier, the Catholic, as the champion of the provincial and Protestant rights. The political world stands naked, indecently exposed.

Laurier holds a solid Quebec that has never forgotten Riel, wins almost half the Ontario seats and forms a government of "All the Talents." Even Macdonald could not have devised a strategy more brazen and successful.

Laurier goes to imperial conferences at London, accepts a knighthood, charms the duchesses in public but in private firmly rejects the centralized empire policy of Joseph Chamberlain who vainly declares that the "proud, persistent, self-asserting and resolute stock" of the British race is "infallibly destined to be the predominating force in the future history and civilization of the world." For Britain's rulers Laurier has proved a shock and a disappointment.

What, in fact, is he doing? He is building, little by little, on the foundations of Canadian autonomy laid by Macdonald. But there are difficulties ahead.

Despite Quebec's objection, eloquently voiced by Henri Bourassa, Laurier sends a military contingent to the South African War.

The barometer still rises so fast that, by 1900, Tupper's final election, the Liberal government, after arranging a weak school compromise in Manitoba and a budget of minor tariff reductions, is safe. Thus Canada enters a new century which, says Laurier, should belong to it. He is wrong on two points. The century will belong to no nation but to a world gone mad. The Manitoba Schools Question, apparently dead, will re-emerge before the century's end. And Laurier is enraged by the Alaska boundary deal, a British sellout of Canada as he judges it.

In the meantime Clifford Sifton, ablest and most ruthless minister in the government of All the Talents, has been filling the western vacuum with massive immigration; the CPR cannot handle the swelling traffic; two more transcontinental lines are chartered, their future bankruptcy ensured by a political party that opposed the first.

In 1904 the barometer still rises, the government wins its third election. Laurier ignores the absent Sifton and promises separate schools for the new provinces of Saskatchewan and Alberta. He is forced to retreat under Sifton's threat of resignation. Sifton remains briefly, tarnished by an alleged private scandal, grows deaf, resigns and, in due course, will twice organize the defeat of his former chief.

Hardly noticed, least of all by himself, the Conservative Party has found its own future man at last. Robert Borden, a cool shaggy Nova Scotia lawyer, has accepted the party's leadership for one year only, is persuaded to remain and, after losing elections in 1904 and 1908, is eager to quit. A vain hope. Fate already has marked him for power in Canada's time of deepest agony.

As the year of 1911 begins, even Laurier sees that the government has lost its best talents, is old and jaded, vainly clinging to its comfortable, sunny ways. To rejuvenate it, he plans a Canadian Navy and grasps an unlikely chance offered by President Taft. The lesson of 1891 forgotten, Laurier calls an election on a Reciprocity deal with the United States, not mainly for reasons of principle as celebrated in the Liberal myth but in the hope of a fifth victory.

Now comes the moment of Sifton's victory if not of truth. He rouses the despairing Borden and organizes the anti-Reciprocity campaign. Political cynicism reaches a new peak. Laurier with his worthless "tin pot" Navy is denounced outside Quebec as a traitor planning to sell Canada to the United States; inside Quebec as Britain's lap dog who will drag Canada into imperial wars.

The Conservative mix of opposites is even more successful than the Liberal mix of 1896. The idolized Laurier's Happy Time ends in electoral defeat and cannot be resurrected.

What has he accomplished? The peopling of the West; Quebec's dawning sense of equality in the nation (a false dawn soon to fade); above all, the nation's growing sovereignty in an empire already turning into the modern Commonwealth of equals, a Canadian invention. On that record Laurier, though defeated and heartbroken, belongs to the ages.

His successor is a captive of the present, now staggering blindly towards war. Borden has hardly taken office before all his plans collapse. The government promises to contribute $35 million, the cost of three dreadnoughts, to the British Navy. Laurier, strangely believing that he can win one more election, blockades the Conservative policy, keeps the Commons sitting and raging day and night for weeks until Meighen, Borden's young lieutenant, devises a cunning trap for the opposition and closure is imposed for the first time in Canada.

But the unacknowledged, unnatural Conservative alliance with the anti-British Quebec Nationalists breaks down. So does Borden's health. He is suffering the misery of carbuncles, sciatica, neuritis and lumbago, and addresses the House swathed in bandages. The Senate rejects the Naval Service Bill. Canada has no defence policy.

Recuperating at a Muskoka resort in the summer of 1914, the prime minister is summoned by telegram to Ottawa, passes a series of orders-in-council without legal authority and, on 4 August, Canada automatically follows Britain into war. Health suddenly restored, a new Borden appears to master Parliament and becomes the nation's first great war leader.

Even this man of immaculate honour cannot eradicate the grafters in his party, cannot get satisfactory information from Britain where, in the autumn of 1914, Canada's original military contingent has arrived on its way to Flanders. In a bungled trench war, 425,000 Canadians will fight and 60,000 die from a population of 8 million. On that record and his own Borden will win the total independence of a colony forged into a nation by the blood of its sons.

The process takes more than four years and nearly kills Borden. Sickened by the news of Canadian slaughter in Europe, he goes home one day, shovels snow and in his diary reveals an unknown poetic side to his nature: "The flakes seem like flowers from heaven strewing the bosom of mother earth, fast asleep until spring."

His relief is momentary. Nothing goes right. Laurier's superfluous railways are bankrupt. Meighen arranging the details, the government-owned Canadian National Railways is established by Conservatives the nation's first large socialist experiment. The megalomanical defence minister, Sam Hughes, is belatedly fired, grafters rooted out, the British government forced to give Borden the real facts of a war almost lost in 1917, the year of Borden's final test.

The facts are so appalling, the need of more soldiers so urgent, that Borden decides to form a conscriptionist union government of Conservatives and Liberals. He invites Laurier to join it, to choose his own

Liberal colleagues and even to veto Borden's Conservative nomi-
nees—an incredible offer from a patriot of generous heart, but Laurier
is not persuaded.

Although the opposition leader has always supported the war with
recruiting speeches that only his magic eloquence can deliver, he
answers that his approval of conscription and the resulting desertion of
his Quebec followers "may rend and tear this Canada of ours to the
very roots." Himself already torn between patriotism, ambition and
the ancestral womb, the old man rejects political union as stage-
managed by Sifton who helps to defeat him for the second time.

Now the Liberal patriarch watches some of his closest friends join a
bipartisan government. By cold logic and oratory of a brilliance seldom to be heard again, Meighen pushes the conscription law through
Parliament (thereby dooming his future) and the government easily
wins the election of December 1917. Laurier, heroic in his tragedy, is
hived with the Liberal Party in Quebec where French Canadian mobs
riot and are subdued by machine guns and bayonets, five soldiers
wounded, four rioters dead.

Is this a newly born, united nation, or still "two races warring," as
Durham found them, "in the bosom of a single state"? No, it is just the
end of Laurier's career. His death early in 1919 comes as a mercy. The
aged Meighen lives long enough to declare that Laurier had been the
greatest of all Canadians.

At the Versailles peace conference Borden finishes his work in a
triumph then little understood. He forces the Big Three victors to
allow Canada's independent signature on the peace treaty and to be an
autonomous member of the League of Nations.

The Rubicon foreseen by Macdonald and Laurier has been crossed
at last and the man who led the crossing is exhausted by his work.
Borden resigns. A narrowly divided caucus selects Meighen in his
stead. Healthy again, Borden can be seen walking the Ottawa streets
with his wife or, in the farmers' market, bargaining for a fat capon.
He, too, belongs to the ages.

Many years earlier, listening to Meighen deliver a speech as clear
and icy as a Euclidian theorem, yet suddenly heated and illuminated
by Shakespearean quotations, Laurier had whispered to his deskmate:
"Borden has found his man." True enough. And true also that the
carefully hidden side of Meighen can be friendly, jolly, lovable. But

the austere visible side of the new prime minister, at the age of forty-six, repels the electorate.

What he does not know (who does?) is that the war has transformed the entire prospects of humanity. So he builds his plans around the structure of a prewar world already becoming irrelevant.

The boy raised in a poor Ontario village has worked hard at his farm chores. He roams the woods rehearsing speeches for a school debating society. Already he seems to know that his future goal is politics. He sells magazines, wins the prize of an imitation gold watch and finds it lacking interior mechanism. It will never tell the time. Nor, in politics, will Meighen.

He graduates with honours from the University of Toronto, meets and instantly despises a chubby, garrulous fellow student named Mackenzie King, moves to Portage, Manitoba, practises law, lives all winter mostly on a barrel of apples, wins a parliamentary seat and quickly makes himself Borden's natural heir.

Now, as prime minister, he commits his first of many mistakes by dismissing King, the new Liberal leader, with searing contempt as a windy "charlatan." Strangely confident of victory, he calls the election of December 1921 and enters the new Parliament with fifty members—less than the Progressive Party's sixty-five, but it allows him to lead the opposition. Where will he lead it, this man of otherwise splendid gifts and total honesty who somehow lacks the interior mechanism, the essential talent of politics?

King, forming a government just short of a majority in the Commons, never doubts where Meighen, given the chance, will lead his party and nation. Yet the new prime minister is not sure of his own plans, either. His interior mechanism will soon fail to work. In the meantime he dictates to a harassed secretary at midnight a repulsive diary of his dreams, fantasies and bodily functions.

King has come by winding detours to the pinnacle. Birth in 1874 in the home of a dilettant lawyer with a mother of strong, rapacious will inherited from her father, the Rebel of '37; normal boyhood of athletics and mischief; graduation from the University of Toronto; discovery, at Hull House, of Chicago's slums and human degradation; official study of the slavelike needle trade in Toronto and dawning secret horror of laissez faire, the Liberal creed—by all these contradictory notions King has quickly reached the first rung of ambition's ladder.

There soon follows his appointment as deputy minister and then minister of labour in Laurier's cabinet. King is now Ottawa's most eligible bachelor, dancer and flirtatious young man-about-town. He buys a run-down farm coincidentally named Kingsmere in the Gatineau Hills, delivers intended speeches to his patient saddle horse, is defeated with Laurier in 1911. His promising career has been interrupted, perhaps fatally.

For the first time King knows real personal poverty, most of his earnings sent to his impecunious parents. Sudden rescue comes from the Rockefeller Foundation which employs him, at the prodigal salary of $20,000, to investigate labour problems in the United States.

But he returns to Canada, expecting and receiving defeat as an opponent of conscription in the wartime election of 1917. Is his career already finished? On the contrary, its success is ensured by his narrow choice as Liberal leader in 1919. What kind of man has the party chosen? It does not know because King is careful to mask his private radicalism for exposure at the right time. Already he knows that throughout his life God will direct him, failing only, by unfortunate error, to provide a wife, after his many half-serious love affairs.

The man who inherits Laurier's ugly old house is a weird conglomerate of opposites, of spiritualism, superstition, worldly greed and otherworldly faith that can never be deciphered, even by himself. But he understands as well as any predecessor how to manage his government and party. In his first bold act of leadership he welcomes home the conscriptionist Liberals of 1917. And soon the world's brief postwar depression had ended (through his wise management, of course).

Clearly, an unseen hand is guiding King, though his government has done little about anything important despite mushy promises of reform in areas unspecified. At least—this fact not then appreciated—he has eased the regional strains of a people angrily divided by war and postwar depression.

In 1925 he is so sure of their confidence that he plunges into his second election and returns with fewer seats than the Conservative Party has won. After an unbelievable recovery, Meighen is in sight of power. But in the following year King raises a constitutional issue and wins his third election.

From now on surely nothing can unseat him. Nothing except the Great Depression. That victorious enemy of governments the world over has found its Canadian field marshal in Richard Bedford Bennett, called "Bonfire" because his speeches are red-hot, sulfurous, never-ending.

Born of poor parents in Hopewell Hill, New Brunswick, in 1870, he becomes a struggling young lawyer, moves to Calgary, makes himself a friend of the future Lord Beaverbrook, is a millionaire by the age of thirty, wins a seat in Parliament and, by 1927, is the leader of the Conservative Party after Meighen's retirement. The new leader is a striking personage—tall and stout, with puffy unwrinkled face, shiny domed forehead and glistening pince-nez, the easy prey of the cartoonists.

When the depression strikes Canada, Bennett knows how to cure it by restraining imports, "blasting" Canadian goods into the world market or "perishing in the attempt." So he is unlucky enough to win, as King is lucky to lose the 1930 election. Now the Liberal leader has time to think and to build his fake Gothic ruins at Kingsmere.

The prime minister is a one-man government. He works twelve hours a day, changes his tail coat at noon, seldom halts his mellifluous burble in the Commons from morning to night, rents a luxurious suite in the Chateau Laurier hotel and usually eats a pound of after-dinner chocolates, the teetotaller's substitute for alcohol, the resulting fat rubbed off by a masseur.

The nation's goods cannot be blasted into the world market, and on the prairies drought completes the work of the depression. In such times the Liberal Party's Beauharnois campaign funds scandal and King's apparent ruin are forgotten, Bennett's amazing restoration of titles of nobility well remembered among desperate urban unemployed and cropless farmers.

By 1935 King knows that he cannot fail to win an election after five years of Bennett's luckless rule. And yet the one-man government is not quite finished. Without warning, in deathbed reversal, Bennett announces a New Deal imitating that of Franklin Roosevelt, explains that capitalism must be totally overhauled, calls an election, returns with 40 seats against King's 173, leads the pitiable opposition and flees "home" to England. There he is ennobled as Viscount Bennett of Mickleham, Calgary and Hopewell before he dies in his bathtub at the age of seventy-seven. A failed prime minister has been a man of incorruptible honesty, Christian faith, lavish charities, mean hatreds, no grasp of a new world already in birth pangs and no luck. He has taught only the lesson that good motives do not guarantee political success and that autarchial bootstrap economics will never work in Canada.

Although neither man had discerned it, a clear line of history must now be drawn between Bennett's single term of power and King's fourth.

Bennett had failed in all his hopes, but not in personal honour. At first the re-elected King failed just as badly. He abandoned his youthful radicalism, attacked Roosevelt's original New Deal and Bennett's imitation (which was largely invalidated by the courts), revived his faith in the flawless market directed by the Invisible Hand.

World war in 1939 changed everything. The depression was cured overnight. Even so, the government found itself in trouble at home. By 1943, after King's easy re-election in 1940, the newly invented opinion polls showed the Liberal, Conservative and CCF parties almost equal in public support. Those figures so alarmed King that he set up a secret task force to study them. When it proposed drastic postwar social reforms he reluctantly agreed and thus committed himself to a welfare state.

The second conscription crisis in late 1944 seemed to disrupt his plans. King's cold-blooded destruction of J. L. Ralston, the selfless defence minister, the appointment of Gen. A. G. L. McNaughton in his place, McNaughton's failure to recruit volunteers, the eleventh-hour resort to overseas conscription—all combined to threaten the government at the peak of its power. But with St. Laurent's aid, King surmounted the crisis.

Then political luck returned in the person of his latest challenger.

John Bracken, the Farmer-Liberal premier of Manitoba, sponsored by Meighen to win western votes, was leading the Conservative opposition, and King knew that his old enemy's final error in choosing Bracken could not be overcome. So it turned out. The government won a summer election by a narrow margin.

From now on, however, King's long path led steadily downward. He was physically depleted beyond recovery, sick, half convinced that the world faced a war of extermination—again an isolationist, comforted only by friends of an unseen world. After resigning he joined them and his two great predecessors on the night of 22 July 1950.

What had he achieved? Not merely a record span of office, in combination of genius, manipulation and luck, but the honest management of a war that made Canada a principal among the victors; the smooth transition to peace, and, in his enduring legacy, a social revolution without violence. A lesser man had matched the work of the humanly greater Macdonald and Laurier.

In the choice of the men around him, King had exercised his most useful talent, or instinct. But he did not choose his successor as generally supposed. When Ernest Lapointe died in 1941 there seemed to be no one else to mend the broken coalition of the two communities that must fight the war together. "Chubby" Power, himself without ambition, suggested Louis Stephen St. Laurent. Who, King asked, was he? French Canada's most distinguished lawyer and finest mind, said Power.

Still dubious, King telephoned an old-fashioned house in Quebec City. St. Laurent took the call and, afterward, told his wife that he would briefly visit Ottawa. Dreading it, she knew what to expect. Next day St. Laurent was appointed minister of justice on the guarantee that he would be released at the end of the war. Politics, at his age of almost sixty, was strange, abhorrent and alien to all his experience. But accident had decided his lifework, though history has yet to judge it fairly.

The father of the son born in Compton, Quebec, in 1882, came of French Canadian peasant stock dating back to 1653. The mother was of Irish descent. Young Louis, working in the family's general store, spoke French to his father, English to his mother, and thought that all boys did the same. His parents hoped he would enter the priesthood. The priests taught him Latin. He preferred the law, graduated from Laval University, joined a legal firm at a salary of fifty dollars a month, loved Jeanne Renault at first sight and married her. By middle age he was Quebec's pre-eminent and wealthy lawyer—a man of ruddy, handsome face, quiet speech and courtly manner. A grand seigneur he looked, and nothing more.

The look did not long deceive the cabinet. St. Laurent had sat with it for only a few days, saying little, before his experienced colleagues realized that a new force had arrived in Ottawa. King was astonished and overjoyed. The essential partner had reached his side. But the new minister found politics as repellent as he had feared. Living in a mean two-room apartment, his wife cooking the meals and keeping her groceries under the bed, he longed for his pleasant Quebec life.

Soon, however, he changed his mind as he managed Newfoundland's entry into Confederation. Politics, after all, was interesting. So was the world which, for the first time, he began to understand, and it fascinated him. With intellectual equipment better than King's, and much more compassion, he was unconsciously making himself the next prime minister. The Liberal Party chose him as its leader against strictly token competitors.

At the end of his first day in office, St. Laurent revealed one of the human qualities that made him a great prime minister. Surprised and indignant to find the elevator attendant waiting for him in the East Block at eight o'clock, as he had always waited for King, St. Laurent told the man not to wait again. A prime minister could walk downstairs. St. Laurent had begun to win not only respect but affection never given to King.

The new leader quickly mastered government and party. He had not yet mastered the nation, the political process or even his own talents. A sudden leap from administration into politics was completed in the election of 1949. Discovering the common people, as they discovered him, St. Laurent became "Uncle Louis" and won the largest majority since Confederation. For some years ahead he was safe in his coalition with C. D. Howe, and later he depended for political advice mainly on Jack Pickersgill, whom he appointed as a cabinet minister from Newfoundland.

The rest followed so smoothly that the public, quite wrongly, took it as the natural course of things—Canada's contribution to the Korean War, the end of appeals to the Privy Council in London, the choice of Vincent Massey as the first native Canadian Governor General, Parliament's power to amend the Constitution in federal business, the St. Lawrence Seaway, expansion of social services and yet surplus budgets with the reduction of war debts. These works, little appreciated at the time, had crowned King's. To be sure, they could not have been done without the Big Boom, St. Laurent's luck and the seeds of his misfortune.

Something much more important than political success had happened to him. At the San Francisco conference of the United Nations he had become an outright internationalist unlike King, the isolationist. As prime minister, St. Laurent persuaded Lester Pearson (who had refused King's invitation) to accept the external affairs portfolio and thereby to launch his unlikely career.

After St. Laurent's second victorious election in 1953, everything seemed to go wrong at once—the tumultuous pipeline debate of 1956;

the prime minister too exhausted in body and mind to lead the government; Howe's clumsy execution of closure; the pipeline scheme approved at the last minute, too late for the planned start of construction; Howe's breach with his leader; the Suez crisis; St. Laurent's "supermen" outburst, misunderstood by friends and exploited by enemies; the Big Boom subsiding; his pathetic campaign of 1957 when he travelled the country almost as a somnambulist; Diefenbaker's minority electoral mandate. Now, at last, St. Laurent was home again in Quebec, defeated but with his honour unquestioned, his work done but yet to be measured.

The work of his successor is more easily measured because it now appears so small, hardly more than a legend remaining. Still, John George Diefenbaker had his usefulness in the cycle of his times. He was a kind of catharsis that the nation required after an unnaturally long Liberal reign.

Almost from his birth into a schoolteacher's poor home at Neustadt, south of Owen Sound, in 1895, the boy intended to be prime minister. Thenceforth his ambition (and his narcissism) did not change.

For the supreme office Diefenbaker had certain solid credentials—a father of German, a mother of Scottish, descent; a strict Baptist upbringing; hard physical work on a Saskatchewan farm where he knew and admired Gabriel Dumont, once the military leader of Riel's rebellion; small-town life in Saskatoon and a chat with the visiting Laurier to whom, as he always boasted, he sold a newspaper in the railway station; then graduation from the University of Saskatchewan in 1916; a lieutenant's commission in the Canadian Army; an accidental injury that forced his return to Canada; a law degree; increasing practice in grubby village courtrooms; successful defence of some three score men charged with murder; a first wife who died young, a second, Olive, who was to play an unassuming though vital part in her husband's triumph.

Since youth into middle age Diefenbaker's mind was on politics. He began his career as a Liberal but ran as a hopeless Conservative in the federal elections of 1925 and 1926. Five defeats in federal, provincial and municipal elections could not discourage him. Already he showed the courage, patience and eloquence that might carry him far. The trombone voice had penetrated the entire West. The glaring eyes were hypnotic. The jowls shook. The platitudes flew like arrows, later to pierce his own heart.

Finally, in 1940, when the Liberal Party swept the nation, he won the parliamentary seat of Lake Centre, no other Conservative daring to run against the tide. Seventeen years in the opposition benches, his defeat by Bracken in 1942 and by George Drew in 1948 for party leadership, had matured and embittered the western prophet not of Conservatism but of hazy populism.

Now he was no longer skeletal in body. The black metallic curls were turning grey. The lean cheeks had fattened. The voice was more strident than ever, the actor's role perfected. Diefenbaker had learned to play Diefenbaker on the national stage.

In December 1956 came the reward for his toil. The Conservative Party's convention elected him as leader, at the age of sixty-one, mainly because it could find no better alternative and little hope of victory. Next year, after a campaign like a prairie fire, he surprised everyone, none more than the government, by defeating it with a popular vote less than St. Laurent's.

Diefenbaker was established as perhaps the greatest campaigner the nation had ever known. But could he long govern with a minority in Parliament when the ego of the hitherto modest man detonated with coast-to-coast reverberation? It seemed improbable until Pearson, the new Liberal leader, plunged into debacle by solemnly proposing that the Conservative government resign in his favour.

Those who witnessed the scene will never forget it—Pearson realizing his folly even as he moved his motion, Diefenbaker gazing, impassive, at the galleries, then rising to inflame or silence his howling followers and leave the opposition in shreds.

The Liberal disaster was worse than it looked at first sight. Diefenbaker came back from the snap election of 1958 with the largest majority since Confederation. He had won 208 seats to Pearson's 49. Best of all, he had broken the old Liberal hold on Quebec. Surely he was set for many years of office? Instead, he squandered his power with astonishing speed.

His impossible promise to divert much of Canada's trade from the United States to Britain; his still more impossible promise of increased spending, reduced taxes and balanced budgets which he drove into deficit; his almost single-handed expulsion of South Africa from the Commonwealth; his blustering, vain attempt to keep Britain out of the European Common Market—these fumbles were perhaps to be expected in a man of such vigour and self-focus.

He rose at 5:30 A.M., drank a glass of milk in the kitchen of the Sussex Drive mansion, reached the East Block by eight, lunched from a tray and worked until midnight. Dief, "The Chief," bestrode his party like a Colossus, or a Bennett.

Against all that, his treatment of James Coyne, the central bank's young governor, who had brashly challenged the government's economic policies, was unforgivable and proved irrecoverable. The public could understand a purely human drama even if it misunderstood the devaluation of the "Diefendollar," as the opposition gleefully called it (not foreseeing a Liberal dollar much less valuable).

The 1962 election campaign opened in the midst of a foreign exchange crisis that Diefenbaker blandly denied. Worse, Quebec already had repented its 1958 vote and reverted to its ancient Liberal preference. The government won only 116 seats to the opposition's 99. Diefenbaker had lost 92 seats within four years, more than any predecessor. And the nation, which he had pretended to govern so well, was begging loans from the International Monetary Fund, Britain and the United States.

Nevertheless, the prime minister, directed, like King, by providence, might survive, given a little bit of luck, despite his jealousy of colleagues and his deepening paranoid suspicion of everybody. But luck turned away from him.

He had installed American BOMARC missiles in northern Ontario and awaited their nuclear warheads. He had quarrelled with John F. Kennedy by seizing his forgotten private memorandum, after a meeting in the Ottawa cabinet chamber, and threatened to use it in an election as proof of the president's evil designs on Canada. Kennedy's counterthreats forced him to retreat. He did not publish the memorandum. Then, uninvited, he appeared at the Nassau conference between the president and Prime Minister Harold Macmillan where, Kennedy said afterward, "We sat like three whores at a christening."

Diefenbaker's irrecoverable blunder followed immediately. Returning to Ottawa, he told Parliament that all NATO planning was to be revised and Canada should postpone the installation of nuclear warheads. This was too much for the American government. While Kennedy slept, officials of the State Department issued a brutal message declaring that Canada had failed "to contribute effectively to North American defence."

Pearson agreed with the Washington message. So did Douglas Harkness, minister of defence, who promptly resigned. The cabinet disintegrated. On the night of 5 February 1963 Parliament voted, for the second time since Confederation, nonconfidence in the government, 142 votes to 111.

Even now Diefenbaker was not finished. In the following election he reached the climax of his oratory, his courage and his malice as he denounced Kennedy's manifest designs against Canada. It was no use. Diefenbaker's inevitable fate struck him down on 18 April. He won 95 seats against Pearson's 129, just short of a majority.

Was this the end of the prairie wizard? Not quite. He led the opposition with skill, lightning flashes and self-destroying rancour until his party excised its old hero in a blood bath, replacing him with Robert Stanfield, a much finer man but a less fortunate politician. And if the public had walked past a modest house on a midnight street in Rockcliffe it would have seen Diefenbaker, clad only in undershorts, his hand clutching a bowl of cereal, as he delivered a speech to an audience of one, his faithful wife.

After his state funeral at Ottawa and his burial at Saskatoon—the most costly and ostentatious on record—the nation could judge his work. What, in all his fury, had he achieved?

A little more, perhaps, than we yet appreciate. He had given us our first Bill of Rights as a changeable statute only, but the foundation of the modern Charter. Whatever his insincerity elsewhere, he had defended the poor, the downtrodden and the ethnic minorities with passionate sincerity. He had detached the Liberal Party from the West (but not from Quebec) for many years to come. He had made his budgets of minor deficit seem models of thrift compared to Trudeau's. He had left behind him the durable legend of a great man struggling with the Big Interests and the gods. That may have been enough to ask of the flaming prophet.

The man who succeeded him in April 1963 was, next to his own successor, the least understood of our national leaders. Lester Bowles Pearson did not look like a prime minister. He did not even look like his real self. The beefy figure, the round pink face and boy's grin, the trademark bow tie and rumpled clothes, the colloquial diction, high-pitched voice, faint lisp and corny jokes concealed a nature that deceived not only his innumerable acquaintances but his closest friends.

Indeed, they concealed such an inner toughness that one of his intimate colleagues and a veteran politician says he was far more tyrannical in government than King or St. Laurent had ever been. He was also more lonely.

Unlike most of his predecessors, he had not planned a career in politics. He had shunned it for the first five decades of his life. Born in Newtonbrook, a village near Toronto, in 1897, he was the son of a hard-up Methodist minister and an equally religious mother. They moved from one town to another, always supporting the Conservative Party.

Without any indication of scholarship, or any career in mind, Lester attended the University of Toronto. There he distinguished himself only in athletics and seemed to lack interest in anything else until the spring of 1915, when he enlisted in a military hospital unit for service overseas.

Bored by hospital work in England, Egypt and Greece, he wangled an infantry lieutenant's commission, volunteered for the Royal Flying Corps, survived his plane's crash, was run over by a London bus and invalided back to Canada.

All he had gained in war, he used to say, was the temporary *nom de guerre* of "Mike" because his commanding officer thought his given name of Lester was too effeminate for a soldier. In fact, he had brought home much more than a nickname. The remembered scenes of bloodshed, death and war's sheer lunacy tormented him, with increasing horror, to his last days.

His young manhood was pleasant enough—brief employment in a Chicago sausage factory; two years' study at Oxford, again distinguished only by athletics as star of the university's Olympic hockey team; appointment as a lecturer at the University of Toronto with a salary of eighteen hundred dollars a year; marriage to Maryon Moody, one of his students from Winnipeg; the casual writing of an external affairs entrance examination; a telegram of acceptance (read to him by a janitor because his eyes were blurred by an occulist's drugs). That telegram changed the whole course of Pearson's life and, later, Canada's.

In Ottawa, in prewar London, in the second war blitz, in the Washington embassy, in every job he tackled, nothing seemed to succeed like his success. By middle age he was the most famous Canadian in the world, the glamour boy of diplomacy, the universal joint of

King's government and a gambler in great affairs more reckless than his chief.

Sometimes the gambles were ill-timed. As St. Laurent's foreign minister, he told an American audience that relations between Canada and the United States thenceforth could never be "easy or automatic." By unlucky chance this sensible warning was delivered on the day of Gen. Douglas MacArthur's dismissal by President Truman. In their troubled mood, the American people wondered if their best foreign friend had deserted them. Was the jolly playboy of Ottawa some kind of radical (as he certainly was) or perhaps a secret Communist (as he was not)?

Drinking nineteen toasts with Nikita Khrushchev in a Crimean palace, and somehow emerging vertical from "conviviality beyond the line of duty," Pearson convinced the Russian dictator that he was a very tough guy despite his soft appearance.

He had to be tough when, lacking any definite instructions from the cabinet, he devised a settlement of the Suez crisis, rescued Britain from a ruinous adventure and won the Nobel Peace Prize, the first capital he had ever owned. But already the Canadian government was ruined by the pipeline debacle and St. Laurent's "supermen" speech that had staggered Pearson.

Inevitably, he was chosen leader of the Liberal Party, with token competition, in early 1958. Then, exhausted and punch-drunk after two sleepless nights, he lurched into his preposterous motion demanding the new Conservative government's resignation. That motion, devised by Jack Pickersgill in a momentary lapse of wisdom, ensured Diefenbaker's record victory. Pearson was left with only a corporal's guard in Parliament, the Liberal Party now little more than a Quebec rump. Had Pearson completed the Party's destruction before he had started to lead it? So it appeared. But Pearson never complained to Pickersgill and found it hard to dislike anyone, even Diefenbaker. Besides, as always, appearances were misleading.

With only Pickersgill, Paul Martin and Lionel Chevrier—the "Three Musketeers"—and, of course, Diefenbaker, to help him, Pearson drove the government towards shipwreck within four years. Yet the legend that he was no politician still persists to this day. Actually, his loss of the 1962 election by a handful of seats was a wonderwork of politics. The following year witnessed the most reckless gamble of Pearson's life.

Alone all night in a Toronto hotel room, he wrote and rewrote the historic Scarborough speech and reversed his long opposition to nuclear weapons because he had discovered, very late, that the government of Canada had contracted with the United States to install them. The reversal split the government and defeated it in the parliamentary vote of early 1963.

The result of the following election was by no means ensured at the start. Diefenbaker, in a campaign of manic frenzy such as the nation had never seen before, staked everything on his anti-Americanism.

Sick with an undiagnosed infection, full of antibiotics, hardly able to stand, Pearson was appalled by a mysterious telephone call from the White House offering him Kennedy's assistance. If the offer became public it would certainly defeat Pearson by confirming Diefenbaker's charges. Happily there was no leak. But, prostrate in bed at Victoria's Empress Hotel, Pearson told me that he was probably defeated anyhow.

Then came luck, the politician's only sure rescue. At Vancouver the following day Pearson was greeted by a clamorous antinuclear audience, howled down as he stood, silent, unshaken, his wife beside him, their hands joined. The next day's newspapers carried from coast to coast a front-page picture of courage.

That tore it. Pearson won the election, just four seats short of a majority, and became prime minister to begin a Liberal rule to last, with one short interruption, for more than two decades. His first successful act was to end the quarrel with Kennedy in a personal meeting at Hyannis Port. His first mistake was to allow Walter Gordon, his finance minister and intimate friend, to bring down an unworkable whiz kid's budget and withdraw it under fire.

Pearson committed more blunders, like the Seaway wage settlement, as recommended by a misguided arbitrator, that heated up inflation; the establishment of civil service unions' right to strike against the state, a policy that split the cabinet; the muddled unification of the armed services to satisfy the erratic defence minister, Paul Hellyer.

Against the blunders some major successes should be counted. First, the Canada Pension Plan enabled workers to save something for their old age.

Second, the Royal Commission on Bilingualism and Biculturalism, Pearson's own idea, convinced Parliament that Quebec, its grievances unrelieved, must split the nation and, as Pearson believed, drive its fragments into the United States. Thus he had laid the basis of Trudeau's career.

Third, without consulting his cabinet, he announced that Canada needed its own distinctive red maple leaf flag and stubbornly fought for it through Parliament, month after month, despite Conservative fury.

Fourth, he greatly increased social services, not yet realizing that they would soon exceed the nation's means, or its willingness, to pay for them. Quietly, insistently, he was edging his party to the Left, to true liberalism as he conceived it.

Fifth, and most important, he understood and conciliated Quebec better than any previous anglophone leader of modern times. King had understood it in electoral terms only, St. Laurent in constitutional terms mainly. Pearson understood it in human terms because he was himself all too human.

Quite wrongly, his flag, the Pearson Pennant, may be his best-remembered achievement when the others are forgotten, above all the beginning of Quebec's re-entry into Confederation as an equal partner.

Meanwhile the supposedly indolent prime minister, so relaxed in public, so jocular with calculated indiscretions at his press conferences, was the hardest-working man in Ottawa. The public could not see him at night in pyjamas and slippers, documents spread on the floor, as he tried to grasp the galloping complexities of government, the unknowable revolution of society throughout the world. For all the waffling and contradiction, his elastic stretched thin but never broke.

Even in a time of deepening trouble everywhere, he enjoyed some light moments. When, for instance, he was in London and called at Number 10 Downing Street, the failing Churchill did not recognize an old friend. At lunch the British prime minister's memory returned. He asked Pearson, as a personal favour, to order the singing of "Rule Britannia" in the Canadian Navy. Pearson agreed but only if the sailors also sang "Alouette." Churchill grunted, unamused. The subject was dropped.

By now, Pearson judged that civilization's chances of surviving the nuclear threat were no better than fifty-fifty. He viewed the war in Southeast Asia as the possible beginning of the end. In this belief he undertook his last big gamble, having previously advised Kennedy to "get out of Vietnam." Again without consulting the cabinet, he went to the United States and, in a deliberately provocative speech, urged President Johnson's government to cease the bombing of North Vietnam while a peace settlement was explored.

Such public manners by a foreign guest and friend were, of course, inexcusable. An outraged Johnson told his officials that the prime minister "has come and pissed on my floor." As Pearson doubtless expected, he was received at Camp David in sullen silence. But after lunch the president's outburst of anger came close to physical violence while the guest stood still and made no reply. American and Canadian officials fled from the scene in horror to walk in the woods.

On his return to Ottawa, I asked Pearson why he had made the Vietnam speech with no warning to his cabinet. Because, he said, the cabinet would have tried to prevent him making it and leaked his plans. There was no reason for regret. The grinning extrovert had become the solitary decision maker.

In 1965 Walter Gordon induced him to seek a majority mandate after less than three years of office. He came back from a premature election with another minority. Gordon, his advice proved wrong, honourably resigned.

For Pearson the great days were passing, but he saw one final task that must be done before he departed. Having failed, so far, to discover a worthy French Canadian lieutenant, he had persuaded Trudeau, Jean Marchand and Gérard Pelletier to enter Parliament as the "three wise men" of Quebec, and then the cabinet.

In Trudeau, who did not yet suspect his destiny, the man of the future had arrived. But for party leadership he was not the first choice of the prime minister, whose judgement of men often faltered. His erring choice (as he told me later) was Marchand, who wisely refused the leadership as exceeding his abilities and knowledge of the English language.

Although Pearson had held office for only five years, by the spring of 1968 he had changed the future of Canada internally and externally, prepared Quebec for the defeat of separatism, established the welfare state beyond any possibility of repeal and, by his diplomacy, made his nation envied throughout the world. A bounteous estate— its economic liabilities still not reckoned—was left to the great internationalist's equally unreckoned heir.

After his retirement and latest travels in Asia, Pearson reached Vancouver thoroughly dissatisfied with his successor, not because

Trudeau had failed to consult him on anything but because he seemed to know nothing of the world and might even be reverting, like King, to a youthful isolationism. What most infuriated Pearson was Trudeau's recent outrageous speech (the work of an erring ghostwriter) suggesting that his predecessor had been too much influenced by the military establishment.

"Me!" Pearson fairly shouted in his Vancouver hotel room where we were alone. "Me of all men! But I'll have it out with him."

He never did. Weeks later, Trudeau knocked on Pearson's door in Ottawa near midnight, looking so exhausted that Pearson could not bear to aggravate his troubles. So passed an incident without public record. Probably Trudeau did not guess how deeply he had wounded his former friend. And now Pearson was dying.

Shortly before his death I talked to him in his Rockcliffe home, both of us aware that we would not meet again. He looked as healthy, pink and cherubic as ever while we gossiped lightly about current affairs. He told me that Trudeau had recently consulted him on the problems of the minority Liberal government resulting from the bungled 1972 election, and Pearson replied only that the prime minister must not, under any circumstances, embarrass the Governor General as King had done in 1926. Of our long friendship and Pearson's approaching end, no word was spoken between us. But I could see that a simple faith, never expressed, had always sustained his life and sustained him still.

The Trudeau years are too green in the nation's collective memory to need much comment here. And yet none in our history were less understood.

Of this extraordinary man numerous books have been written already. More will follow to clarify or confound the truth. We may be sure, at least, that no contemporary book is likely to penetrate far past the surface of such a mysterious personage.

As the old English rhyme puts it, "Ne'er of the living can the living judge, too blind the affection or too fresh the grudge." Trudeau won the affection of his idolators and the grudge of his enemies in more abundance than any predecessor, except perhaps Macdonald, had ever received. One doubts that even history in the long aftertime will make a fair judgement.

For what they are worth, my occasional talks with Trudeau convinced me that he was more ambivalent than the six other prime ministers of my acquaintance. He could be charming or brutal, sensitive or indifferent, polite or vulgar. But he dominated any gathering. The weather of his handsome-ugly face changed from sunshine to storm as fast as a day in April. He was resolved, as he had written in a youthful book, to defy other people's opinions, to swim against the public tide wherever it flowed; he rarely lost an argument and in matters important or trivial he was always a bad loser.

None of these qualities were apparent to me when I first met him, in 1959, on the veranda of his mother's old-fashioned Montreal house. The man who opened the front door was dressed in sweat shirt, uncreased slacks and sandals. He clutched a bottle of whiskey in his hand. "Have a drink?" were his words of greeting.

We did so, and he talked with rash candour. That he might become prime minister was unimaginable to me or him. Neither of us was very perceptive at our first meeting. My only impression was that the young professor of law had about the toughest mind I had yet encountered and used the toughest language.

Towards the end, while understanding humanity in the abstract, the finest mind in politics never understood individual human beings, not even his colleagues, and they, of course, never remotely understood him. Some of them, notably John Turner, always disliked him. So, in general, did the West, blaming him for all the nation's trouble. Certainly Trudeau deserved much blame. He mismanaged Canada's economy to the point of ruinous budgetary deficits, close to the point of catastrophe, because his interests were focussed on constitutional or larger, worldwide concerns. He broke the historical political coalition between the two cultural communities when he allowed his leading anglophone ministers, including Turner, to depart, unwanted. He recruited little new talent of quality.

Unlike his successful predecessors, he neglected his party, treating it as a vehicle of his own authority with occasional gestures of mild interest. It ceased to be truly national and it bored him. Although himself scrupulously honest, he used patronage blatantly to reward his favourites and thus gave his enemies a handy weapon of moral outrage before they repeated his methods. Between leader and nation understanding was never possible. He was given only blind admiration or its opposite.

These liabilities were balanced, or outweighed, by Trudeau's achievements. The homemade Constitution; the Charter of Rights and Freedoms; the entrenchment of the French Fact; the defeat of Lévesque's party and its design for national suicide; the return, with unconscious irony, to Pearson's internationalism, and finally the peace mission that no successor could afford to abandon—all combined to place a creature *sui generis* on history's record beside the Canadian giants long after affection and grudge have faded. No successor can afford to neglect the lessons that he taught—or the fallacies that he abandoned.

He taught the nation and himself that, contrary to his youthful dream-book, a leader must frequently abandon his "opposition to accepted opinions"; that consistency, or even candour, are seldom the hobgoblins of great minds; that a leader's neglect of his party cannot be repaired by a last-minute deluge of patronage appointments tarnishing his record; that the people will recognize real achievements like the new Constitution while resenting the abuse of power, and that brilliance of mind, which Trudeau certainly had, can be flawed by the use of dirty tricks.

Against him, what chance had Joseph Clark? To all appearances, none. But the bodily awkward politician from High River, Alberta, with no trade except politics, narrowly won the Conservative Party's leadership at a distrustful convention and slowly proved himself a better man than the "wimp" described by the giggling newspaper columnists. Their leering lampoons of his tall, loosely knit figure, his receding chin and the loss of his baggage on an Asian tour (as if he were responsible for it) did not stop his steady climb despite an addiction to formal, ponderous language.

In 1979 he unhorsed the smug Liberal regime, and this in itself was a feat so remarkable and unexpected that Trudeau decided to retire. He changed his mind at the last moment, undercut the ambitions of Donald Macdonald and clung to the party's leadership.

In the meantime Clark formed a minority government, groped for new policies and delayed them too long. When his finance minister, John Crosbie, finally introduced a sound budget of necessary tax increases, the opposition denounced them, defeated the government in a snap parliamentary vote and won the resulting election of 1980. Back in office with a majority, the resurrected Trudeau government imposed taxes higher in the end than those it had rejected.

The continuing and deepening financial crisis showed how right Clark had been in refusing to surrender his budget, though he knew in advance, contrary to accepted gossip, that Parliament might vote against it. Having lost the election and now demanding stronger support among his gloomy followers, he called another leadership convention and lost again, this time to Mulroney, whose methods were decidedly rough. A party given to frequent regicide had turfed Clark out like many previous leaders. But he survived to become minister of external affairs. In Conservative politics he was not expendable.

Clark has his own modest, respectable place in history, above all his place as the only bilingual Conservative prime minister up to his time who understood Quebec. His lesson to successors is that a leader must not exaggerate the scruples or misread the tactics of his enemies, the temper of his colleagues and the volatile mood of the voters.

In 1984 the Liberal Party chose a leader who could not have been more different from Clark or Trudeau. Since his university days, John Turner had wanted and hoped to lead a government. For this ambition he seemed to have promising credentials—poverty in childhood after his father's death, education at Oxford, skill in athletics, a law degree, bilingual speech acquired in Montreal, political savvy, handsome looks, piercing, frigid eyes and masculine charm.

Although a Liberal convention rejected his first bid for leadership in favour of Trudeau, all went swimmingly with Turner until his career in government was assailed by sudden doubts towards the end of 1974. As minister of finance and second man in the cabinet, he had tried to curb its extravagant spending, borrowing and ever-increasing debt, but he failed. If he had resigned on a clear issue of policy, as urged by some of his intimates, he might expect a future call to leadership when his stand was vindicated and the party needed him. That call was delayed by nine years. Then it came too late for electoral victory.

In the meantime, at the critical point of 1974, he yielded, despite his misgivings, to the advice of friends, the pressure of colleagues and his own ambition and introduced, the next year, a budget that did not significantly alter the government's financial course. Finally, tiring of a hopeless struggle, he asked Trudeau for a change of portfolios. A brief meeting between the two men altered the course of both and the politics of Liberalism.

Trudeau, in a moment of folly and arrogance, offered his chief lieutenant a judgeship or a senatorship. Angered by this contemptuous insult, Turner walked out of the prime minister's office and wrote his own resignation. It could not disturb Trudeau who was riding high and regarded Turner, like all his lieutenants, as expendable. While Turner said nothing in public, the bicultural coalition was ruptured and Trudeau saw no need to repair it. That was his mistake, its cost postponed for almost a decade.

When Turner left politics to practise law in Toronto, he had little money and a large family to support. His rise was again rapid. As a wealthy lawyer and director of many big corporations, he was soon a board room insider, a faithful Catholic regularly attending Mass, an affectionate husband and father, an outdoor man daring perilous northern rivers on summer canoe trips with his family.

Success had not changed the goal of his youth, only blurred it for the time being. In the conscious half of his mind he intended to remain out of public life for good. In the unconscious half he was eager for the highest office if the breaks of the game offered him the chance. That chance came in the spring of 1984. Trudeau, keeping the government and the nation on tenterhooks while he continued his peace initiative, seemed likely to retire without any designated successor. But Turner was available and far more popular than his chief.

Since Laurier's time the Liberal Party had alternated its leadership between an anglophone and a francophone and this old custom was a barrier to the hopes of the ultraloyal Jean Chrétien who had stood with Trudeau in many portfolios through good days and bad. Even when Trudeau did not bother to consult Minister of Finance Chrétien before announcing his own policy of budgetary restraint (which he soon abandoned), Chrétien accepted this outrageous treatment in silence. His fine character and simple humanity were admired everywhere, but loyalty received scant gratitude from his leader.

While Turner knew he probably could win the leadership of the party, his intimates warned him that neither he nor any man could re-elect it. The opinion polls showed beyond doubt that the nation wanted a change of government and would be satisfied with nothing less. All right, said Turner, he was prepared to lead the opposition and await a friendlier climate. He did not underestimate the odds against him. He did underestimate Chrétien and overestimated his own appeal to the voters.

All Canadians remember the dénouement of this drama. The party assembled in convention. The minor candidates were eliminated by a series of votes. On the last of them, Turner beat Chrétien by a surprisingly close margin. Their personal disagreement had long preceded the final clash but, at first deeply wounded, Chrétien later accepted defeat, remained in politics and threw his powerful influence behind the new leader who certainly needed it.

Not yet prime minister, Turner was asked by Trudeau to guarantee that he would appoint various party stalwarts to the Senate, the courts and foreign embassies. Otherwise Trudeau would appoint them before he resigned. The ultimatum was crude and irresponsible, Trudeau at his worst. Although its full results were not anticipated, it was enough to wreck the party.

Because many of Trudeau's chosen beneficiaries were members of the Commons, Turner feared he would lack a working majority if he delayed the election until autumn or winter. The ultimatum could not be resisted, or so Turner believed in a mistake soon to prove disastrous. He guaranteed the appointments and took office. But his government, already damaged by the Liberal record, could not survive the patronage scandal.

Even if Turner had wisely refused to make the appointments, he could not beat Mulroney's newly reorganized Conservative Party. Refusing to make them, he could hope to lead a respectable opposition.

Encouraged by temporarily favourable opinion polls, he plunged into a September election, a Commons majority unneeded after all. The unprepared Liberal machine was rusty and collapsed. There was no time for repairs. Turner was also rusty, too long absent from politics, a game drastically changed since his earlier days in government. On television, now the decisive lever of political campaigns, he looked uncomfortable, tense and unsure of himself, not the confident, charismatic figure of public memory.

In a harrowing test of courage, he doggedly struggled on, all hope of victory lost, to emerge with a seat for himself in Vancouver and thirty-nine parliamentary followers—an outcome even worse than Pearson's debacle of 1958.

The original creator of the Liberal defeat in 1984 was not Turner with all his mistakes. It was Trudeau whose economic mismanagement had doomed any heir. But Turner must share the blame and accept more than his share. Wounded to the quick, he maintained a confident public look and grimly began the revival of his shattered party, knowing that it could go the way of its Liberal parent in Britain, crushed between the political Right and Left.

A chastened, sadder and wiser man handed government to Mulroney, a former personal friend. At last Turner found time to examine his whole political philosophy, to synthesize and articulate what he had always called his thrifty financial conservatism and generous social liberalism. At this writing the synthesis had yet to appear. The party still searches for a workable overall policy not without some help from its successor whose budgetary stumbles and retreats gave the opposition a wonderful, undeserved break of luck. The Liberal Party was not dying after all, as the opinion polls plainly showed.

Defeat was a good thing for the Liberal Party. It had overstayed its natural span of power, become ever more arrogant, reckless and depleted of ideas. It needed some years in the chilly, cleansing air of opposition to rethink its purpose before it could become a truly national party again.

Brian Mulroney's career is so well known that it needs no lengthy recapitulation here, but it raises questions that probably he himself could not answer. Is he at heart a conservative or a liberal? The truth, of course, is that he is both. His motives, like most men's, are too complex and contradictory for simple definition. They will evolve and clarify when he does in office what he has to do, not what he hoped and planned. All prime ministers go through the same evolution, growing or shrinking under the pressure of the days and years.

The son of a poor Quebec electrician of Irish descent, Mulroney began work as a truck driver and a mechanic in a paper mill. There he learned to understand working people. Later he studied law and soon afterward became a man of Big Business, director of various companies and of a major bank. In 1976, full of premature ambition, he made a brash stab at the Conservative Party leadership, and his failure seemed likely to blight his political future. But lucky to have time for seasoned thought—and still luckier in his Liberal opponents—he captured the leadership from Clark, then he went on to electoral victory and problems even worse than he had expected.

The Mulroney era opened with high and unrealistic expectations, for the new government had made unnecessary promises that no government could deliver—economic recovery, massive private investment, "jobs, jobs, jobs," no general tax increase and yet, miraculously, the reduction of an inherited budgetary deficit, now intolerable.

If he regretted the promises, as he surely must, Mulroney knew that the public did not believe them anyway in the heat of a campaign. He appeared unruffled and innocent as he rewarded his friends with enough cushy jobs to equal or surpass Trudeau's patronage which he had attacked with moral wrath. He defended his wholesale appointments by comparing them to the Liberal record as if two wrongs could make a right.

Whatever the public thought about him, Mulroney immediately gave political Ottawa a new style. His smiling good looks, happy domestic life, purring silk-smooth voice articulate in English or French, quick retorts friendly or acidulous as occasion required, homely jokes, a knack of compromise and conciliation learned in his legal and business career, a full understanding of his native Quebec— these assets are formidable. Canada had found a born politician and natural queen bee.

But counterbalancing the assets, and the luck of a depleted opposition, he bore some onerous liabilities. His first act was to appoint the largest cabinet and Prime Minister's Office on record, after condemning the inordinate size of Trudeau's establishment. If the public did not understand this *volte-face*, Mulroney knew what he was doing. He surrounded himself with a bodyguard of trusted political operators for protection against bureaucracy suspected of Liberalism.

From the start he demonstrated his control of the government. Like all successful prime ministers, he will be the boss. And in Ottawa there is never any shortage of royal jelly.

So far, so good. But what long-run system of ideas and philosophy lies behind such a captivating exterior? It is still too early to guess. The nation will not know its leader for several years at least. By then he, and it, will be changed by unpredictable events and mere accidents.

Meanwhile a key question remains: Does Mulroney have the essential inner stuff for the hard days and the long voyage ahead? Where will the unchallenged captain on the bridge find safe anchorage? Is he steering by a reliable chart or by the Gallup Poll?

Of greater moment than the government's first budget are its relations with the United States. They alarm many citizens even if nothing could be worse than a powerful, unfriendly neighbour. Some loyal Conservatives and perhaps some of Mulroney's cabinet worry about his "continentalism," his subserviance to President Reagan. Deploring it, the Liberal opposition tries to make itself the accepted champion of the nation's sovereignty. As Turner explains, Canada should be open for business but not for sale. Mulroney replies that he is hardening sovereignty by "enhancing" foreign trade and increasing Canadian defence forces at home and abroad.

The NDP, hoping to replace Liberalism as the alternative government, is thoroughly protectionist and logically so. A party determined to plan the national economy, if it ever reaches office, could not allow the competitive foreign imports to disrupt its plan.

The history and adventures of individual men who won and lost the supreme office should have taught many lessons of future value to the nation. If they are forgotten, they must be learned all over again, democratic government being for the most part a learning process without end. And now it is deeply infused by an element of unofficial power yet to be measured.

17

WORDS, WORDS, WORDS

The art of communication, as it is pretentiously called nowadays, had a strange beginning in Canada and it is still evolving—or exploding.

When two ragged, starving American expeditions marched on Quebec in the autumn of 1775, they hoped that Canadians would join their revolution against Britain. A man greater than the commanding generals had installed in the Chateau de Ramazay, Montreal, the first printing press ever brought to New France. It was a crude hand press but, as Benjamin Franklin thought, better than none. Until now the French regime had excluded all printing machinery lest it corrupt the minds of the King's loyal overseas subjects.

That, precisely, was what Franklin planned to do. He would indoctrinate the Canadians with the ideal of liberty and persuade them to fight for it beside their neighbours in the rebellious thirteen colonies. Before such a word came into common use, he was a master of propaganda and many other crafts.

For once the skilled printer, author, statesman, inventor and philosopher failed in his mission. The American armies attacked Quebec and were driven off by Guy Carleton and his little garrison of English sailors and French Canadian militia in a New Year's Eve blizzard. Thenceforth Britain held Canada, its geography and wealth yet unknown. But if Franklin's efforts had proved a failure in Quebec, he had launched a process which, long after his time, must transform the future of the Canadian society, as well as his own, beyond the scope of his powerful imagination.

Thomas Jefferson believed that a free press was the spark of a revolution not limited to the newly born American Republic. If it came to a choice, the pre-eminent democratic sage would prefer newspapers without government to government without newspapers. He exaggerated, of course, because there could be no such choice. In a free society government and newspapers must live together, inseparable. Neither can exist without the other.

While Franklin and Jefferson were meditating revolt in America, a contemporary giant, Dr. Johnson, regarded this enterprise as nothing more than "abortions of folly." But the Great Bear understood the press and was then inventing and publishing, for small wages, the orations of a London Parliament to which unofficial reporters were not admitted. Already he had made the reputations of some pretty mediocre statesmen.

Edmund Burke, one of his friends in The Club, had said that Parliament consisted of three estates. Wrong, said Carlyle in the next century: "There sat a Fourth Estate [the press], more important far than they all. It is not a figure of speech or witty saying; it is a literal fact—very momentous to us in these times." And, it may be added, still more momentous, for good or ill, in our times.

Momentous, clearly, when we now gasp, writhe and drown in communications, in numberless trillions of words through every hour of the day, immune to them only in sleep. Let the present readers who, perhaps, never look at a newspaper, listen to radio or watch television pause here. What follows can be of no interest to them.

For other people a momentous question arises: What is being communicated by a system that girdles the world entire with results still unforeseeable but profound? How many momentous ideas have been communicated since humankind articulated words long before it invented writing and then printing? Very few.

With our wonderful communicating apparatus we have discovered no truly new idea for centuries, merely repeated variations on themes as old as civilization, or older. Two ideas only—the existence of a purposeful universe and the opposite—have dominated all thought in philosophies, religions and antireligions too numerous to be counted. For such mystical ideas contemporary journalism has little time, or none. The name of the craft is well derived from the French word *jour*, since most journalism lasts for a single day. Today's newspaper is generally useful tomorrow only for lighting a fire or wrapping a wet fish. As the late Cyril Connolly, a leading British journalist, sadly admitted, his work "by its very todayness is excluded from any share in tomorrow."

But there are exceptions. Real literature, though temporarily ignored, may be written in the newspaper for future disinterment. Certainly historians will find the paper an essential source of information because it records, as nothing else does, the common round of society.

In earlier times the paper enjoyed a longer life than its current successors can expect. The pioneers of Canada depended on it, starved for alternative reading material. A copy of weeklies like William Lyon Mackenzie's *Colonial Advocate* in Upper Canada, Joe Howe's *Acadian* in Halifax, Amor de Cosmos's *British Colonist* in Victoria, George Brown's *Globe* in Toronto would be passed from hand to hand, every word read and pondered.

By the end of the nineteenth century the Canadian institution founded by Franklin had travelled far to produce the daily paper, usually the organ and kept woman of a political party. The views of the party were faithfully advocated, its heroes celebrated, its enemies denounced, the laws of libel disregarded. The paper became more influential than any we know today. In those times people believed what they read unless, of course, it was printed by a partisan enemy. Whoever prints it, a majority of readers now doubt what they read. That fact, too, is momentous in our politics and society.

When I entered my trade in the spring of 1918 as the ostensible and unfit sports editor of the Victoria *Times* (only because most of its trained newspapermen were fighting in Europe) nobody used the word *journalism*. To us anybody calling himself a journalist was likely to be tattered, unwashed, drunk and thirsty. He invariably sought a loan of five dollars, a large sum when the distinguished editor, Benjamin Charles Nicholas, received a wage of fifty dollars a week. Mine was twelve dollars.

Still, a certain glamour clung to the trade and our dingy cluttered workroom. The myth of newspapering—a reporter in shirt sleeves and vest, a compulsory fedora on his head as he pecked out the big scoop on his typewriter, the frantic scramble at deadline and then the thunder of the press—remained a mighty myth. It was celebrated on the stage and in flickering movies, almost as glamorous and spurious as the western myth of cowboys and Indians. To me, and even to old-timers, the myth was true. And it helped to compensate us for our poverty; also for our ignorance.

Before the myth died the newspaperman must know a little about everything and nothing much about anything in particular. He had yet to call himself a generalist (another word then unknown). His educated successors are making themselves specialists in some fields and often know more than the experts, assuredly more than the typical cabinet minister knows about his department. All this knowledge does not necessarily make a good journalist. Something else is required, as no doubt it is required, in every trade. In mine only an insatiable curiosity about things important or unimportant will serve.

For reasons obscure, the public, while skeptical of the press, never seems to lose interest in its workers as if their work held some mystery. It does not. Or at least no more mystery than all trades do. Their skills come only from experience, mainly from mistakes. The greatest newspapermen and women will be lucky indeed if they are right half the time. After more than sixty-seven years of it, I would rate my batting average at .300. (Readers might ask themselves if they have done better in their unreported lives.)

As in all trades, the craftsmen must learn many tricks. To begin with, they must learn to listen, and that is not easy. In your next private talk among friends you will find that they often fail to catch your meaning and repeat, as their own, what you have already told them.

The journalist, interviewing some celebrity, cannot afford such lapses. The real substance of the conversation flashes by in a second or two, the person interviewed unaware that he has said anything newsworthy. The trick is twofold—to ask the provocative questions and to remember, usually without notes, the few replies that count. Then you have your story.

Nothing said specifically off the record must be printed, no confidence ever broken. The journalist who breaks confidences will soon get none from politicians or his fellows. Much better to lose a scoop than to lose your reputation and prime asset. It can seldom be recovered. Not many journalists cross that line. Those who do are contemptible. The majority guards a store of secrets which, publishable long hence, when the confidants have departed, will often amend our prevailing view of the nation's history.

It would be absurd, however, to suppose that journalists are free of prejudice and absolutely fair in their commentaries, since they remain human beings even if they sometimes appear to be of another species. Inevitably, personal friendships and enmities affect their trade as in others, despite every honest precaution.

But our trade is different from the others because its product, unlike those of most industries, can be remodelled, improved or debased each day and because talented workers need not await promotion until they fill a retired veteran's shoes. Talent rises very fast, regardless of its possessor's age, sex or background. The success of women has been especially marked in recent times because the average female intelligence (as I privately suspect) is superior to the male's.

The apprentice of either sex learns new tricks, fads and fashions all the time. At present, for instance, "investigative" reporting is the general ambition of the young who fancy themselves as the investigators of some hidden Canadian Watergate, fed by a native Deep Throat. This is perilous ground sown with booby traps and libel suits. Only experienced professionals should be allowed to tread it.

A second ambition is to become a syndicated columnist, since reputable columnists are highly paid, famous and powerful. Here again experience is required and promotion should not be too rapid lest the youths of talent let success go to their heads.

It often does when columnists of the new breed are becoming as influential as the old-time editors. They inform, amuse or mislead the reader with cogent political diagnosis, moral indignation (easiest of all tricks), humour (the most difficult) and, in some cases, brazen effrontery.

A more practical and essential ambition is to learn the modern writing style of simplicity, brevity, vividness and punch that fortunately has replaced the old-fashioned, wordy news "lead." But in straining for effect the apprentice is tempted to bury the facts in extravagant metaphors and cute images, thus irritating the reader and driving the busy desk man crazy when, like a general in war, he is at the mercy of his subordinates' blunders. Tricks, in short, are the mere beginning of craftsmanship.

Even the veteran never knows what story will catch the public's fancy. It is easy to write some ponderous comment on politics or an editorial on the approaching destruction of the world. In my time I must have written thousands of them. The "light" piece, the whimsy of human touch, if possible a glint of humour, demands the heaviest work and challenges the finest craftsman.

As a pretty dreadful illustration, my preposterous interview with Zsa Zsa Gabor in Hollywood—she too clever to misunderstand my intended ridicule of a love goddess—was more widely read than anything else I ever wrote. If journalism holds no mystery, public taste is always mysterious, fickle, occult.

In mentioning some great and forgotten fellow craftsmen, I speak with the prejudice of friendship and rather long experience.

Greatest among all Canadian journalists, by general consent, was John Wesley Dafoe of the Winnipeg *Free Press*, last of his breed, the breed of Greeley, Dana and Watterson in the United States. But what the books written about Dafoe do not seem to understand is that, while some of his views were already outdated, he was growing and changing right up to the end, losing his early quirks, becoming more liberal in the true, nonpartisan sense of the word, whereas, in youth, he had been a partisan and bitter Liberal.

Only those who saw him slumped in his favourite leather armchair at the Manitoba Club like a tired old lion with reddish mane and wary eye, suspected that growth. I was fortunate enough to guess it when I wrote a piece about him in *Fortune* magazine. He talked candidly for several days in his office and home but did not ask to see my copy and correct any errors. Instead, he would take a chance, he said, and soon hired me, just before his death, alas, and before he could write his memoirs. A vast area of our secret national history was forever lost.

With him, though not above him, I would rate Walter Lippmann who was more famous because he occupied the larger American pulpit. Like Dafoe, Lippmann wrote classic English and talked in colloquial idiom. Relaxed in his Washington home, in frayed sweater and baggy flannel pants—a once handsome man, his face now lined and ravaged by disillusionment—he would discuss, without using such a stilted word, the broken American Dream, the dream of his own youth.

Beginning life as a rich boy but a left-wing radical, he had become, unlike Dafoe, a right-wing political agnostic, all passions and all faith spent. (The doomed President Johnson actually called him a Communist.) When I last met Lippmann in his New York apartment, not long before his final illness, he was, I thought, a tragic, and in some of his notions a mistaken, prophet.

At the opposite pole of journalism I found Christopher Morley, a columnist, essayist, novelist, artist of the English language, poet, playwright and, for all his laughter and worldly talk, a shy mystic. As the perceptive reader will see, his masterpiece, *Thunder on the Left*, was a ghost story under faint disguise. Getting to know Morley in New York, I realized that fate had placed him in the wrong age. He should have been a member of Dr. Johnson's Club or even a regular client of the Mermaid Tavern.

Such talents are rare in any profession, but I worked in Canada with men and women just as able as their American counterparts, though less famous because their country was smaller and poorer. They, not the famous, made the Canadian press. Their names listed together would record journalism at its best over more than six decades—so many names that escape an old man's memory, not his gratitude. But two colleagues are unforgettable.

The late Grant Dexter, who had long been Dafoe's eyes and ears in Ottawa, later succeeding him in Winnipeg, taught my first political lessons and gave me "a friendship as had mastered time." In his own work he mastered politics better than any of his contemporaries and has few equals today. My debt to him can never be repaid.

Nor can I repay the late Richard S. Malone who came home from war in Italy, France and the Pacific with grievous wounds and a brigadier's rank to become my employer, benefactor and wise counsellor. Among other things he built F. P. Publications. This organization of leading papers from Montreal to Victoria did not long survive his retirement, but he had well earned his leisure and friends throughout the world before his sudden death.

All my fellow workers searched for the truth, the whole truth and nothing but the truth. They strove to find and agonized to find and failed in striving. Failure was preordained. Journalism can tell only that part of the truth visible in the day's events, a small part. The news and the comments on it must be rushed into the world before their time, scarce half made up. Long afterward, historians with time to spare and records to read will discover more of the truth, but even restrospective books, in the end the most accurate medium, will never grasp it whole.

Until middle age at the earliest I did not realize the limits of my trade. Looking back now, it is amazing to think how long it took to understand them. More amazing, the companies that employed me put up with my work and especially my stubborn refusal to leave my hide-out in Victoria despite their tempting offers. But none tried to dictate my printed views. What instructions the publishers received from head office I did not know or want to know. Enough that they were perhaps too charitable for my own good and theirs. Not once in those years was I asked to change any opinion, however mistaken, in my copy.

Apart from the publishers, whose job was to take full responsibility for everything in the paper, to manage, not to write, the friendships of a lucky working life included too many good fellow journalists for remembrance and mention here.

It is the habit of old men to tell themselves that everything in their trade was better in earlier times. On the contrary, I believe that most things were much worse.

Peter Newman, already a glittering star of journalism, disagreed with me at a friendly public confrontation. As I realized afterward, we had argued about different periods. He was thinking of his young days and since then, as he said, some papers have declined in quality. I was thinking of days long before his birth and since then some papers have greatly improved their quality. Both of us failed to see that the rise and fall of journalism continues in all times at different speeds in different cities.

Newman lamented the disappearance of illustrious editors like Dafoe, and there, of course, he was right. But Newman is still too young to recall the newspapers of half a century ago. If he looked into their faded files, he would see that they offered far less nourishment to the reader than the average newspaper contains today—little world news, no reports from costly foreign bureaus, no instantaneous photographs of remote wars, revolutions, riots and personalities, no unbiased commentary on politics from Ottawa, no reflective writing on society, manners and morals by independent contributors.

Still worse, the political news was always slanted in favour of one party or the other (and the recollection of my own youthful slants fills an old man with remorse). Nor did papers struggling for existence dare to offend their advertisers. Today, while advertisers are eagerly sought and get full value for their money, they cannot buy the editorial support of any respectable newspaper. It can afford to offend them and their views on public issues and often does. Advertising is a salable commodity, open to all buyers, including political parties and pressure groups of every sort, but editors, though influenced by their own prejudices, in their columns ignore the advertisers.

Despite many flaws, the old papers did report the debates of Parliament, legislatures and city councils at a length which no modern reader, with plenty of alternative entertainment, would tolerate. Something of great value to the democratic process has been lost because the general public, the market of the press, no longer wants it.

In contemporary Canada, I judge, the average paper is as good and honest as any of similar size in the world—far superior, for example, to the scabrous popular press of Britain where the quality papers have relatively small circulation. (How British democracy survives its papers of mass circulation I always wondered as I read them in their own territory.)

Newman's mistake, and that of most readers, is to compare the average Canadian paper to the *Times* of London, the *Times* of New York or the *Post* of Washington that control almost unlimited resources. Lacking them, the paper in any metropolis or town is the outgrowth of its changing local circumstances and must change with them. On the whole, the change in my time has been a vast improvement.

Certainly the average paper is more honest than it was in my youth, not necessarily because its workers are more virtuous, but because it can now afford a standard of honesty that it could not afford then. On the other hand, the press, like every human institution, has fallen behind in the race between the world's problems and their solution. No one understands this time lag as well as newspaper people who, reading the day's product, are always dissatisfied with it. So they should be.

In some ways, Newman rightly contends, the age of the great editors was superior to ours. Such a man could give his paper a distinctive personality echoing his own. Today the press, like just about everything else, is too uniform, too much depersonalized and undiversified. No group of journalists, assembled over their beer, fails to weep into it, mourning the loss of individual character in their trade. All of us would like to restore the good old days, every town equipped with two or more locally owned papers. The age of industrial giantism, including the press, excludes that possibility. Small is beautiful, said the late economist and philosopher E. F. Schumacher in his notable book, and bigness, pressed too far, may be inefficient as well as ugly.

While the so-called economies of scale are the objective of most business everywhere, it does not follow that the long-term result will be satisfactory, and in some cases could prove to be the opposite. Many factors besides efficiency are involved, and at present small business as a whole is the largest creator of jobs.

In the press of Canada the factors are much more complicated than in business as a whole. Many of them result from the nature of the country itself. Since its inhabitants are few, a mere handful by world measurement, and spread over continental distance, Canadian newspapers developed as local enterprises and so remained for most of a century.

A small island like Britain could support a national press whose product moved in hours to all cities, towns and villages. In Canada this was physically impossible until technology learned to bounce signals off satellites outside the planetary atmosphere. Now it is possible to print the same newspaper simultaneously in different cities and deliver it anywhere between the Atlantic and the Pacific.

The Toronto *Globe and Mail* has used the new method to publish Canada's first national newspaper. Most publishers cannot begin to do the same. They must cater to their own communities where the readers' prime interest is local. No more than a minority of them will buy a paper that neglects the local news and plays up the news of the world as circulation figures demonstrate.

Many editors would prefer less trivia, entertainment and lengthy feature stories than they print, and some papers greatly overdo this "soft stuff" at the sacrifice of hard, factual reporting. The market wants a product that dissatisfies the more thoughtful journalists and can never fully satisfy all the readers. It keeps changing and its economic requirements may also change, but in the foreseeable future mass circulation will belong to the local market.

The audience for many national papers, good or bad, like those of Britain, Europe and Japan, is not yet available to Canada. Apart from public taste, geography alone forbids Canadian imitation on any large scale.

The same is true also in the United States with a population ten times that of Canada. There a few great newspapers enjoy a national circulation relatively small in so large a country and limited to a minority of serious readers. But the minority is increasing on both sides of the border.

So are the solid contents of the successful Canadian papers. Even if their attempt to see the world and its problems as a whole often fails, even if the front page features stuff of less importance, the reader searching for national and international news, or depth studies of the human condition written by experts, will find more of this material on the inside pages than the general public ever reads, far more than any paper contained until recent times.

A common criticism of the Canadian press is that it depends too much on services, mostly American, outside its control. The world is seen, we are told, through foreign eyes, and events are analyzed by journalists who know nothing about Canada. Why, the critical reader asks, should this be necessary?

The reason is simple, economic and, for the present, unalterable. Few Canadian papers can afford to maintain expensive foreign bureaus though the richer among them do so at heavy immediate cost but long-term gains not to be reckoned in money. To cover the world, the press has to make use of foreign services, the most extensive of them based in the United States. They pour out a torrent of news and features eagerly read in Canada where most editors try to select the best stuff but much inferior stuff is printed because so many customers demand it, just as they watch American television which is sometimes excellent, often banal.

Negative legal barriers could have little effect against cultural penetration (not restricted to Canada). They will never halt the movement of ideas, even if that were desirable.

On the positive side there are encouraging signs. The Canadian Press, co-operatively owned by all the leading papers, has greatly expanded its foreign coverage and improved its quality, assessing the news from a native viewpoint. Reuters, based in Britain, is widely used in Canada as a competitor of the pre-eminent Associated Press. Undeterred by geography and subsidized by the taxpayers, the Canadian Broadcasting Corporation and the unsubsidized private networks serve the public with television and radio. For Canada's needs they have become indispensable. Fortunately, the CBC, nonpartisan in its news treatment, is untouchable by politicians, as some of them have learned after damaging experience.

Canadian books, about three thousand new titles annually compared to a tenth of that number a few years ago, prove that the nation has ideas of its own worth reading and preserving long after the daily paper and the electronic picture have disappeared.

Do governments try to manipulate the press? Of course they do at every chance. Delaying unfavourable news if they can, announcing favourable news with a flourish or leaking biased versions of it to chosen reporters, they may briefly improve their images, but these tricks often backfire on the tricksters. And hell has no fury like a reporter misled.

On the other hand, the honest reporter with friends and sources in high places can hardly avoid their influence even when they are honest, too, though prejudiced in favour of the government that employs them. For conscientious journalists such an association is bound to be difficult and at times a critical test of integrity. Some of them meet it at the cost of friend and source if necessary. Some do not.

Whether the test is met or defaulted, no government can manage the news for long. By searching the written documents, by consulting experts, the government's political enemies and the official records in Ottawa, sometimes in Washington, by laboriously accumulating forgotten details, the press eventually uncovers most if not all secrets and scandals.

The job is never done and cannot be in the political world. But think for a moment of what that world could hide without the media to investigate and publish the facts. To be sure, government and press are inadequate everywhere like other human institutions. Both need criticism and it is never lacking. If it were, no free society would survive.

In serving it, the press has to maintain its adversarial though symbiotic relationship with politicians of all stripes. By and large the relationship is vigorously maintained and occasionally pushed too far when a small group of reporters, or a single individual, breaks a politician's confidence and publishes his off-the-record conversation.

In these cases the offender's more scrupulous companions are as outraged as the victim. The entire craft suffers while all but a few members of it obey the rules so easily broken. Integrity pays off. Journalists who disregard it may succeed for a time, make big money and enjoy their fame, but in the end they will nearly always get their deserts.

In the English language journalism works against a varied background. Government is much more open in the United States than in official Britain, reflecting the different attitudes of the two societies. Canadian government stands somewhat between them.

As in other countries the journalism of Canada has gone through many phases. The latest is the newspaper chain. It was made by economic calculation or necessity, as judged by its owners, not by political or social theories.

The chains so alarmed the Trudeau government that it appointed a royal commission to study them. The commission, a second shot at the same target, issued a report which was never implemented because its main recommendations, whether sound or unsound in theory, were clearly unworkable in the real newspaper world. They would have limited the ownership of chains, given tax incentives to encourage wider news coverage (thus placing newspapers under obligation to partisan governments) and set up committees of local citizens as editorial advisers without any experience in the business. Legislation was drafted to carry out some of the recommendations but it died, by general consent, or fear of the press, on the parliamentary order paper.

In the visible future the chains are here to stay, though they probably could not expand much in the larger cities without realarming Parliament and public. They have their advantages and disadvantages—the advantage of sufficient financial resources to improve their products, the disadvantage of at least the possibility of overcentralized control.

Here, in new form, is a question long disturbing all free societies. Where should control of public information, the ultimate safeguard of freedom, be safely placed? If it rests with government, there can be no free press, only political organs like those of authoritarian societies. If it rests with private owners, will they abuse their powers?

So far, I believe, that power has not been abused in any fashion dangerous to Canadian society, though newspapers, each with its own strengths and weaknesses, continue to make mistakes of fact and opinion. But they do not suppress the opinions of their enemies in politics. Thus, for example, the Socialist New Democratic Party finds no reason to complain that the news columns ignore or distort its speeches and policies. They are played up day by day, often overplayed in the opinion of competing parties.

The left wing of politics has no right to complain when its views are attacked in editorials or signed commentary. If the NDP ever takes national office, it surely will not attempt to nationalize or restrict the freedom of the press, unless it prefers to sit again in opposition.

What concerns the thoughtful, nonpartisan critics of the press is the fact that newspapers belong to private owners who can manage them for the public's benefit or damage.

Newspapers are business enterprises, in many cases big business, with their stock widely held, and are finally governed by profit or loss. Already loss has extinguished some of the best among them. Under that mandate some improve, others deteriorate. So do all segments of the economy.

To suppose that the owners of newspaper chains are joint conspirators seeking control of the state is to overrate their influence and underrate their intelligence. No conspiracy exists. If such an unimaginable act of folly were ever attempted, Parliament would rightly crush it in the bud.

Aside from this impossible notion, the public would be naive to suppose that the owners, in an excess of altruism, desire an economic system unfavourable, perhaps fatal, to their interests and the interests of society as they see them. The owners have more practical business to occupy their time. They leave editorial decisions to their publishers and editors. Within the chains the decisions vary from town to town in support of different political parties and causes. But the owners do not knowingly appoint men or women who disagree with them on fundamentals.

No Communist, outright advocate of socialism or of Canada's annexation to the United States, for example, is in charge of any important paper. Why should this surprise anybody besides idealists and revolutionaries who expect to inhabit a world without greed, profit or sin? Are the owners obligated by some higher law of morality to choose executives who aim at the destruction of the business? As Bernard Shaw remarked in another context, it's not bloodly likely.

It is likely, indeed certain, that publishers and editors do agree in general with their employers, or they would be following a different trade. This does not mean that there is always agreement on political and social problems. There is widespread disagreement inside the business. These personal strains and office politics are common to all organizations, from the giants of industry down to the little enterprise with a dozen employees.

In human life the struggle for power, status and money will never end, and newspapers are not immune to it. Sometimes, from a safe distance, I have watched the struggle get very rough as competent journalists were demoted, inferior men and women taking their places. Errors of judgement and personal favouritism are not peculiar to the press.

Often forgotten is the fact that newspapers, however rich in their local monopolies of print, must compete with new electronic rivals for public attention, advertising and profits. The competition is increasingly fierce and a good thing for all the media.

Concerning the economics of the newspaper industry I know little. But I do know that in all my jobs I never received instructions from head office about editorial policy, no suggestion that it take a certain line in favour of some political party or cause. How other editors fared I do not know, but on the firing line we could not guess whether the proprietors ever read our copy. If they did, we suspected that they frequently disagreed with us. We made independent choices, wise or unwise, but our own.

As many papers learned on the eve of their demise, prosperity, even survival, depends on readership that alone builds advertising, lifeblood of the industry. Without it, the reader would probably get a weekly paper of half a dozen pages, not worth the price of a dollar, or more, per issue. The typical paper is the best bargain on the present market, a lucky tub, its contents, serious and trivial, so bulky and varied that readers can take what they fancy and ignore the rest.

Like me, most journalists seldom concern themselves with the business problems of a newspaper, a product that demands huge capital investment, ever-changing machinery and yet, with all its complex gadgets, is delivered by a boy on a bicycle. This weird mix of automation and obsolescence will be superseded, some day, by an electronic delivery system not yet perfected. Or so the experts assure us.

Whatever form the system takes, the paper cannot be an ordinary business. Granted complete freedom within the laws of libel and decency, it must justify that privilege by providing truthful news, offering its own comment thereon (carefully labelled as such) and giving civic leadership that the public may follow or reject. Always it tries to satisfy the readers' taste, its market. For, after all, it is a commercial enterprise as well as a public responsibility. The alternative, too familiar abroad, is a state-controlled press and the destruction of everybody's freedom.

All this is journalistic shoptalk of small interest to press readers. What they want to know is how the "media" touch their lives. To newspaper people such a word is offensive. It recalls Leonard Brockington's memorable crack when, investigating Mackenzie King's spiritual advisers, he said that, for the first time, he was tempted "to strike a happy medium." In fact, the printed medium is never happy, perpetually discontented with itself.

The media, if they must be so called, deeply touch everyone's life, though their effect is generally misunderstood. Here an odd reciprocal process is at work as Brian Tobin, a wise old Victoria editor, observed to a gathering of journalists. The paper, he said, must satisfy the public taste, and it has changed itself for that purpose. But it has also changed the public taste so much that no reader would be satisfied today with the paper published in Tobin's youth.

Long before some tasteless lexographer christened it a medium, the paper influenced the social environment mainly through editorials reflecting the mind of its editor. Now its influence is more diffused and osmotic, exerted by many different persons mainly through the news, the features, the signed columns. Let no readers suppose that they are immune to a daily drumbeat and overwhelming tide of information, entertainment, opinion and controversy. Anyone who even glances at a paper or listens to electronic impulses is conditioned by them, willy-nilly. The "play" of the news, as we call it, the emphasis on the important or trivial, the accurate or innacurate headline, the columnist's praise or derision have a total effect beyond measurement.

Although it is enough to frighten those who wield such intangible power, they generally underrate the continuing power of the editorial because it is read by a minority. They forget that all communities are governed and shaped, no matter what constitutions say, by about 10 per cent, at most, of their inhabitants. Persuade this group on a given proposition and you have persuaded the community. The process takes a long time. As Dafoe used to say, it requires endless repetition until, slowly, the drips of water wear away the stone of resistance.

Politicians cannot wait so long when they seek immediate votes. What they most need is not editorial support but "media attention." Once the media take a politician seriously, he is in business even if the editorial writers scorn him. No politician understood that fact better than Franklin Roosevelt who won four elections, with the quiet backing of the reporters around him and against the opposition of their editors. As a corporate citizen a newspaper must vote, but its editorial votes do not settle elections. They are settled by the public's judgement of candidates and issues presented, accurately or inaccurately, over time, in the media.

The electoral power of the photograph should not be underestimated. By a shot of some politician's awkward stance or momentary facial twist, the photographer can do him grievous harm. Alternatively, a politician of mediocre ability may be made to look like another Churchill or Roosevelt if the camera happens to catch him at the right fraction of a second. Trudeau was the classic exhibit of both postures as hero and slob. Mulroney has been luckier, or more gunshy, on parade. But no public figure can hope to escape the pitiless lens forever.

The cartoonist has still less pity and a long history in Canada. From the time of Bengough, who vainly spent his talent on Macdonald's destruction, the cartoon was, and remains, a formidable weapon of politics. It can tell at a glance more than the writer usually tells in a thousand words.

Until modern times the paper enjoyed a virtual monopoly of the news, but the monopoly is now broken by competitors other than the electronics media. Weekly American news magazines and the excellent *Maclean's* in Canada have a major advantage over the daily press. While the daily product must be put together in a few hours by a miracle of men and machinery, the magazine has days for background research, writing and rewriting up to the moment of deadline. In some ways its product is superior to ours, in other ways inferior. It is generally better written but too often written in a hyped-up style of pop, crackle and snap. It mixes news with comment, the reader unwarned of the mixture.

Both daily and weekly publications have their valuable place in the information apparatus of a free society. Television, the latest competitor, is a different thing entirely, perhaps the most revolutionary communicating device since the invention of movable type. Its effects, good and bad, are yet unknown. Its proprietors have not fully learned to use it for the benefit of a society which, like the press, it can gravely damage. All we know for sure is that its competition for audience and advertising is strong enough to complicate the whole newspaper industry in content, product and profit.

The camera, roaming the world at leisure, brings into every home motion pictures more dramatic, vivid and commonly violent than the printed word can convey, and it has almost doomed the old-fashioned scoop. It can also explore unmapped mountains and jungles, the life of animals, birds, insects and vegetation beyond the reach of print. On the other hand, television cannot equal print as the explorer of ideas. It tries to do so with seminars, debates and think-tanks, but they are weak competitors in the field of thought.

For purposes of democratic debate, television has a grave built-in flaw. When a statesman is allowed half a minute or, at most, a minute to explain infinitely complex problems, the explanation will often be worse than silence. By its nature, television is the prisoner of time calculated in seconds to fit an iron schedule, even if a victim's words are cut off in midsentence, left dangling or distorted. The newspaper can expand or contract space to fit the importance of the story.

If thoughtful citizens, searching for the truth of things, see the world only through an instantaneous kaleidoscope, they will get an unbalanced, topsy-turvy view of it. The televised program, necessarily built around pictures rather than unpicturable ideas, must oversimplify, overdramatize and overhype the news.

It has great and frightening power all the same. Listen to your neighbour across the fence and nearly always you will find his political judgements based on last night's utterances by an actor whose script was written by someone else, unidentified. As Peter Newman puts it, with excusable exaggeration, any man may become a pundit of the tube if he is handsome and has the right voice. A woman needs only a beautiful face and the right hairdresser.

Here a distinction should be drawn between television and radio, though they are usually under control of identical owners, public or private. Radio, too, is time-imprisoned but much less so than television. Its programs are not built on the day's available pictures, and they can be altered at the last moment to cover the breaking news. One of the most distinguished electronic journalists of the United States tells me that the Canadian Broadcasting Corporation's radio performance is by far the best in America.

More and more young journalists are lured away from print to the world of Marshall McLuhan because the pay there is high and they like to see themselves on the screen, larger than life, nationwide.

Now and then I ventured into McLuhan's world and was always glad to escape its weary repetition of camera takes, its inflexible time limits,

its vagrant cuts that left a thought unfinished, bleeding like an amputated limb.

The riddle of our trade, and society, remains: Is McLuhan's world to be the end of the world known to human beings in print for some five centuries? Will newspapers of real paper and type be replaced by gadgets that read aloud to the householder in his living room, summoning up information from everywhere at the touch of a button? Will printed books become scarce museum pieces not long hence? Is the faithful jobbing gardener outside my window today, with a portable radio in his pocket to soothe him with music or bore him with shouted commercials, the symbol and wave of the future?

We need expect no answer to such questions for some time yet. The immediate present has raised another question of interest to journalists and readers alike: Why are newspapers, according to the opinion polls, less trusted than they used to be, even less than television, when most of them strive so hard for accuracy, beat their breasts and confess their errors to independent press councils? The answer, at least among the intellectuals, is that they have become rich, fat, arrogant, indifferent to the public welfare.

Such an answer is too glib. In fact, the newspaper, with all its virtues and sins, is caught, with every human structure, in the worldwide social revolution and cannot see the end of it. But already, long before the end, we must see that our generation is more informed, or misinformed, more dominated or penetrated, by the so-called media than any other generation in history. No free society can resist the tide. If dikes are built against it, then society ceases to be free. Hence the ultimate question: How truly free is our Canadian society, and where is it going?

18

THE
HUMAN
MENAGERIE

King Edward VII was more of a rake than an intellectual, but he had one sound idea. A society, he said, is not made. It *grows*.

His own British society did not grow as the King had hoped. Nor has the Canadian society grown as its older inhabitants expected. Least of all could they expect to live in an age of revolution, peaceful here, often violent elsewhere. What they still fail to understand is that constructive and enduring revolutions are not led mainly by the authoritarian and so-called revolutionary nations like Russia and China but by the free societies of the west. They are the true revolutionists of our time, Canada among them. Freedom's nature keeps it always in revolt. And for those who live through it, the experience must be hazardous, the way dark, the end unseen.

In Canada our social growing pains have been relatively mild because we happen to possess more natural wealth than we know how to use, manage and conserve. Our half-continent of lavish resources, with only some twenty-five million people to enjoy them, makes us, in material terms, the luckiest people on earth. But somehow luck has not made us as happy as we are rich. Certainly it has not prepared us for our present change of fortune.

As this final chapter and rambling, repetitious summing-up will try to argue, so many things have happened so fast that we have yet to accommodate ourselves to them, even to glimpse their shape, meaning or future result. Of course no generation ever understands the events around it, but in Canada they are confused by peculiar native elements.

It is easy for historians, reciting the obvious, to explain that humans are social animals in a curious menagerie. Easy for Emerson to say that "society everywhere is in conspiracy against the manhood of every one of its members"; for the dismal German philosopher Oswald Spengler to write, incomprehensibly, *The Decline of the West;* for an aged, bewildered Canadian to realize, too late, that he knows much less about our society than he knew, or thought he knew, in youth.

When I was young, in various country towns and later in the capital city of Victoria, the word *society* did not mean what it means today. With us humble folk Society (as reported by the newspapers in capital letters) meant the rich, their mansions, shiny coaches and sleek horses, their exclusive clubs, the gentlemen in London-tailored clothes, the ladies in silk and ostrich plumes for the balls and garden parties at Government House. Like the observers of Ozymandias's monument, we looked on the mighty and in bad times were inclined to despair. In all times we envied.

That was before society became a science, the professor a sociologist. He tries to teach youth the unteachable in a university, teachable only in the rough kindergarten of private life since every human being lives inwardly alone, beginning as an egg, and is surrounded by a shell of solitude until death cracks it. But the sociologists do the best they can. The politicians, invariably following in the wake of events, add their transitory contributions. And society grows according to no plan or prophecy.

All old men still living have witnessed the arrival (with trumpets and headlines) of the Just Society in the early Trudeau years, the Good Society in the United States, the Fair Society, the Square Deal, the New Deal, the New Frontier, Reagan's wistful Old Deal and God knows how many other grandiose labels, soon expunged.

Throughout our time Canadian society was being changed by such factors as these:

Massive immigration that diluted the original British and French bloodlines, with consequences unfathomable and irrevocable. (This foreign inflow will continue when, the demographers warn us, Canada's falling birthrate is insufficient to maintain, let alone increase, its population in the next century. But demography is a science as unreliable as economics, both dependent on the people's uncertain living and breeding habits.)

The homemade Constitution and the Charter of Rights and Freedoms that force the Supreme Court to make political and legislative judgements clothed in legal idiom.

The final establishment of the French Fact against stubborn opposition.

The rise of the sky-scraping megalopolis and the schizophrenia of a pioneer breed torn between the sweet security of streets and the wilderness of their forefathers.

The structural unemployment and poverty uncured by any economic theory.

Canadians' slow discovery that they are no longer a safe part of an empire or of an impregnable Fortress America but of John Donne's "maine," of humanity entire.

Before this dizzy spectacle most of us stand frozen on the other side of the street and watch a new house being erected or an old one burning down, reluctant to help builder or fireman.

Nevertheless, a free society, with all its imperfections, is stronger than it looks to those who live in a society of compulsion. It resembles a finely woven Indian basket, stretching but not breaking, not even in the Great Depression and two world wars. Not breaking, though all societies live under a pretty thin veneer of law and order. Everything considered, I would judge that Canadians possess, with scant gratitude, the most fortunate society yet known to the present generation of mankind.

But their society has now entered a phase without precedent in their experience. It doubts its leaders, its political institutions, its organization of power. Suddenly it even begins to doubt *itself*. There is the nubbin of our peevish temper as vaguely reflected in the blurred mirror of politics. There is the still imperfect Unjust Society bequeathed to our children. There is the origin of our discontent and, worse, our apathy.

Instead, this time of trouble should be the source of our hope. For if we are discontented enough, we will try to correct our old mistakes (while undoubtedly making new ones).

At the moment the Western world, and especially North America, are said to be in a "conservative mindframe," society everywhere in retreat from "liberal" ideas. Even if this be true—a moot question below the surface—the rightward motion of politics is reform of a sort. It means that society, after various detours leftward, is seeking the middle way, the way of compromise, the only way to preserve balance and freedom.

Without pausing to define it in those simpler times, Canadians groped for the middle from the beginning. The French regime could not limit its colonists to the Laurentian Valley as planned in Paris. They paddled and walked to the Rockies, to the North, to the Gulf of Mexico. Then English-speaking settlers broke the Family Compact and its ludicrous aristocracy in Upper Canada. But they were doing nothing new.

More than two millennia before their time, Aristotle (himself no democrat) had laid down the rule that still guides us now: "The best political control is formed by citizens of the middle class. Those states are likely to be well administered in which the middle class is large and larger, if possible, than the other classes . . . the middle class turns the scale and prevents either of the extremes from becoming dominant." Such was his Golden Mean applied to governments.

Today, like its American neighbour, Canada is a middle-class society dominated by what the sociologists call the bourgeoisie. That class, from the frontier sod busters to the scientific atom splitters, has grown steadily with the faltering but overall growth of the economy until millions of so-called blue-collar workers belong to it. They use much the same vocabulary, accent and idiom as the so-called upper class. In my youth the line between gentility and those below it was clearly and firmly drawn; now a "gentleman" or a "lady" may come from any parentage, any class.

Your plumber may be sunning himself in Hawaii beside your doctor and your lawyer when you need him. Your electrician is in the woods shooting moose. Your carpenter, painter or garage mechanic has gone to Las Vegas for a long weekend to play the slot machines.

Since these skilled workers are the producers of our collective wealth, why shouldn't they enjoy their full share of it? The lack of such a thriving class, the essential balance wheel, puts freedom beyond the reach of most societies. The human majority is governed by powerful minorities, more often by single tyrants.

In Canada we like to pretend that our society is classless, but of course it is not, never was and never will be. No more than the children's Santa Claus is this notion believed by any adult. In fact, Canada supports many distinct classes, but they are "mobile," as the sociological lingo describes them. They constantly reshuffle themselves like a pack of cards. The ambitious man or woman moves upward from one class to another, the weakling or the handicapped downward. But that process is uneven and in too many cases unfair. The victims of personal misfortune or the state's economic mismanagement should never cease to trouble the conscience of a good society. The test of a good society is its just treatment of the unfortunate, not the fortunate who can look after themselves.

Although a broad egalitarian trend is clear, the unacknowledged aristocracies of wealth, luck or merit exist in every class. Always mankind is ruled by an elite (now a dirty word deplored by the elitists themselves), as boys in a school playground have their natural leaders, and chickens in a barnyard their pecking order. It has been said, indeed, that in each generation a dozen individuals of genius save mankind from a return to its primeval cave. The hyperbole may be excused since it is invariably the few, their number unreckoned, who protect, or abuse, the many.

In the free nations privilege, though never absent, is not imposed by a state bureaucracy of armed and naked power, as in the authoritarian societies. It flourishes without clearly defined rules. Thus, the Western world has spawned a jet set too rich, repulsive and pathetic to matter, except in the scandal sheets. For Canadians what matters is a different privilege. The right to live in Canada, with all its injustices, is so great a privilege that countless millions of the world's desperate peoples would come here tomorrow if they could.

Thence arises a question to haunt our posterity: Can a handful of privileged inhabitants forever hold their empty land against the thrust of an overcrowded planet when mankind, like nature, abhors a vacuum? Not unless Canadians deserve their fair estate and give it better management than they have recently exhibited. The present generation may seldom ponder that question. Its children and grandchildren must. The vacuum remains a magnetic goal for the underprivileged, a very utopia.

It falls far short of these people's imagination. But at least it is to Canada's credit that all attempts to perpetuate the rigid, comical aristrocracy of the frontier have failed. When Mackenzie King abolished titles of nobility, R. B. Bennett restored them at the depth of an ignoble Great Depression. Back in office, King abolished them again, this time for good. They simply do not fit our society, geography or cultural mix. Only a few nostalgic old Canadians lament their disapapearance.

Yet nobility of character, talent and spirit, recognized or unrecognized, has not disappeared. It lives on because humanity, lacking it, would become subhuman again. For its own reasons Britain still defines its classes by title, birth or wealth, and they are too rigid, as foreigners see them, for the nation's prosperity in a world of savage competition. That is Britain's exclusive business, not ours. But even there a woman of humble origin broke the class barriers to make herself the leader of a Conservative government.

Here we have more than enough social problems to test our intelligence, our tolerance and our right to own such a treasury as Canada. In that test some of our recent marks are inexcusably low.

The shame of poverty in a land so naturally rich, the soup kitchens of our cities, the jobless youth eager to work (a time bomb audibly ticking), the misery that slips through our welfare safety nets, the shambles of our governments' budgets, the confusion of our politics— all tell a humiliating story and should impeach our conscience.

Power to solve these problems, if they are solvable, has been largely concentrated in the three familiar citadels of Big Government, Big Business and Big Labour, a tripod whose legs and relative strength are always shifting. Each of them sometimes abuses its power to the disadvantage of the powerless.

Abuse by government provides, next to the weather, our favourite topic of conversation. We seem willing to trust any experts but the managers of the state.

After the age of the industrial robber barons (who built the modern economy by methods now deemed barbarous), their successors were rescued from the Great Depression by government and various New Deals. Then the biggest corporations, some bigger than foreign states, usually denounced the rescuer. In later slumps many of them sought rescue again, and some got it after warmly extolling the ruthless competitive market in weekly luncheon speeches.

Labour, organized in unions, some more powerful than their employers, helped to preserve free enterprise by compelling a fairer distribution of wealth and thus of purchasing power. For their efforts in earlier days, they received little credit or understanding, more often the employers' brutal strike-breaking goon squads. Today the total and sometimes recklessly misused power of unions is declining, but without them, behaving responsibly, the free enterprise system as we know it could not exist. Instead, it lives, with fluctuating success and failure, under the law's protection and the state's frequent intervention, wise or unwise, while other systems are failing everywhere.

Like all organs of society, the system is in deep, if erratic, change. Against today's imperatives the old adversarial attitudes and enmity of the bargaining table become obsolete and unworkable. Until owners and workers accept their interdependence, and the overriding public interest, society will remain at the mercy of industrial warfare. The wiser union leaders and industrialists increasingly recognize the fact that they are, or should be, partners and not enemies in a joint undertaking. But the recognition is slow, belated and still far short of society's needs.

Another fact must be understood—the last thing that union members want is equality of status among themselves. Trained plumbers will not accept the wage level of their apprentices, nor airplane pilots the level of their flight crew. Inequality is as natural to the human work force as to animal and vegetable life. It also prevails within the unions whose members frequently decide to strike or not to strike by narrow votes, a large fraction of the membership absent, leaving the result to the more active group. Only when some unions claimed more than the economy could provide did serious trouble follow during the boom years. Wages driving up production costs were a major element of the inflation which priced thousands of workers out of their jobs and gravely damaged Canada in the domestic and world markets. The full cost of this folly has yet to be paid.

Lately average wages in the unions and outside them have not risen as much as retail prices, and average hours of work have begun to increase, but many industries remain uncompetitive in all markets. And despite the comforting assurances from government, inflation, even at about 4 per cent annually, is still an uncured economic disease that steadily erodes all fixed savings. The necessary readjustment of costs including wages, interest rates and taxes is painful, frequently unfair to workers and employers alike and far from complete. Yet both sides in the free enterprise system must prepare themselves for still more change. So must society as a whole.

Meanwhile the strike is the union's legitimate weapon in the private sector as the lockout, according to law, is the weapon of the employer, even if both weapons are sometimes used irresponsibly. Used in the civil service, the strike is a different weapon aimed at the state and society. One of the divided Pearson government's worst mistakes was to allow the use of that weapon to disrupt services vital to the public when fair arbitration was the proper, damageproof method of settling these disputes.

While Acton's warning against the misuse of power was disregarded by all the Big Three in the boom, the unorganized national majority, including small business concerns that are collectively the largest employer, fell prey, with their workers, to the quarrels of cabinet office, board room and union hall. Then each member of the presiding triumvirate blamed the others for the trouble.

The same trouble, immediate or looming ahead, threatens every nation whatever its ideology may be. Each faces a social imperative second only to the ending of the mad armaments race. The satisfaction of work and, with it, dignity in place of charity, must be found for the men and women idle through no fault of their own.

No society can long endure today's unemployment level and remain content, even peaceful, unless it compels obedience with guns and prison camps. In a free society like ours such methods are intolerable. But no Canadian government has found a sure answer to this many-sided economic riddle. All that society has received up to now are excuses and promises.

In the pursuit of a social balance, the Big Three are not the only power citadels. Besides government, business and labour, society has its professional class of doctors, scientists, lawyers, university intellectuals, farmers (whose votes are few but concentrated where they decide elections) and organized women's and ethnic groups that have already transformed Canadian life beyond an old-timer's recognition.

In the endless flux of classes, something else should be remembered. It is not merely the flight from the land to the city but the loneliness of urban life. Nothing, as a countryman sees it, can be lonelier than a metropolis, its inhabitants sealed off from one another by concrete apartment walls unknown to the pioneers. They knew and helped their neighbours. Hungry or benighted by storm, they dropped into any house along the way for potluck and lodging, always welcome. City folk nowadays must arrange a lunch or dinner days or weeks in advance, like a head of state programmed by a weary calendar.

Most pitiable of all are the urban rich as they toil after pleasure at the horrid make-believe cocktail hour with its buzz of meaningless, unheard chatter, alcohol, tobacco smoke and tomorrow's hangover. No Mermaid Tavern here, no Dr. Johnson's Club, just brief escape from swarming solitude.

The countryman (full of prejudice and quirk like everybody else) is never entirely himself in the metropolis. He can only pretend to like it for the reassurance of kindly hosts. Detached from the land, its teeming life and emanation of forces stronger than his own, he feels denatured. The human juices run out. They can be renewed nowhere but in the soil, the forest, the plains and the mountains.

Do city folk ever look up to see the geese in flight, that black wedge against the sky, hear the swish of wings, the clamorous message of travellers guided to their destination by a chart invisible to human eyes? Do they never feel a terrible earthbound longing if they watch these creatures that need no maps and defy the boundaries of men and nations?

Although urban people separate themselves from nature and apparently enjoy the separation so long as they have a pot or two of house plants beside them, they are the pioneers of the new society. But how little any of us really know of it outside our own tiny niches! How confidently we entrust our lives, and lives more precious, to a doctor, a chemist, an airplane pilot or a farmer who feeds us! Their skills are removed from ours by distance immeasurable, as if we inhabited different planets.

All this, of course, is merely the countryman's fantasy. But do not let him imagine that, in wilderness or metropolis, he is forgotten by the managers of society. His name is recorded somewhere in the electronic memory bank of government as a social security number, in the business index as a possible customer. Rich or poor, male or female, white, black or yellow, each of us is a statistic, enrolled for society's inscrutable purpose.

Soon, no doubt, all men and women of a free democracy will carry identity cards for inspection by the police, the tax collectors, the customs officials, the health authorities, the census takers and additional snoopers yet to be invented. The state may have been pushed out of the nation's bedrooms, but it penetrates all the other rooms from attic to basement.

Its search is yet far from complete as it proclaims individual freedom by law while spreading collectivism by action and threatening to homogenize the free citizens against their will. The process is not deliberate in most governments. It is driven by the subtle, intangible, osmotic forces of all societies when they reach a certain point of maturity and, nowadays, by the new forces of technological advance—this despite the opposite centrifugal pull of discordant interest groups.

Thomas Jefferson's abiding conundrum remains unanswered: Can an elected government be strong enough to govern without destroying the liberty of the electors? In modern times, how can we keep demanding more state services but less of the state's taxes and presence needed to provide them? How can we expect to have it both ways? How far can the basket of the society be safely stretched?

These are among the contrary trends for sociologists to explain. The layman has not seen any explanation so far. But he can see that social fragmentation is not restricted to ethnic, industrial and legal disputes. It goes much deeper and spreads wider.

As he travels North America, the layman observes another and parallel process. In the United States it denies all prophecy. In Canada it confirms an opposite assumption. In both countries one of the most striking social movements is the fast-growing power of the ethnic minorities. The United States had assumed that, in an affluent society, hordes of immigrants would quickly slough off their old habits and memories, smoothly adopt those of a better land. Education, law and native custom would surely work this miracle. There was no room in his country, said Theodore Roosevelt, for hyphenated Americans. The hyphen would be removed, lifeways transmuted, by an imaginary "melting pot."

Since Roosevelt's day the miracle has not worked. Instead, the ethnic enclaves, above all the blacks, have rediscovered and proudly rejuvenated their racial roots, organized their potent pressure groups and controlled so many votes in vital areas that few politicians dare to offend them.

The melting pot itself has melted. The social contract, or whatever you choose to call it, is strained by forces unsuspected by the Founding Fathers or even by Roosevelt only some eight decades ago. The United States now faces an ethnic problem far more difficult than Canada's.

After some contrary attempts had failed in earlier days, Canadians abandoned the notion that immigrants could be quickly absorbed into native lifeways, much less that the people of Quebec (so strangely misconstrued by Lord Durham) would adopt those of the majority. The children of parents from Britain, Germany, Holland, Italy, the Ukraine or other European countries, and some from Asia and Africa, may eventually become like us, but full absorption must take a generation at the earliest. As a convenient label we called our policy the national "mosaic," though nobody knew what it really meant. Anyhow, we had no use for an unworkable melting pot.

In recent times, only in recent times, the word *racism* entered our common speech, and it was a dirty word for an age-old evil. To cure it, our legislatures passed laws and later framed a Constitution punishing anyone who discriminated against fellow citizens of different sex, origin, culture, colour or religion. The laws are wise and generally approved, though sometimes more honoured in the breach than in the observance.

Human nature will not be changed overnight or over a single generation by any law, regulation or antiracial piety in the mouths of politicians. But the fight must go on. Even if we cannot prevent murder, we must punish and discourage it. Even if we cannot eliminate racism this side of Heaven, we must punish and discourage it also. We have made more progress in the fight than our children are likely to realize since the anti-Oriental riots of the early century and the exile of the Japanese from the Pacific Coast in the years of the Second World War. Today many of the exiles are successful and distinguished in business and the professions, respected among the elites.

Witness, too, the conscience money, adequate or inadequate, lately paid to Indian and Inuit communities for our wholesale breach of treaties, our inadequate but costly foreign aid programs. We may not be wiser but we are a kinder people than we used to be. Ugly, depraved racist incidents are not restricted to Canada. They erupt the world over, nowhere more frequently than in the nonwhite countries, but offer no excuse for ours.

For all past evils there was, by unanimous consent, a sovereign remedy—they would be cured by public education. So we put our faith in the schools and universities, forgetting that Germany and Japan, two of the best-educated nations of the world, had almost destroyed their civilizations; forgetting, too, that Canada's urgent need was not more and more graduates in higher learning but skilled craftsmen whom we imported, perforce, from abroad. Education alone, it turned out, was not a universal cure, only a necessary tool among many. And we have still to learn its true use.

But we have learned certain other things. Perhaps the most notable is our discovery that government, no matter how much power we give it, cannot solve all our problems. The present conservative swing away from government involves nearly all countries, even Communist China. It brought Reagan to the White House. It hardened the British iron in Margaret Thatcher. It softened the socialism of France. It forced Canadian Liberalism to rethink its earlier credo.

What the reforming politicians of North America (including the once radical Trudeau) have grasped is that this continent's natural economic system is predominantly a system of free enterprise. Historical experience, trial, error and folk instinct produced an economy and society of capitalism mixed inseparably with socialism, government with private enterprise.

On the preservation of the system, however described, both sides at the industrial bargaining table agree, even if they disagree on the system's reform. The wise labour union, while never satisfied with its rewards, knows that in a fully state-controlled economy there can be no room for unions or enterprisers, only for tyrants, bureaucrats and flawless plans seldom workable. Big Business and Big Labour may quarrel and spill their quarrels on society, but in America they are sisters under the skin.

Besides, as it seems to a lay observer, the rightward swing is greatly exaggerated. A few simple figures should demonstrate the exaggeration: Canadian government, at its three levels, now spends 41.7 per cent of the gross national product, according to the latest figures, and this expenditure continues to rise (along with taxes). In the United States and Japan the expenditure is somewhat lower; in Britain (44.7 per cent) and Germany (45.2) it is higher. Such figures are marginally disputable because they have been calculated by methods differing from nation to nation. Some experts calculate that the spending of all Canadian governments has risen already to 48 per cent of the GNP. The International Monetary Fund reports that average spending in

Western nations rose from 36 to 43 per cent in the decade before 1981. Everywhere government, despite its contrary vows, expands its territory.

Another set of figures, the figures of election results, should demonstrate a fallacy prevalent in all the various schools of economic planners, psychologists and even practical politicians. They had generally assumed that bad times would radicalize politics. On the contrary, recent bad times made people more cautious, preferring the ills they had to those they knew not of. Hence the rightward swing. But the social pendulum will swing in the opposite direction later on if conservative policies fail.

Wherever the pendulum may next swing, a towering continental fact is avoided by most politicians: North America has been living on its capital like a farmer who eats his seed corn. The infrastructure of roads, bridges, railways, waterworks, sewers, urban housing, breathable air and productive soil, the essential apparatus of society, has deteriorated so far that the cost of its repair, not to mention its improvement, must be reckoned in billions, more likely in trillions, of dollars.

Where will the money come from? Only from taxes, honestly collected or hidden in the price of goods and services. For who but government, however remote it seems, can deal with such problems, directly or indirectly? Who but the state, through its various agencies, can cleanse the polluted earth, the acid rain in the fresh water, even the multitudinous seas fouled by our chemicals and garbage? Who else can rebuild the decaying cores of our cities and replant our depleted forests?

Who else already finances the weapon factories with their millions of jobs, recruits the armed forces and tries to negotiate disarmament? Who, among contemporary statesmen, has been as ironical as Ronald Reagan when he resolved to limit the state while expanding the military-industrial complex, the state's costly offspring, far past the limits that horrified Dwight Eisenhower, himself a soldier?

The complex provides millions of jobs. Canada shares them in building components of weaponry for the United States, and it hopes to get still more as the complex keeps proliferating. The economies and hence the societies of both nations have become enmeshed in the vast apparatus of defence and potential overkill.

If this seems unavoidable for military reasons, it is mad economics when the money spent on weapons could be used in a sane world to repair the neglected infrastructure, create new jobs in the process and safeguard the human future. But the societies of the world are not sane.

Apart from defence and the dubious ongoing armament negotiations, when will the world's governments realize that other vital tasks cannot be done unless they work together because pollution, poverty and madness recognize no boundaries, population no international control, raw resources no national monopoly?

And where does all this lead in the free societies? To less government as imagined by the conservatives of all political parties? Surely it leads to more government under assorted misleading slogans as the nonpolitical taxpayers must see it. Already they see that if an industry or financial institution is sufficiently big, the state cannot allow it to go broke along with its workers. Bankruptcy, the original safety valve of capitalism, has become outmoded except for small business, the largest single economic sector, where it is rife and devastating in bad times.

The next step does not lead to a clear choice between government and private business as menders of the infrastructure, since each has its own special talents and defects. Our mistake in the past was to suppose that one or the other could do the entire job, if given the chance, when in fact neither could do it alone. The division of their costs, responsibilities and methods of co-operation is today's urgent need. Unfortunately, those decisions have been delayed and bemused by political expedients and ideological nit-picking.

To most citizens the prospect of increased government is horrifying when they find too much of in their lives now. On the other hand, they want government to give them more services and they remember, too, that private managers have frequently been as misguided and error-prone as the politicians, at the cost of the whole society.

For the citizenry the worst mistake would be to expect anything like foolproof behaviour in government, business, labour, other groups— or in the people themselves. We are all huddled in the same leaky lifeboat far from shore, all weighted down by our humanity, all forced to live with some problems that cannot be solved or, if solved, will breed new ones equally or more stubborn.

The choices before us are not confined to politics and economics. Much more important, and difficult, is our own performance as citizens. That task, if we are to accomplish it, compels a realignment of total consumption and conservation, of immediate demand and future supply.

America has been a consumer society since the introduction of machines, the building of railways and the opening of the West. On ever-increasing consumption the economic system was built to the point where living standards, full employment and many other things of value now seem dependent on it.

To restrain the public appetite with its hope of still more consumption is so difficult and unpopular a feat in politics that few politicians venture to talk about it. Instead, we are promised the old inexhaustible pie in the sky, consumed but always growing bigger. This promise, or sophistry, is measured by the production of goods and services, whether they be good or bad for us, from an automobile to a cigarette, from a haircut to a bottle of whiskey.

According to the gross national product measurement, the living standard of the United States, once the highest ever known, has slipped below those of several minor nations. The standard of Canada, once the second highest, has slipped still lower. Is the measurement reliable? What does it actually measure? Certainly not the life and happiness of the average citizen. Few North Americans would choose to live in countries with supposedly higher standards, in some temporarily oil-rich desert sheikdom, for instance, or even in cozy Scandinavia.

The doomed Robert Kennedy (whose family owned a substantial chunk of the American GNP) began to grasp these facts shortly before he was assassinated on his way to the presidency. Beyond the statistics the most intelligent and least understood of the Kennedys saw a larger fact. Like President Carter, he saw a "malaise of the spirit" that no statistic could measure; saw that the GNP included expenditures on "air pollution and cigarette advertising and ambulances to clear our highways of carnage, special locks on our doors and jails for people who break them . . . and television programs which glorify violence the better to sell toys to our children."

What the GNP did not include, he said, were "the health of our youth, the quality of their education or the joy of their play . . . the beauty of our poetry or the strength of our marriages, the intelligence of our public debate or the integrity of our public officials." In short, the GNP measured "everything except that which makes life worthwhile."

Kennedy also saw "the plain nuttiness" in society that ensured his murder as it had already murdered John Fitzgerald, his brother.

What else does the GNP fail to measure? Professor Jonathan Wisenthal of the University of British Columbia has distinguished a missing piece in the social jigsaw puzzle—the cultivation of thought as an end in itself. "The main reason that we hold ideas in such low esteem," he wrote, "is that thinking does not appear to be a useful activity. Apart from physical well-being just about everything in our society is seen as instrumental. We reduce everything to the level of utility."

But even at this level, not the most important, we do not see that the private labour and pleasure of the mind have what we call practical value to be measured, later on, by a more reliable GNP, for the hard-thinking nations, says Wisenthal, will eventually out-compete the thoughtless in measurable production and consumption.

Right now North American society appears to be more concerned with its "plain nuttiness" than with ideas for their own sake. Washington, which was a pleasant, manageable southern city not long ago, has become so obsessed with "security" that you can enter its government buildings only with adequate indentification. Inside, you must wear an official badge to reassure the ubiquitous guards. The White House is protected by concrete barriers and rockets against air attack.

Ottawa, where Borden used to ride a bicycle and Mackenzie King and St. Laurent frequently walked to their offices, is tightly guarded. The prime minister rides a bullet-proof limousine. At the doors of Parliament, the East Block, the Langevin Block, the Bank of Canada and similar haunts of power you will be politely stopped and the guards, if they are satisfied, will pin a safety label on your coat. No longer can innocent citizens freely enter their own collective premises to see how their servants are performing. Even the latest measures of security are being strengthened and a new antispy, antiterrorist intelligence system has replaced that of the Mounties with powers not yet specified.

Since organized espionage and terror are worldwide, bullets and bombs universal, Washington and Ottawa have good cause for their precautions. Cause, too, for grim merriment, since the age of "social security" with its escalating costs is the most insecure age yet experienced by mankind. How can it be otherwise when social revolution spares no country in varied forms and the Bomb hangs over them all?

No wonder that the citizen feels like an atom in some chemical experiment conducted by inhuman scientists, by power concentrated in the hands of a few uncontrollable men, some apparently deranged.

No wonder that the citizen asks whether democracy can survive such an age. After nearly three centuries when we had no doubt on this score, we are tempted, or forced, to reconsider the view of John Adams, the second American president, who, in a letter to his son, another president, said that democracy always committed suicide wherever it was tested. Adams may have been wrong in his foreboding, but certainly Alexander Hamilton was right in his admonition: "Give all power to the many, they will oppress the few. Give all power to the few, they will oppress the many." That warning still holds for our time.

We are also tempted to ask (in the heresy of heresies) whether universal suffrage, an equal vote for everybody, informed or ignorant, virtuous or malicious, can work in a complex, technical society that becomes ever more interdependent, brittle, difficult to govern and obscure in its direction and purpose.

Even the scholarly Walter Lippmann could not answer this question in a series of confused books and articles. He saw, as we all see, that when society gives the same voting right to the educated and uneducated citizen, it takes grave risks. He knew that all societies are governed, and must be governed, by an elite of some kind, since the details of governments nowadays are too complex for the average voter's understanding, and the risks grow with the growing complexity.

Where, then, can a trustworthy elite be found and how dismissed when it inevitably becomes corrupt and dangerous? No political scientist having yet devised a better method of choosing an elite, univeral suffrage that often makes its own bad choices is the only safe method. Its alternative, as Churchill, a philosopher of conservatism, once said, would be far worse, freedom's taproot severed. Where, in short, is Aristotle's Golden Mean applied to politics and dividing liberty from licence? Philosophers have quarrelled over that shifting line since Athens's great days and have reached no agreement.

Perhaps, as a gruff old fellow craftsman, the late Percy Rawling, told me in my youth, the search is not worth the effort. "Forget philosophy, forget history," he said. "They're just the inflammation of some professor's gall bladder." Perhaps they could be so dismissed with a chuckle in simpler times but not now. A wiser man than my old friend put the human predicament in a contemporary nutshell.

Alexander King, president of the much-underrated Club of Rome, concluded, after his long experience in the world, that its managing methods had become archaic, unfitted for modern times, its "government policies, in general, not coherent. They are the sum of all sectoral policies, whether industrial, agricultural, foreign policy, the whole lot, rather than an integrated result of all these. Consequently, some policies reinforce others, some conflict with others.

"There is a very bad need for long-term thinking in government," King warned. "Government policies are constrained by the needs of the next election. So they [governments] are dealing often with immediate issues . . . and neglecting more fundamental things which are just around the corner or over the horizon, and this is leading us to a sort of government by crisis."

The crisis that most alarmed King as a scientist and man of practical affairs was the unequal distribution and looming shortage of the world's food supply. "How," he asked, "are we going to provide food to fill the bellies of six billion people who are going to be on earth at the end of the century and probably seven billion a few years later?"

He did not know. Nor does anyone else today when thousands of human beings starve in Africa and millions throughout the world are underfed. But it is time, and very late, for the well-fed to think about the consequences of hunger, disease and desperation that threaten the peace and the whole human future, even if nuclear war is avoided.

Another side of the predicament and its consequences look equally uncertain. Technology, King said, could give mankind the chance of a richer, freer life, but it is "a perfect instrument for Big Brother to control everyone, centralize everything and, in the end, to find out what the thoughts of the people are."

What will emerge from these mingled hopes and horrors? Again, he did not know, but it will be something "beyond capitalism and communism." That something has begun to emerge already and demands longer thoughts than it has yet received from governments and citizens alike. Here is room for endless argument, permitted only in a free society.

Apart from urgent physical needs of all kinds, the hub and moral pivot of freedom will not be found in a majority of electoral votes, as if 51 per cent of the voters must be right by some arcane law of arithmetic and 49 per cent wrong, when the reverse is often true.

The ability of the democratic process to correct such mistakes is its virtue and strength. It should be judged, above all, by its treatment of the minority striving to become the majority. The minority's right to strive and succeed is the final justification of democracy's right to live and pursue an experiment still young in human affairs and never without enemies, foreign and domestic.

Over the long haul the minority will usually be the source of most useful ideas and reforms. Today's heresy is tomorrow's norm. But until tomorrow, practical politics must be an agonizing task for honest democrats—agonizing because the citizenry does not, and cannot, grasp the complexity of the vital issues requiring decision today.

At best in these issues only a few oversimplifications get through to the public, filtered or warped by the communications media. More than ever nowadays governments have to govern with knowledge incommunicable if they understand it themselves. And many citizens do not even bother to vote while deploring all governments—little above half of the electorate in the United States, but more, fortunately, in Canada.

As the sardonic Aldous Huxley once wrote, "the human mind has an invincible tendency to reduce the diverse to the identical . . . We shall never succeed in changing our age until we give up our ambition to find a single cause for all ills."

Thoughtful or not, even in the free nations the majority would mistreat the minority, and the minority would have no protection, without some code of discipline generally accepted by both. It is the present widespread violation of the Western world's long-standing code that leads towards social disorder, even if the struggling groups invariably confuse their self-interests with the good of society at large.

In fact, the free and, for us, the only tolerable society must be a microcosm of the universe which, so far as humans can understand it, is a system founded on disciplines. A man falling downstairs will recognize one of them called the law of gravity, though he cannot see it. There are many other invisible laws, and when they are violated punishment of some kind eventually follows.

For collective and individual purposes we describe our self-imposed disciplines as morality. Every great issue facing society, whether it be political, economic or military, is moral at bottom. But nowadays, when the superpowers wrestle just short of war, Gresham's law debases morality as it debases money, the bad driving out the good.

It was easy for the nagging moralist Macaulay to sneer that "we know no spectacle so ridiculous as the British public in one of its periodical fits of morality." Burke, a greater man, did not think these things were ridiculous. But he saw that the morals of a politician could not always be the morals of a philosopher because "the latter has only the general view of society; the former, the statesman, has a number of circumstances to combine with those general ideas and to take into his consideration . . . A statesman, never losing sight of principles, is to be guided by circumstances."

Too often principles are sacrificed to what W. E. Henley, the British poet, later called the fell clutch of circumstance. The politician, with high private morals, sometimes becomes immoral in his public life, promises the impossible, wins office and deranges a nation's business. Between principle and circumstance the war never ends for those in power and even for the humblest citizen in his unreported domestic affairs.

One eminent American thinker and diplomat (but no politician) has always been supported, and also tortured, by principle. No man of my acquaintance is more intellectually honest than George Kennan, or more sensitive to the human ordeal. He thus explains it:

"In the West, both in the traditions of Christianity and Judaism, we were brought up to feel individual responsibility. There is in the United States no one to hold the people to that today. The churches have lost the power to do so, the state cannot attempt to do so, and our two political parties would not know how to begin to do so. They cater to what is basest in the American electorate." (An earlier American historian, William James, held the same general view and protested against "our national disease—the bitch goddess, success.")

A democrat (in no partisan sense), Kennan apparently has travelled far from Jefferson's faith in the "goodness and wisdom" of the common people living in "perfect harmony." Jefferson might travel far, too, if he were alive now. As social animals all of us have travelled far. And looking back, we behold a road travelled by a multitude of others.

In some respects, haunting and perhaps a little terrifying, even as a much-used cliché the current state of the Western world resembles that of the Roman Empire in the years of its decline and fall. The congested, ill-planned cities with the mean housing of the poor, the comfortable apartments of the prosperous and the mansions of the rich, the restive unemployed, the angry street demonstrations, the suffocating bureaucracy, the neglected farmlands, the bread and circuses (nowadays known as welfare services and professional sport), the death of the old gods, the religious vacuum, the broken moral code, the luxury beside destitution, the hedonism and the misery—these things recur to students of history in a vivid *déjà vu*.

Is it an accurate view or a misreading of history? Does it foretell the West's destiny in repeated cycle? No one can be sure about that when libraries of divergent books have been written to explain Rome's fall without explaining it. The Western fall is too glibly predicted, just as its future resurgence is too lightly promised by politicians. Either way, the historical parallel must not be too simply drawn.

We do not watch lions eating Christians, though we demand a night of satisfactory violence in hockey and football. We profess the sanctity of human life, though one highly civilized nation of our time murdered six million Jews, another starved unrecorded millions of its people to death and put extra millions in slave camps to perfect the Communist society. Few of us indulge in Roman orgies, though our spirituous liquor is stronger than Roman wine and Rome had not discovered tobacco or habit-forming narcotic drugs. We accept, even boast about, our sexual revolution as if it were a new thing under the sun and forget that it was old before Rome fell. So were polygamy, legal homosexuality and organized prostitution which remains a problem with us, far from solution.

But the imagined historical parallel breaks down under a truly new thing appearing only four decades ago. When the atomic bomb was dropped on Hiroshima, most Roman experience, and human experience everywhere, became largely irrelevant for our guidance. Like no previous generation, we know, in a too familiar platitude, that we have the power to destroy all life, good and bad, on a trivial planet.

If Julius Caesar or Nero had possessed the Bomb and its delivery system, there might be no written history, no one to write or read it. Yet the parallel recurs unmistakably in a different context. Shortly after the time of Julius, the spiritual vacuum of Rome was permeated by various "mysteries" from the East. The educated Roman treated them with contempt as possibly comforting to the mob but unworthy of a gentleman's attention. Nonetheless, one of the mysteries had come to stay, to control Europe and much of the then undiscovered New World when Rome was a heap of rubble left by its barbarian invaders.

Unlike Hiroshima, Nagasaki, Dresden, Berlin, Coventry and others, most Western cities have not been ruined by modern invaders. Like the Romans, however, we live in a new spiritual vacuum, awaiting a new mystery.

Until recent times American and European societies portrayed themselves as Christian (with minority enclaves of different faiths). In truth they have not been Christian, in more than euphemism, since the turn of this century or long before then. To use the argot of the sociologists, they are *secular*. In plainer terms they strive, at their best, for improved behaviour, success varying from place to place and time to time. Often they confuse morality with religion, two separate things. A person can be strictly moral, a paragon of virtue, but not religious.

The great divide in all human thought, since mankind began to think, was symbolized by the Greek philosophers Plato and Aristotle. In his unforgettable metaphor of the cave where the prisoners saw only the shadows of different creatures moving through the sunshine outside, Plato committed himself to a second real world impalpable to the ordinary senses. For Aristotle the palpable world was sufficient.

On one side or the other of the divide, humans must take their stand. Alternatively, taking no stand, they can declare themselves atheists who deny any universal purpose, or agnostics who say, usually with pride, that they have no conviction and need none. So a jury, as G. K. Chesterton once remarked, might boast of its impartiality because it could reach no verdict. To the minority of believers this is simply flight from the supreme issue, a cop-out.

The secular societies do maintain some relics of a lost Christian faith, like daily prayers in Parliament, and Christmas, now a pagan feast, a commercial proposition and an annual headache for most of us. The manger and the Child are replaced by a jolly old St. Nicholas with padded belly and white beard in every department store. Instead of the star overhead we have coloured electric lights. Instead of the wise men bearing gifts we see governments bearing weapons and collecting taxes.

To be sure, Christian churches are still open, but with generally shrinking congregations. The Lord's Day is devoted mainly to amusement and weekly shopping. If the Child were here and saw what has become of His teaching, He would learn that, like all faiths, it has been mocked and parodied by its supposed believers. Apart from perpetual war in His native land and mass hunger in distant lands across the world, no more depressing sight could meet His eyes than a beautiful Norman church in the English countryside on Sunday. About a dozen old folk attend the service with a sprinkling of the gentry who are there not to worship but only because gentility requires their presence before a lunch of hearty fare and vintage French wine to entertain the jocund vicar.

The stranger roaming England can hardly believe that this nation was built around the Bible; that it fought wars innumerable, and also futile, on the Bible's precise meaning while innumerable heretics were burned at the stake to proclaim the faith as taught by the Man of Peace.

If Britain's religious faith has declined, the faith of most people in their institutions, customs and themselves remains strong, though it is derided, as in other nations, by a squalid minority. The vast majority was shocked and shamed by the violence of a long coal miners' strike and by riots at soccer games culminating in 1985 in Brussels where thirty-eight people died fleeing from a mob of British fans.

"What's wrong not just with British football but with Britain?" the usually unflappable London *Economist* demanded. It is not for strangers to say what is wrong with Britain, especially when they find much wrong at home. Let them remember the opposite side of the equation. All the bloodletting of the First World War and the blitz of the second when they stood alone never doubting the outcome, all the wounding loss of an empire, all the stresses of a social revolution and the blunders of government, business and labour unions could not break the spirit of the British national family. If it should break, the world would suffer an irreparable loss. I cannot believe this will ever happen.

By contrast, the United States is historically more violent than Britain and yet more religious, at least on the surface. Harvey Cox, an eminent American social scientist, observes among his people a revolt against the secular society because it fails to advance the Pursuit of Happiness.

A foreigner will observe that reviving frontier fundamentalism, carried into politics, sometimes becomes itself an obscurantist secular drive and crosses the wise constitutional barrier between church and state. Around this issue, apparently settled long ago, debate suddenly rages again. The American people, in their subconscious, can never forget the frontier, even if it has disappeared in all but myth and movies.

These religious movements have come and gone over and over again. They vexed but did not halt the march of society. Concerning it, a wise Englishman, Michael Howard, professor of modern history at Oxford, wrote recently in *Harper's Magazine,* after a prolonged tour of the United States, that "America leads the world in every branch of science, technology, every field of scholarship and the arts."

Such a judgement from such a man (though few of his fellow citizens may agree with it and fewer know or understand the Americans) helps to keep things in balance, to counteract the ignorant anti-Americanism rife in Britain, Europe and Canada. It should be remembered, too, that the United States was the first country where the Constitution forbade any law touching religious beliefs.

Canada, always less violent than the United States, has lately witnessed the worldly reforming zeal of churchmen, inspired by some bishops of the Catholic Church, once the bulwark of conservative thought. This protest against social injustice (somewhat confused in economic theory) should not surprise us, for it was Laval University, named for the first Quebec bishop, that turned out many earlier political reformers.

But to non-Catholics it is surprising that worldwide social reform finds an eloquent spokesman in a courageous Pope from Poland where Communist atheism has not extinguished the faith. If his Church is divided on such issues as birth control, which he condemns and many Catholics practise, so are all human institutions divided on other issues at a time of uncertainty and increasing terrorism that challenges all faiths.

The result of these stirrings in the Western world's present vacuum is a mystery as it was in Rome. For clarity we must look elsewhere. In the Middle East and all the way through Pakistan to Indonesia, the Christian faith as a whole meets a resurging Islam with its 800 million followers who used to have no doubts about anything of importance. But when Iran erects a grim theocratic state on a single idea, and its armies, welcoming martyrdom, fight Islamic neighbours in a holy war, they, like Christians, are also divided, and threaten to provoke larger unholy wars. Religion and politics make a dangerous compound.

As Jesus could not recognize His teachings in their organized version today, so Mohammed would be amazed by contemporary Islam. It was the Prophet who said, among other warnings, that "three things in this life are destructive: anger, greed and self-esteem." It was the philosophers and poets of Islam—such men as the sublime Rumi and al-Ghazali—who preached, in the Middle Ages, the same inner mystical doctrine already preached by Jesus. Has it been lost amid modern weaponry as Christianity has been traduced in the West?

Have religions of all sorts forgotten that their starting point was identical, a belief in the other, invisible world? If so, an unlikely claimant to the opposite belief seems to have forgotten and learned nothing. Marxism, despite its rejection of God, showed at its beginning the vitality of a bastard religion. Now it, too, is failing to satisfy its disciples, even to succeed in the material realm.

Of course religion does not necessarily dwell in any church. The most religious men and women I know never attend it. They do not think they need an outward vehicle or public rite. It may be useful for others, for them a distraction. For all people the church is no true measure of religion and can be its enemy.

Why anyone should be afraid to declare a faith, churched or unchurched, I do not know. But reticence, except perhaps in a minister of the Gospel, is required of the decent citizen in the secular society. It lives on Matthew Arnold's darkling plain where ignorant armies clash by night.

An exceptional case and the least likely of my friends to discuss such matters is George Ball. But then, he is an exceptional man well worth close foreign scrutiny. Until his remarkable career had passed the mark of three score and ten, the American lawyer, politician, economist and diplomat had refused to worry about the purpose of humanity in the general scheme of things. If our species had any purpose, individuals like himself, he decided, were not equipped by nature to understand it. Ball lived, worked and travelled the world on his country's business as a classic agnostic.

All of a sudden, in his age, he could not escape the question of questions. Writing the final naked chapter of his memoirs, he was forced to move past the immediate human prospects that had long gripped him on the edge of despair. He wondered in print if any society could succeed and endure without faith in a being of some indescribable sort above humanity's physical senses. Like the latter-day Romans, he had perceived a mystery.

The question asked by the classic agnostic was a personal revelation to amaze his friends. Evidently the answer still eluded him and may have eluded most of his readers. For some others the answer was clear—no society can succeed or long endure without faith in something infinitely higher than itself. As Voltaire put it, if God did not exist, He would have to be invented. But a flash of Gallic wit is not good enough. It begs the question of ultimate truth, for the question is not who invented what or which came first, egg or chicken, God or man—it is whether anything at all makes sense in this world and countless worlds beyond the reach of the strongest telescope.

The great divide in human thought remains unbridged, forever unbridgeable, to divide our society, our politics, our economic systems and everything else confronting us in the trouble-time of revolution.

All things considered against a background of nearly four centuries, how should we judge our Canadian record of success and failure? How reckon gains and losses in the nation's ledger? What, as the financiers would ask, is the bottom line? There is no bottom line. Unlike an insolvent business corporation, a society lives out its allotted span regardless of its immediate balance sheet. But at least we can detect some significant trends, positive and negative. Every citizen will rank their importance or unimportance by individual judgement, experience and prejudice. Make your own list.

On mine, after a long journey, the first positive is the Canadian people's emergence as a distinct nationality and creaturehood unlike all others, even unlike their neighbours a few miles distant whom, on the surface, they so closely resemble.

Canadians have been increasingly identifiable since Champlain landed at Quebec to make himself, unwittingly, the first citizen of a state yet unimagined. To the contemporary layman nothing is funnier than the sociologists debating the existence of a distinct national character when a nation could not have been built without it. But like most things of true value, that character is difficult if not impossible to define in words. You might as well analyze a human life by measuring its bodily organs, weight, size and chemistry. The important qualities of a people defy such measurement and appear only in action, often surprising its possessor.

If Canadian qualities must be listed for lack of better measurement, I would include a hard-working competence, practicality, improvisation and disregard of theory, a way of doing the job at hand as learned in the first days of settlement when the struggle against the wilderness separated the strong from the weak; a stubborn patience when the task looked hopeless; a dumb courage that issued in frontier or overseas wars and coloured all life at home (though Canada has been spared the ordeals of modern war experienced by many other nations); a certain reticence unlike the exuberant manners of the Americans or the British sense of inherited superiority; a respect for authority less than that of Britain and greater than that of Canada's neighbour; an open-minded willingness to consider any idea, however improbable; an inbred habit of thrift mixed with generosity; above all, a common decency and gentle behaviour noted by all foreign travellers.

Any list of virtues, in itself almost meaningless, should be counter-balanced by our national defects. Among them we must acknowledge an old inferiority complex and self-doubt, an underestimate of Canada as a factor in the world and the unlimited opportunities of its people in their own land; an excessive awe of older cultures and sometimes, in reverse, a national pride verging on arrogance and xenophobia; an individual frugality turning to collective waste that produced our current economic malaise; a regionalism, local interest and prejudice natural enough in a land so vast but often delaying or even prohibiting agreement between the disparate segments.

No list of particulars—all lists disagreeing—adds up to a whole character in single humans or in nations. But at least we can say that no foreigner is likely to understand the Canadian identity and no recent immigrant shares it.

The quality that made Canada and sustains it perhaps can best be described as a will to independence and native lifeways, good and bad, only felt, never fully articulated. Many visitors from the United States, for example, go home to report that Canadians are "refined" or "conservative" Americans, "peaceful, decent, diffident and dull." The British people welcome Canadian travellers and usually respect them as a superior type of American. Of course they are something quite different, as only they can know but never adequately explain.

Nor, it must be admitted, can they explain their folly in recent years. If the undefined identity is the largest Canadian positive, the mismanagement of the nation's joint business is the largest negative.

Why did we let sound Keynesian theories go to our head until—the free lunch syndrome—they drove us into a kind of economic lunacy? The origin of this un-Canadian botch should be clear now. We took for granted, as a right, not a privilege and responsibility, the treasures of a half-continent, demanded more than it could immediately provide and squandered both income and capital.

The result is many-sided—industrial products too costly to compete in the world market or, in some cases, at home; a weak currency in American terms that helps to sell exports but raises the price of imports; a struggle between owners and workers, damaging them and all of us dependent on the same source of livelihood; the expanding role and taxes of the state always bewailed by those who benefit from its expansion and receive regular cheques from the governments they always berate; the collapse of socialism, here and everywhere, as a panacea when no satisfactory alternative is yet in sight.

These things are obvious to us all. Less understood in its consequences is the advance of the computer, the dehumanizing march of the robot. They and many additional factors pose a long-term unemployment problem solvable only by a redistribution of wealth, work and leisure in a better-managed economy.

The nation's conduct in the easy, booming times was both uncharacteristic and contradictory. On the one hand, the people who wasted their heritage were saving their money at a rate about three times that of their American neighbours, a rate among the highest in the world, that limited public purchasing power when it was badly needed. But if Canadians had been less thrifty, the deficit-ridden governments could not borrow enough at tolerable rates in Canada to finance their deficits.

Another fact of nature, not government, should be noted— Canadians as a people are living longer than their parents did. By the end of the century the working young will have to support an increased population of the old, unforeseen when the various pension schemes were established. Despite the massive savings vested in these schemes, we approach an actuarial crunch that the computers already foresee.

Looking candidly at such negatives, we must confess that we managed economic affairs up to now worse than our neighbours did. Naturally, therefore, business recovery in the United States has been faster than in Canada, the federal government's deficit, and the unemployment rate, proportionately lower.

The more arcane theoreticians of government blame much of its failure on its structure. If authority were better distributed between federal and provincial governments—perhaps with a reformed Senate as a kind of national arbitrator—then we could begin to solve our problems. So goes the popular argument of the day, but it is here that an odd notion has long misled us.

Power, we are told, is too concentrated in Ottawa, too weak in the provinces. Actually power has flowed steadily outward since the Second World War until the provinces are now ten semi-independent baronies far more powerful than the fifty American states. This has happened to strain the federal system at a time when we should be pooling our strength to use it, with maximum effect, internally and externally. In a shrunken world such problems as the ravaged environment, the poverty, the hunger and, above all, the Bomb can be solved, if they are solvable, only by the co-operation of strong national governments, each speaking for its united people.

The excessive concentration of power is always dangerous and, pushed too far, could destroy freedom as it has done in many foreign societies, but our Canadian internal feuds are a luxury we can no longer afford. Nonetheless, our governments continue to pursue them as a handy excuse for their own mistakes. It is commonly said (the grand cliché of our time) that governmental structures are primarily at fault. Undoubtedly the structures need basic repairs, but even fully repaired they alone will solve nothing basic. The real need is a restructured public mind.

Looking back again at the opposite side of the ledger, we find some definite positives, or at least some signs of progress, in our collective thought. Among them count these:

The honesty of our courts when we are increasingly litigious. While the judiciary confronts a massive backlog of work, and makes mistakes, its integrity is unquestioned as it begins to interpret the Charter of Rights and Freedoms.

A new understanding of ethnic groups and sympathy for their troubles as sometimes exacerbated by native bigots. Despite the nation's changing bloodlines and lifeways, these Canadian problems are easier to solve than the corresponding problems across the border.

A crime rate appallingly high but a ninth that of our neighbour's. They always note the difference when visiting Canada.

Only one political assassination, more than a century ago, no civil war, no political execution since Riel's death on the Regina gibbet,

no Watergate, no Richard Nixon, no Joseph McCarthy (but no Washington, Lincoln or Roosevelt, either).
A wholesale embezzlement of Indian lands, but no massacre like Wounded Knee; racist abuses, some of them irrational and depraved, but nothing like the rioting mobs of earlier times; unfair treatment of women but their steady penetration into business, politics, the Supreme Court and Rideau Hall; male chauvinism on the wane.

While the list of positives may be comforting, it should not be overdrawn. It is commonly said, for example, that nonwhite people are treated better in Canada than in the United States. Yes, but we have no large black population, no heritage of slavery and comparatively few Hispanics or Asiatics. Long ago we took precautions against them. In the days of mass immigration before the First World War our governments, always denying any racial prejudice, kept most of such peoples out by twisting or ignoring the statutory rules of entry.

If the nonwhite population were large, how impartially would we treat it today? And how large, how sudden, a mixture of foreign bloodlines can we afford in practical politics, which is to say in human nature? These are questions worth asking though seldom publicly asked. Although our laws have become more enlightened, prejudice and local violence against such groups occasionally appear. But nothing like the organized persecution and bloodshed in the first decade of the century has been known in recent times.

A vivid proof of our improving attitudes and declining xenophobia was documented by Pierre Berton in *The Promised Land.* He recalled, in many shocking and forgotten incidents, the shabby, often brutal welcome accorded to European settlers on the western prairies. They were lumped together as "Galicians" or "Bohunks" and usually regarded as an inferior species hardly better than the native Indians. Today their children and grandchildren are leaders in business, the professions and politics. Names derived from the old empire of Austria-Hungary, the Ukraine, Poland, Germany, Holland, Scandinavia and other once mysterious lands are now familiar in our governments, family origins no longer questioned.

If we are a more tolerant and kindly people than we used to be, something intangible and important has yet to appear. With all our success in the science of medicine, the arts of painting, music, ballet, architecture and literature, we have found no adequate voice to articulate our native longings, no Jeffersonian Declaration, no Gettysburg speech, no Whitman singing when lilacs last in the dooryard bloomed.

Let us not boast too soon. And let us not be deceived by the myths of our Peaceable Kingdom.

For yet another example of self-deception, observe how Canadians have been persuaded that they are a folk so thrifty and timid that they refuse to gamble on any risky venture. In fact, they spend more than a billion dollars annually on lotteries, still more on race track betting and unrecorded sums on games like bingo for purposes of "charity."

Again, Canadians are supposed to be a grim, silent, northern species, though they talk more by telephone than any other people in the world; supposed to be stay-at-homes, though the cost of their travel abroad is one of the main elements in their recurring net foreign exchange deficits; supposed, in the stranger's eye, to be dull and humourless, though their family jokes are too comic, too subtle and too outrageous for strangers to understand; supposed to be uniform and homogenous, though an evening with any regional group will show a wide, boisterous diversity. The foreigner might well conclude that the inhabitants of Ontario, Quebec or Newfoundland are the truly typical Canadians or, among a company of prairie natives typically retired in Victoria, that all of us came originally from Moose Jaw.

Whatever else has happened to us in myth and reality, a profound change of recent origin is too often ignored. Up to now we have thought of Canada as an Atlantic nation bound by old ties of sentiment to Britain and Europe. Rather late, we discover that we are equally a Pacific nation.

Across the western sea our customers have been purchasing more of our goods than Europe does. The Asiatic market grows so fast that we must build new railways and ports, and open new mines, to serve it in competition with many strong exporters.

At the same time we must deal with the frictions of the North American border that will never end. They will continually re-emerge in new forms to demand the wisdom and patience of both sides. But, to keep things in perspective, observe that the frictions of a Europe supposedly united by a Common Market are much more rancorous than ours in America. Besides, the Europeans' ancient grudge against the United States has never entirely melted. Underneath their civil manners, the English people still hold vestiges of their anti-American bias while the French cannot quite forgive two American rescues in this century.

No matter how the nation's books are finally audited, one asset outweighs all the liabilities—Canadian society is as free as any ever known in the record of an always tormented world.

One achievement plainly distinguishes Canada in such a world—it has managed, despite its frequent blunders, to preserve a dual state, a unique example to mankind. And one high responsibility will forever test its worthiness to enjoy a unique fortune—it must accept and nurture the double destiny that life from old time has laid upon it or lose the right to live as a nation at all.

Why, the stranger may ask, do Canadians flout the laws of geography, history, sound business, continental logic, the mandate of nature itself in a rugged land hard to subdue, cultivate and govern, only to be themselves? Are they driven by necessity?

No, by their own free choice. They choose this land because it is spacious, infinitely varied, full of wonders and unlimited choice.

Those who know it best have seen the splendour of mountain and plain, the noble rivers surging east, west and north to drain half a continent, breakers pounding on lonely beaches, white spring orchard foam, scarlet autumn woods, vast sky, dawn and sunset on a boundless horizon. They have heard the clamour of geese in arrow-flight north and south, bird song, tympanic frog music, all the sounds of summer growth and howling winter gale. They have breathed the scent of wild rose, cedar, pine, crushed nettle, mossy rock, parched prairie, old barns, clean wood smoke, fragrant kitchen and steaming vittles at day's end.

Compressed in sight, sound, scent and the nation's secret heart are certain memories, regrets and hopes known to us alone, to strangers incommunicable. Even if they are far from perfect, we love our native ways and homemade home. There can be no better reason to keep, safeguard and cherish anything of true worth.

So ends an old Canadian's last fond look at his still Unknown and Unfinished Country, all the great questions asked, none answered. He cannot see through a time of darkness and promised light, but the eyes of the young will be clearer. It is the young everywhere who have the right to remake a world they never made. They alone deserve better, and may God forgive us, what a world we are leaving to them!

INDEX